Bilingualism Matters Series

MYTHS AND FACTS about MULTILINGUALISM

Julie Franck, Federico Faloppa, Theodoros Marinis

(Editors)

CALEC – TBR Books

New York – Paris

an international, multidisciplinary multisectorial training network on multilingualism

The research leading to this book has received funding from the European Union's Horizon 2020 research and innovation program under the Marie Skłodowska-Curie grant agreement No. 765556 (MultiMind project).

Copyright © 2024 by Julie Franck, Federico Faloppa, Theodoros Marinis

All rights reserved. No part of this publication may be reproduced, distributed, or transmitted in any form or by any means, without prior written permission.

TBR Books is a program of the Center for the Advancement of Languages, Education, and Communities. We publish researchers and practitioners who seek to engage diverse communities on topics related to education, languages, cultural history, and social initiatives.

CALEC - TBR Books
750 Lexington Avenue, 9th floor
New York, NY 10022
USA
www.calec.org | contact@calec.org
www.tbr-books.org | contact@tbr-books.org

ISBN 978-1-63607-484-9 (Paperback)
ISBN 978-1-63607-425-2 (eBook)

Library of Congress Control Number: 2023950433

Cover illustration: iStock.com/melitas

Back cover photo © Luca Prestia. *MultiMind researchers and coordinating team.*

Table of contents

Preface. *Antonella Sorace & Katarzyna Przybycien* i

Introduction. *Julie Franck, Federico Faloppa, & Theodoros Marinis* 1

Part 1: Myths on multilingual minds 19

Chapter 1. 'Verbal salad' is good for you: Demystifying mixing of two languages *Michal Korenar, Jeanine Treffers-Daller, & Christos Pliatsikas* 21

Chapter 2. Is it only about language? Implications of multilingualism in other domains *Sofia Castro & Zofia Wodniecka* . 32

Chapter 3. Language and music: Are they so different? Preliminary insight from research on multilingualism *Dávid György, Doug Saddy, Antonella Sorace, & Julie Franck* 43

Part 2: Myths on language learning and the brain 57

Chapter 4. Multilinguals reveal the brain's capacity for lifelong transformation *Jia'en Yee, Ngee Thai Yap, & Christos Pliatsikas* 59

Chapter 5. It's never too late for the brain! Evidence suggests neurological maturation cannot explain observable differences in non-native language *Sergio Miguel Pereira Soares, Tanja Kupisch, & Jason Rothman* 73

Chapter 6. Can we learn and master a new language as adults? Absolutely! *Sarah von Grebmer zu Wolfsthurn, Leticia Pablos-Robles, & Niels O. Schiller* 86

Part 3: Myths on multilingualism and language acquisition 99

Chapter 7. "I hear, I hear, with my little ear": Multilingual and monolingual children perceive speech sounds differently *Theresa Bloder, Tanja Rinker, & Valerie Shafer* 101

Chapter 8. Bilingualism and vocabulary: Why speaking two languages doesn't mean fewer words. *Daniela S. Avila-Varela, Gonzalo Garcia-Castro, & Nuria Sebastian-Galles* 114

Chapter 9. When learning two languages from birth is *not* confusing *Grazia Di Pisa & Theodoros Marinis* 125

Part 4: Myths on multilingualism and education 137

Chapter 10. Fostering multilingualism to support children's school success *Jasmijn E. Bosch & Francesca Foppolo* 139

Chapter 11. A vademecum on multilingual pedagogy for skeptical teachers *Solange Ariel Andrea Santarelli, & Federico Faloppa* 152

Chapter 12. Breaking the language barrier: Why embracing native languages in second/foreign language teaching is key *Konstantina Olioumtsevits, Julie Franck, & Despina Papadopoulou* 164

Part 5: Myths on multilingualism and clinical populations 173

Chapter 13. When less is not more—Multilingualism as a resource, not a burden for children with developmental language disorders *Maren Eikerling & Maria Luisa Lorusso* 175

Chapter 14. Don't fall for it! Multilingualism is not a risk factor for dyslexia *Juhayna Taha & Maria Teresa Guasti* 185

Chapter 15. The benefits of exploring a foreign language in psychotherapy *Isabel Ortigosa Beltrán & Azucena García Palacios* ... 198

Conclusion. Embracing the multilingual mind *Julie Franck, Federico Faloppa, & Theodoros Marinis* 208

References..211

About the authors 243

About TBR Books..255

About CALEC..257

Preface

Antonella Sorace and Katarzyna Przybycien

Multilingualism is the norm in most cultures and societies across the world. Yet, in modern industrial societies, growing up with more than one language or learning a language later in life is often regarded as 'special.' Bilingualism is still surrounded by false beliefs and misunderstandings, even among the otherwise educated and scientifically-minded. Many people are ready to believe that handling two languages at the same time is too much of a burden for the infant's brain, or that the languages compete for resources in the brain, at the expense of general cognitive development. The contrast between these false beliefs and the amazement often expressed by people at how easily children pick up two or more languages has been termed the 'bilingual paradox.' Part of the problem is the fact that people find it difficult to think scientifically about language; therefore, everyone feels entitled to have strong opinions about it. In this sense, the world is full of linguistics experts. With regard to bilingualism, opinions are unfortunately not restricted to the domain of academic discussion, but often inform decisions—by parents, teachers and educators, health professionals, policymakers—that end up affecting both children's and adults' lives. Given this general context, it is particularly important to create stable and effective links between research on bi-multilingualism and society, which can make research findings accessible and comprehensible to different communities and enable them to make decisions based on evidence, rather than misconceptions. This is why Bilingualism Matters exists.

Bilingualism Matters is a not-for-profit membership organization created in August 2021 as a University of Edinburgh spin-out. It builds on the work of the Bilingualism Matters Research and Public Engagement Centre, founded in 2008 at the University of Edinburgh by Antonella Sorace. BM currently affiliates over 30 branches and over 500 individuals across the world. The main aim of Bilingualism Matters is bridging the gap between research and different sectors of society by (a) enabling people to make informed professional or personal decisions on multilingualism and language learning that are based on facts rather than prejudices, misconceptions, or misinterpretation of current research findings; (b) supporting research on multilingualism and language learning and making it relevant, available, and accessible to wider audiences; (c) inspiring dialogue and impactful collaborations within its growing multidisciplinary and multisector membership; (d) developing skills, tools and opportunities enabling academics, professionals, policy makers and community members to effectively communicate and collaborate with each other. Moreover, public engagement feeds back research at least in two ways. First, Bilingualism Matters trains researchers to communicate research findings in a comprehensible way, adapting contents, terminology, and level of details to very different audiences. Second, engaging with society allows a deeper understanding of the different contexts for bilingualism, which in turn can enable researchers to appreciate and evaluate bilingual diversity in its multiple forms, and to widen research horizons in an interdisciplinary way.

This book, based on the results of the EU-funded project "The Multilingual Mind," is our first attempt to draw directly from a research project, contextualize its findings within a wider disciplinary context, and tailor its content and style to appeal to non-academic audiences. The process of creating the book involved new researchers working together with senior academics, practitioners, and book editors. As such it offered an excellent opportunity for the younger researchers to master their communication skills and for all involved to enhance their experience of working across disciplines and sectors of society. Both these experiences align directly with the mission of Bilingualism Matters. We hope this book becomes a springboard for future publications that aim to bring research closer to society, not only as sources of information but also as frameworks to inspire society's understanding and trust in academic research.

Introduction

*Julie Franck, Federico Faloppa,
and Theodoros Marinis*

Language is what makes us human. It enables us to think, plan, and communicate. Languages across the world are windows to different ways of thinking, planning, and communicating: windows to different cultures and perspectives on the world. Importantly, languages are resources that enable children and adults to learn through sharing the vast amount of knowledge humans have accumulated, but also to develop new knowledge, allowing us to better understand the world and ideally make it a better place.

Language and cultural diversity result from the heterogeneity of coexisting populations, which have been shaped by the extensive history of human migrations. Despite this long history, there are still plenty of myths and misinformation about multilingualism that, sometimes, set barriers to the range of benefits that it can actually bring to our societies. This book aims at dispelling some of the common myths about multilingualism by bringing research evidence and facts from the EU funded project 'The Multilingual Mind' (MultiMind), a 4-year project that conducted research on multilingualism whilst training a new generation of researchers in world-leading labs using cutting-edge methodologies. MultiMind was an international project, bringing together researchers from 14 different countries in Europe and beyond. The research teams brought expertise from the disciplines of linguistics, psychology, neuroscience, education, and speech and language therapy, and applied them within the education and health sectors to investigate the influence of multilingualism on language learning, cognition, creativity, and decision making, on brain function and structure, and its role as a reserve in atypical populations. Understanding the benefits and challenges of being multilingual is of prime importance for the future construction of shared and successful cultural, educational, and health settings across Europe and beyond.

The fifteen chapters are distributed in five parts, each targeting a more specific topic and sometimes also audience including parents, teachers, speech therapists and psychotherapists. The first three parts present findings from what is referred to as 'basic research' or 'fundamental science,' i.e., pure research about how multilingualism impacts the functioning of the mind and the brain, and how it influences language acquisition. The last two parts are dedicated to applied research, i.e., research that has an impact on issues regarding individuals and societies, aiming at providing evidence-based recommendations about 'best practices.' By reading these parts, you will learn what we know about the impact of multilingualism on children's and adults' education as well as how it affects clinical populations and the therapeutic settings developed to help them. The book is written in such a way that it can be read without necessarily following the order in which the chapters were arranged. This allows you to follow the order that matches your interests best. References across chapters addressing related questions enable you to jump across chapters to follow up on what you just learned. Readers interested in knowing more about some of the questions addressed in a chapter can consult the references at the end of the book. To guide you in your reading, we recommend that you read the description of the chapters provided here, in order to have a clear idea of what you will find in each of them.

Part 1 of the book, *Myths on multilingual minds*, provides a wide angle on some of the major findings invalidating the myth that multilingual minds are two monolinguals in one operating independently. As you will discover, multilingualism turns out to impact a wide array of domains, well beyond language skills. These domains include creativity, the ability to regulate our behavior to achieve goals, and even social skills and musical skills. The three chapters reveal a number of highly exciting results, showing that multilingualism enriches the minds of children, adults, and the elderly.

In Chapter 1 *'Verbal salad' is good for you: demystifying mixing of two languages,* Michal Korenar, Jeanine Treffers-Daller and Christos Pliatsikas discuss the advantages of 'code-switching,' i.e., the shifting from one language or dialect to another within a conversation. Code-switching is often denounced as a sign of laziness or low overall language proficiency, as reflected in the pejorative terms used to refer to it, like 'verbal salad' or 'gibberish.' Yet, research shows that code-switching brings advantages not only for communication but also for creativity and brain plasticity. Through code-switching, multilingual speakers can indeed communicate effortlessly but also constantly train their brain to suppress the language they are not currently activating. This training improves specific brain networks that underlie switching, creating better and stronger connections between different brain regions. Research shows that it has an impact on brain plasticity throughout the whole life cycle and even suggests that the multilingual brain may be more resistant to ageing! What is even more interesting is that this plasticity does not only benefit language processing and communication skills, but also other thinking abilities which do not have much to do with language, such as attention, the ability to resolve conflict, retain a thought longer, and... being more creative. By using neuroimaging and psychological tests, scientists have in fact recently come up with evidence that multilingualism can influence even such a complex and seemingly elusive concept as creativity. This happens for instance when young bilingual children use unconventional language by applying function words, such as articles (*the, a*) or negation (*not, no*) from one language in sentences that mainly consist of words from another language. Far from being a 'verbal salad,' Korenar and colleagues conclude that code-switching is indeed an opportunity for the speaker's brain to maximize resources when using languages, keep training itself, improving its plasticity and last but not least being more inventive, which definitely debunks the myth of a laziness and sloppiness for long time associated with code-switching in the multilingual brain.

In Chapter 2 *Is it only about language? Implications of multilingualism in other domains,* Sofia Castro and Zofia Wodniecka review the implications of multilingualism on a set of functions that allow us to regulate our behavior to achieve our goals. These functions, called 'executive functions,' involve for example the ability to focus on what is relevant and ignore what is not, or switch our attention to something new. Multilingual speakers turn out to train these skills all day long when focusing on the language they are using while ignoring the other language(s) they know, which are simultaneously activated. Although the question is still debated, some studies suggest that this daily practice may enhance multilinguals' executive functions. Multilingualism appears to delay the onset of the symptoms of dementia in the elderly, providing them with a greater 'cognitive reserve.' Research suggests that even short language training can have positive effects on this reserve, and even at a later age! Interestingly, multilingualism also affects our social skills through two major functions. The first one concerns how we categorize people, for example by their age, ethnicity, or sex. Categorization is a core cognitive mechanism that allows simplifying and structuring the highly complex environments in which we evolve, by grouping units that differ within a single category. Recent studies suggest that multilinguals are, on the one side, more efficient at categorizing people, but on the other side, less prone to develop stereotypes and prejudice about these categories, i.e., beliefs and negative evaluations that typically lead to discriminatory behaviors. The second social function affected by multilingualism is our ability To understand a situation from the point of view of another person, and more generally to understand that our knowledge, thoughts, feelings, or intentions might differ from those of other people. Studies show that regularly using a second language, switching between languages, and having experienced multiple languages during childhood all have a positive impact on the development of these skills.

The myth that language and music are independent functions located respectively in the left and right parts of the brain is debunked in Chapter 3 *Language and music: are they so different? Preliminary insight from research on multilingualism* by David György, Doug Saddy, Antonella Sorace and Julie Franck. Language and music actually both involve some rhythmicity carried by variations in timing and amplitude: vowels or notes can have different lengths, be separated by pauses of different lengths, and can be more or less salient or accented. Numerous relationships have been found between language and musical rhythmic skills, in both typical and atypical children and adults. György and colleagues discuss the directionality of these relationships: is it musical skills that influence language, the other way around, or both? Most studies have explored the impact of musical rhythmic skills on a subsequent language task, reporting significant influences. Rhythmic 'priming' studies for example show that participants are better at deciding whether or not a sentence they hear is grammatically correct after listening to a short sample of rhythmically regular music compared to when it is rhythmically irregular, noise or silence. In rhythmic 'cueing' tasks, participants are better at detecting a particular speech sound in a sentence if it is preceded with a short musical sample whose pattern of weak and strong beats matches the pattern of weak and strong syllables of the target sentence. In contrast, very little is known about the possibility that language influences musical rhythm processing. Interestingly, research shows that exposure to multiple languages may lead to better musical rhythmic skills, pointing towards a significant influence of multilingualism on musical rhythmic skills. Although these bidirectional relations between language and music pave the way to the development of potentially relevant diagnostic, therapeutic and educational tools, the authors call for caution in regard to the multitude of commercial products that have not necessarily been validated through adequate evidence-based protocols.

Part 2 of the book challenges the common misconception that the human brain is an organ that does not change once it reaches adulthood. This myth is ingrained in both popular culture and in the scholarly assumption that the adult brain becomes hard-wired and unable to grow new neurons, and therefore, learn a new language upon reaching maturity. It is supported by the common observation that adults typically find it harder to learn a new language than children. However, this comparison does not rely on what is called 'minimal pair' comparison in science: comparing adults to children does not only involve differences in age, but also a wide array of differences in terms of the learning conditions and the amount of language input the two groups have access to. While babies acquire language implicitly as they are exposed to it through their environment, adults usually acquire it through explicit teaching and much limited exposure to language through their environment. Recent evidence, both from behavioral studies and from studies of the brain itself, shows that under some conditions, adults are fully able to reach native-like knowledge of a new language, invalidating the myth of a 'critical period' for language learning.

In Chapter 4 *The brain continues to change beyond childhood and adolescence,* Jia'en Yee, Ngee Thai Yap, and Christos Pliatsikas start by reviewing scientific evidence showing that the mature brain is still "plastic": it can change in terms of its activity, shape, and volume, which enables it to regain functions after brain injuries, but also to change when learning new skills. The authors discuss recent studies showing that the adult brain continues to grow new neurons as well as create and prune away connections between neurons when adapting to new demands in our day-to-day experiences throughout our lifetimes. Importantly, this plasticity turns out to be more pronounced in bilingual or multilingual brains. This plasticity at the brain level is assumed to arise from the competition in choosing to use one language over the other: having to suppress the unselected language(s) is argued to train a set of complex cognitive skills (executive functions already referred to in Chapters 1 and 2) like attentional control, monitoring, and conflict resolution. Research has shown an increase in grey matter density in a network of regions that underlie these skills. Interestingly, studies show that both cortical regions (the superficial part of the brain) and subcortical regions (deeper regions within the brain) also increase in volume when learning a new language in adulthood. Notably, the degree of growth in these regions correlates both with the quality of performance in that language and with the amount of effort adults invest in language learning! Intensive training in a new language also influences white matter structure, particularly in areas known to be essential for language processing and control. All these observations provide a remarkable demonstration of neuroplasticity. The brain, Yee and colleagues conclude, has an extraordinary ability to modify itself functionally (when learning a new language) and structurally (changing at the cortical, subcortical, and white matter levels), even beyond childhood or the 'sensitive' or 'critical' periods in life.

Sergio Pereira Soares, Tanja Kupisch and Jason Rothman follow up on the debate about the 'critical period' for language learning in Chapter 5 *It's never too late for the brain! Evidence suggests neurological maturation cannot explain observable differences in nonnative language.* The 'critical period hypothesis' states that around puberty, regions of the brain 'crystalize' into specialized functions and language learning becomes challenging as a result of this maturation process, leading to the common observation that the earlier a language is learned, the better. The authors provide scientific evidence suggesting that this age effect is actually the by-product of differences between children and adults in the conditions that favor optimal language learning. In line with that view, the recent literature in neuroscience suggests that brain plasticity only minimally decreases over the lifespan (until the last years of elderly life). In order to understand that literature, Pereira Soares and colleagues guide the reader into the technicalities of two methods used to investigate the brain: electro-encephalography, and more particularly the tracking of neural activity in relation to a specific event (event-related brain potentials), and magnetic resonance imaging. Research based on these methods suggests that as adult language learners become more proficient, their brain progressively shifts towards highly similar mechanisms to those of native speakers, and overall similar brain regions are activated in language comprehension and production. Moreover, the learning of a new language increases the volume/size of areas involved in language and triggers white matter adaptations, sometimes after only a few weeks of training in the new language. To conclude, current evidence fails to support the claim of a cut-off point around puberty after which reaching native-like skills in a new language becomes impossible.

In Chapter 6 *Can we learn a new language as adults? Absolutely!* Sarah von Grebmer zu Wolfsthurn, Leticia Pablos-Robles and Niels Schiller survey knowledge accumulated about language acquisition by babies and then focus on the brain mechanisms that underlie later language learning. A notable feature of how children acquire language is that it arises without the need for explicit instruction.

Children exposed to multiple languages from birth go through the same automatic process of becoming highly proficient speakers of all the languages they are exposed to. Late language learners go through different processes since they are already equipped with a fully developed language system when they come to learn a new one. Whereas some learners will remain low-proficient in the new language, others, even at a later age, will become remarkably similar to native speakers. The authors present scientific evidence showing that adults learning a new language can become highly functional exactly like children. A number of studies explored the neural activity of adult learners' brains when presented with a grammatical error in the new language. Although some studies show that late learners do not manifest the typical brain signature in reaction to grammatical errors, others show that this signature is actually there, but delayed, or even show that late learners have identical brain signatures as native speakers. This demonstrates that at least some adults are able to process the grammar of a language learned late in a native-like fashion. Similar results were found when investigating another brain index of language processing triggered by an unexpected word like 'dog' in the sentence 'I drink my coffee with milk and dog.' Here too, research suggests that the brain of adult late learners reacts to such incongruencies in a similar way to native speakers, although with slightly weaker and slightly delayed responses. Overall, brain evidence leads to the conclusion that adults can achieve high proficiency levels in a new language.

Part 3 of the book presents the current state of knowledge about how children exposed to multilingual environments acquire language, and more particularly knowledge about speech sounds, vocabulary, and grammar. Chapters 7 and 8 review studies comparing bilingual to monolingual children while Chapter 9 explores how bilingual adults with a migration background master the grammar of their 'heritage' language, i.e., the language they acquired in the home, which differs from the language of the society they live in. Although small variations are commonly found between monolinguals and bilinguals, research overall shows that language processes are essentially the same across all groups and highlights the importance of exposing children to linguistically rich environments to promote optimal language acquisition.

In Chapter 7 *I hear, I hear, with my little ear: Multilingual and monolingual children perceive speech sounds differently*, Theresa Bloder, Tanja Rinker, and Valerie Shafer discuss how multilingual children develop knowledge of the speech sounds of the languages they are exposed to. Since changing one of these sounds may change the word's meaning (for example changing /p/ with /b/ in **p**ear / **b**ear), the ability to perceive speech sounds is crucial for the development of vocabulary. Children are born with the ability to discriminate between hundreds of speech sounds of the world's languages, but they lose that ability for sounds they are not exposed to by the end of their first year of life. How do children exposed to multiple languages develop knowledge of the speech sounds of these languages? The authors review recent studies capitalizing on a typical brain signature of sound discrimination that is observed when a repeated speech sound is interrupted by a different sound. While discrimination is automatic in adults, babies and young children need to pay attention to show discrimination of subtle sound differences. The authors compared this brain reaction in 4- to 6-year-old children growing up in Germany and exposed to both Italian and German to that of monolingual German children. They tested their perception of sounds that exist in both Italian and German, but that slightly differ in their pronunciation. Whereas monolingual German children showed robust brain discrimination of the German speech sounds, Italian-German bilingual children showed a weaker brain response, depending on their exposition to German. Even bilingual children exposed to German much more than to Italian failed to react like children who were only exposed to German. This shows that children exposed to a multilingual environment do not show the same level of automaticity in speech sound perception as monolingual children. The authors invite clinicians and teachers to not expect bilinguals to behave like two monolinguals in one and be cautious when interpreting differences between multilingual children as indicators of a language disorder.

Families of bilingual children sometimes worry that their children's linguistic development may be delayed compared to their monolingual peers. This topic is addressed by Daniela Avila-Varela, Gonzalo Garcia-Castro, and Nuria Sebastian-Galles in Chapter 8 *Bilingualism and Vocabulary: Why Speaking Two Languages Doesn't Mean Fewer Words.* The authors focus on the development of vocabulary which plays a key role in later academic performance, and thus, in professional success. The chapter questions the position that exposing children to multiple languages may cause them to have smaller vocabularies compared to children raised in monolingual environments. This position is based on studies that measure vocabulary in only one language, and thus, fail to take into account the words known by multilingual children in the other languages they are exposed to. When children's total vocabulary is measured, the vocabulary size of multilingual children turns out to be similar or even larger than that of monolingual children. Moreover, research shows that similar processes underlie monolingual and multilingual linguistic development. For example, vocabulary size correlates with the amount of input children receive, such that children exposed to multiple languages tend to know more words in the language they are most exposed to. The authors report a recent study they conducted on a wide sample of children between 1 and 3 years old in Barcelona, comparing the vocabulary of those raised in monolingual environments (exposed to only Spanish or only Catalan) to that of children exposed to both languages. Results show that the total number of words understood in Spanish and Catalan is the same for the two groups of children, which is in line with the conclusion that bilingualism does not penalize early vocabulary development. The chapter highlights the importance of exposing children to rich and diverse experiences in the various languages they are acquiring in order to promote successful vocabulary development in all these languages.

In Chapter 9 *When learning two languages from birth is not confusing,* Grazia Di Pisa and Theo Marinis address the question of how bilingual adults master their heritage language. The authors report a study they conducted on second generation Italians who grew up in Germany, that is, heritage speakers of Italian. The study focused on grammatical gender. Whereas the phenomenon is present in both Italian and German, nouns in Italian are either masculine or feminine, whereas in German they can also be neuter. Moreover, nouns that have one gender in Italian may have a different gender in German. Are these differences confusing for a speaker who has to juggle both languages? The authors studied this question in three different tasks: reading sentences, judging the correctness of sentences, and producing sentences, which they describe in detail so that the reader can have a precise idea of how such questions are addressed in the lab. Results overall show that heritage speakers of Italian tend to read and judge sentences more slowly and make overall more errors than Italian speakers living in Italy, so-called homeland speakers. However, both groups make more errors with feminine than masculine nouns, suggesting that despite being slower and making more errors, heritage speakers of Italian process gender similarly to homeland speakers, using the masculine as a 'default' gender. An important observation is that heritage speakers have more difficulties knowing the gender of a noun, which is a purely arbitrary property, than agreeing adjectives with nouns, which is a property of Italian grammar. Crucially, their performance depends on their proficiency and on the amount of exposure to Italian they had in the home. All in all, the results show that bilingual heritage speakers process gender in a similar way as homeland speakers, and that increasing exposure to the heritage language at home would allow them to be maximally efficient, that is faster and more accurate. The authors end with providing numerous tips for parents about how to preserve their heritage language in a fun and meaningful way for their children.

The three chapters of Part 4 challenge the misconceptions commonly entertained by teachers that multilingual practices negatively impact learning and school success. Chapters 10 and 11 review studies on teachers' attitudes and present current research showing that supporting native language development and multilingual literacy at school has positive effects on academic outcomes, contributes to enhancing engagement and motivation, and facilitates social inclusion. Chapter 12 focuses on language teaching and argues that pedagogical 'translanguaging' practices—by which students are guided to systematically compare the languages they speak—benefits language learning, and contributes to developing positive emotions in the classroom, especially in learners with a forced migration background.

In Chapter 10 *Fostering multilingualism to support children's school success*, Jasmjin Bosch and Francesca Foppolo debunk the myth that the use of the native language at school negatively affects the academic outcomes of multilingual children. In contrast to the mastery of high-prestige European languages, such as English or French, seen as an enrichment, the multilingualism brought into the classroom by students with a migration background is often seen as a problem, and the native languages of these students are typically not valued to the same extent. Also, it is widely believed that school performance of multilingual students can be improved by maximizing the amount of input in the school language and by rejecting the use of native languages. As a consequence, many teachers do not allow children to use their native language in class and avoid making reference to the cultural or linguistic background of the students while teaching. As Bosch and Foppolo demonstrate, though, current research shows that supporting native language development and multilingual literacy has various positive effects on children's school success. First, using children's native language in education is beneficial for content learning. Second, involving the native language supports linguistic development and improves children's metalinguistic awareness. Third, the use of the children's native languages in primary education supports early literacy acquisition: understanding that specific symbols correspond to certain sounds and meanings is undoubtedly more straightforward in a native language, in which the phonemic categories and lexical meanings are more precisely defined and more strongly established. Reading development is also strongly related to oral language proficiency, and specifically vocabulary knowledge, which tends to be stronger in the dominant language of multilingual children. Moreover, it is argued that taking a multilingual approach may enhance the children's sense of belonging, self-confidence, and motivation, all of which are crucial for learning and for developing social skills.

In Chapter 11 *A vademecum on multilingual pedagogy for skeptical teachers*, Solange Santarelli and Federico Faloppa provide some recommendations to teachers willing to engage with multilingual pedagogy. Teachers do not normally believe that multilingual teaching can be implemented in class, as they are not familiar with the language(s) of their students, and they feel unprepared to deal with linguistic and cultural variety. Even when they have come across multilingual pedagogy, they are often inclined not to apply it in class, as they often believe that multilingualism can impede the achievement of didactic goals. Moreover, they do not usually feel responsible for the maintenance of the native language(s) of their 'foreign' students. In this chapter, Santarelli and Faloppa argue that teachers may have an active role in fostering their students' multilingual competence and resources, enhancing their motivation, and learning experience, facilitating their social inclusion, and contrasting injustice and discrimination at school and in society, particularly for speakers with a migration background. Through dynamic practices of translanguaging, it could also promote cooperative learning and increase participation. As the authors show, multilingual pedagogy would be particularly beneficial in multi-level classrooms of non-native adult speakers, in which students normally have different levels of literacy, competence and meta-competence, and motivations. By creating a learning space for negotiating language use, acknowledging their students' linguistic resources, softening boundaries between languages (and cultures), promoting peer interaction among students speaking the same 'foreign' language, and challenging the monolingual ideology that still permeates school systems, teachers can be agents of social change and enable their non-native speaking students to both better perform in the classroom and enthuse their social participation outside the classroom.

Konstantina Olioumtsevits, Julie Franck, and Despina Papadopoulou present evidence against the popular belief in the field of language teaching that the language classroom should be an 'island' keeping away the learners' native languages, in Chapter 12 *Breaking the language barrier: Why embracing native languages in second/foreign language teaching is key*. The banishment of native languages from language classrooms dates back in the 1970s and has been implemented through a variety of pedagogical practices throughout Canada, Europe, and the USA. Intriguingly, no empirical basis seems to support the 'island' principle, which appears to be based on the erroneous interpretation of two real phenomena. First, the more learners are exposed to the new language, the better they learn it. Second, learners sometimes make mistakes due to transferring from their native language(s). The authors show how these two sets of observations actually fail to support the island principle, and present studies showing that language learning can actually benefit from the systematic comparison between the native language and the new language. For example, pedagogical translanguaging capitalizing on children's knowledge of Basque, Spanish, and English was shown to benefit children learning the 'pieces' of words (e.g., de-, colony-, and -ize in the word 'decolonize'). Children exposed to exercises highlighting similarities and differences about how a word is formed across the three languages were found to develop better awareness of words' structure compared to children exposed to exercises within a single language. Moreover, grounding the new language in learners' native languages was shown to be enjoyable for the teachers and may contribute to developing positive emotions in the classroom, especially for learners with a forced migration background. A recent study conducted by the authors on vocabulary teaching to refugee children highlights the benefits of the use of the native languages in the classroom on motivation, engagement, language learning, and in the development of a bond between teachers and learners.

Part 5 addresses questions related to clinical populations evolving in multilingual environments, busting the myth that multilingualism will penalize their condition, either by worsening or even causing persistent language difficulties in children (developmental language disorders or dyslexia), or by reducing the effectiveness of psychotherapy if a non-native language is used in populations suffering from psychological disorders. Although multilingualism comes with some challenges, it also provides significant resources for children with language or reading difficulties, as well as for patients suffering trauma.

In Chapter 13 *When less is not more—multilingualism as a resource, not a burden for children with developmental language disorders*, Maren Eikerling and Maria Luisa Lorusso come back to the myth that exposure to multiple languages is a source of confusion for children and discuss the challenge multilingualism poses to children who manifest language difficulties. The process of language acquisition is characterized by its high automaticity, and evidence points to the conclusion that it is effortless for children, even when they are exposed to multiple languages. However, evidence shows that it is crucial for children to be exposed to hearing a rich and good-quality language in order to fully master all the languages they are in contact with; this will enable the establishment of adequate social relationships, both with the family and the society, and access to education. Although multilingualism is not a burden for children, it is a challenge to clinicians and educators, especially in the context of a developmental language disorder. The challenge lies in teasing apart language difficulties due to a real language disorder to those simply due to reduced exposure to the language, which tend to manifest in a similar way. In order to do so, practitioners should ideally test children in all the languages they speak. This is often not possible because there is a lack of multilingual practitioners who speak the languages spoken by the children. A wide-scale study conducted by the authors shows that even though clinicians are fully aware of the risk of misdiagnosis when tests are conducted in a single language, this awareness does not transpire in their work. Eikerling and Lorusso propose a number of ways to bridge this gap between theory and practice. For example, they found that concrete experience with multilingual children is actually the best way to ensure speech therapy work is sensitive to the specificities of children with multilingualism. The authors conclude that in the context of multilingualism, the saying 'less is more' is not true; rather, families should make use of the full repertoire of their linguistic resources.

The issue of diagnosis also arises when multilingual children learn to read, as explained by Juhayna Taha and Teresa Guasti in Chapter 14 *Don't fall for it! Multilingualism is not a risk factor for dyslexia*. Determining if reading difficulties are due to dyslexia or simply to lack of exposure to the language is again a challenge for clinicians and educators. Dyslexia is characterized by impairments in accurate and fluent reading, but also reading comprehension and also spelling. To avoid overdiagnosis, it is therefore crucial to know how multilingual children develop all these skills when they learn to read in their new language. For example, research shows that while multilingual children starting to learn to read in primary school will often show no difference compared to monolinguals on most reading skills, lower skills can be found when they start secondary school. Interestingly, the literature suggests that multilingual children often show similar and sometimes even better cognitive skills involved in reading, like the ability to play with parts of spoken language (words, syllables, and sounds) or the ability to inhibit irrelevant information in the environment. In contrast, the authors review different studies, including theirs, showing that poor readers (monolinguals or bilingual) underperform good readers in tasks targeting these skills. Hence, assessing children on these cognitive skills that are prerequisites for learning to read and that are deficient in poor readers provides a new diagnostic avenue. The authors also highlight the relevance of 'dynamic assessment' tools, which measure the child's learning potential rather than their current attainment. Research suggests that the child's ability to learn, for example, new letter shapes associated with sounds and then to new words made of these letters, predicts further reading skills. Taha and Guasti conclude with important recommendations for clinicians in charge of evaluating reading skills of multilingual children.

In Chapter 15 Popular *Myths related to people doing therapy in a foreign language context*, Isabel Ortigosa and Azucena García Palacios challenge the idea that, for multilingual speakers, psychotherapy is only effective in the native language and not in one of the other languages they speak. For a long time, common sense has suggested that using a non-native language in a psychotherapeutic process was an obstacle for the efficiency of the therapy. As a consequence, most multilingual speakers do not even discuss the possibility of using another language with their therapist and even multilingual therapists tend to discourage the option of using the patient's foreign language(s) in therapy. However, new research shows that psychotherapy could indeed benefit from a multilingual approach.

For instance, several clinical cases collected over the last decades demonstrate that dealing with painful or traumatic memories in a second language might shield from highly emotional experiences, allowing patients to put some distance from themselves and the trauma. Therapists also noticed that switching languages during therapy could be an asset not only for articulating distress but also for regulating emotions. Evidence has in fact shown that the use of a foreign language elicits lower emotional responses than the use of the native one. But to what extent and how may the so-called 'foreign language effect' affect psychotherapy? Garcia Palacios and Ortigosa provide an answer by discussing the results of a series of experiments on emotion regulation processing, such as fear conditioning, fear extinction, and reappraisal. They argue that the use of a foreign language is not an impediment to the effective development of the processes of extinction of fear and reappraisal. Using a foreign language in psychotherapy is in fact not a handicap. On the contrary, it shows benefits, such as protecting patients from emotionally engaging in uncomfortable situations or providing them with a flexible choice of communicative tools.

Through a variety of topics and approaches, these fifteen chapters aim to shine a light not only on theoretical strands, but also on possible applications in education and continuous education, therapy and wellbeing, and language policy, to enhance knowledge, participation, and social inclusion. By presenting state-of-the-art research in an accessible way, they provide both experts and the wider public with an informed introduction to the main questions surrounding multilingualism in 21st century's societies; at the same time, they open up to further investigation and practice by— hopefully— inspiring a new generation of scholars and practitioners.

Language and linguistic studies have never been so key to fostering intergenerational and intercultural communication and— from an ecolinguistic perspective—reaching a better understanding of the world we live in, and of its diverse environments and contexts. Although it cannot alone be seen as the solution of any global problem, debunking myths and misconceptions on multilingualism as well as on the speakers' language competence, repertoire, and resources can definitely be considered a good starting point to create and disseminate counter-narratives to prevent and combat discrimination, xenophobia, and nationalism in an era of fake news, chauvinistic propaganda, and misinformation.

Part 1:
Myths on multilingual minds

Chapter 1. 'Verbal salad' is good for you: demystifying mixing of two languages

Michal Korenar, Jeanine Treffers-Daller, and Christos Pliatsikas

Multilinguals often mix their languages in one conversation. This is called code-switching. Code-switching is often perceived negatively and is referred to in pejorative terms, such as 'verbal salad' or 'gibberish'. But does code-switching deserve such names? In fact, code-switching is far from trivial, and our minds need to work hard to mix two languages in one conversation. This hard work might be why code-switching appears to improve our attention and creativity, and even change our brain.

In English, we call an animal that has four legs, a tail, meows, and hunts mice, *a cat*. In Czech, we would call the same animal *kočka* and in Portuguese *gato*. If someone speaks all these languages, there are three different names in their brain representing the same animal. So, when a polyglot sees a cat or when, perish the thought, they want to name it, there is a conflict in their mind about which of the given words is the most appropriate to use in the given situation. And this challenge goes far beyond words. Successful communication requires more than just vocabulary. Languages also differ, for example, in grammar or what sounds they use. Last but not least, other cultures also express anger, requests, or, for example, rejection in different ways. In the Czech Republic, a Czech speaker can go unnoticed if they give to their colleague at work, a direct command like "close the window, Peťa," which many people in an English environment might consider rude or inappropriate, at the very least. Multilingual people thus need to solve many conflicts in their heads daily, on many fronts, to communicate effortlessly.

Interestingly, effortless communication among multilinguals speakers does not necessarily mean that they always choose to use solely one language within a conversation. Multilinguals often mix the languages they know together in one conversation or even in one sentence! Consider (1), where Malay words are given in italics, and English words in regular type font[1]:

(1) *Suami saya dulu* slim and trim *tapi sekarang* plump like drum.

Before my husband slim and trim but now plump like a drum.

"Before, my husband was slim and trim but now he is plump like a drum."

This specific multilingual act is called code-switching, and it happens often if multilinguals meet with people who have in their repertoire the same set of languages. Mixing two languages in one sentence is often denounced as a sign of laziness or low overall language proficiency. This negative attitude is also reflected in pejorative terms by which code-switching is called, such as *verbal salad* or *gibberish*. But is it really easy to mix two languages like that? Or is it just one of the strategies multilingual people use to achieve fluent communication? And if multilinguals are good in deciphering such subtle cues as what tone they should use in what language when they give commands, can it be that code-switching has its social function too? In this chapter, you will find out about how multilingual people deal with their languages in their mind so that they can communicate effortlessly. We will focus on code-switching and scientific evidence which suggests that mixing two languages is not that easy for our brain. Instead, it presents our brain with *different* challenges than if we decide to keep languages strictly separate and use purely one language within one conversation, and the other in other situations or when we speak with other speakers.

Multilingualism as mental training

Research shows that all the languages we know are activated in the brain whenever we use at least one of them.[2] Yes, it means that even though you read these lines in English, your, say, French or Malay are also activated and, to some extent, even your German, which

---

[1] Cook, 1992.
[2] Kroll et al. 2012.

you may have learned 40 years ago. Many people mistakenly believe that when using a foreign language, our brain must laboriously mine the foreign language from its guts. But, in fact, the brain spends a huge amount of effort on suppressing the non-relevant language so that it does not manifest itself so prominently if we do not need it. This training in suppression is then accompanied by training in choosing between several alternatives, because in our minds we must continuously evaluate which of our languages to use in a given situation. This internal conflict also constitutes training that helps our brain to work more efficiently.[3]

We can think of the brain as a muscle. If we plan to do a few push-ups every day as a New Year's resolution, it might be difficult for us to do push-ups on the first day of our training. You could say that it might even be painful. However, over time, we will train our muscles and we will feel that push-ups come easier and easier. Our improvement will be faster the more often we do push-ups. It is similar to languages. Learning additional languages, and how to control using them, puts additional strain on those parts of the brain that are responsible for language processing. The effects of language use on the brain are often studied using magnetic resonance imaging (for more information on this method see Chapter 5 and Chapter 4 in this volume). At first, this task seems challenging and difficult, and the brain needs to find a way to deal with this challenge. One way for the brain to become efficient in carrying out a challenging task is to improve those networks that underlie the task, usually by creating better and stronger connections between different brain regions. And we have evidence to show that this is exactly what happens in the multilingual brain: studies using magnetic resonance imaging have shown that the brain's function is "enhanced", expressed as improved communication of the said regions. Moreover, we now know that the structure of the multilingual brain continuously changes in order to deal with this challenge, an effect that indexes the steady creation of new brain connections until the optimal ones are found, followed by the

---

[3] Grundy, Anderson & Bialystok, 2017.

removal of any superfluous or underperforming connections.[4] There are even suggestions that these efficient connections, which are continuously utilized by multilinguals for long periods of time, are very resistant to ageing—in other words, it may be the case that the multilingual brain takes longer to get old! In all, what this evidence provides is a reminder that the brain is a plastic organ, and this plasticity is triggered by challenging mental experiences, such as multilingualism (for more information on neuroplasticity, see Chapter 5 and Chapter 4 in this volume). This plasticity is harvested to achieve efficiency, but it is in itself dependent on how continuous and sustained the mental challenge is. This is particularly relevant to language use in multilingual environments, when the task of switching between languages, and/or suppressing one of them depending on the context, is not an optional one, but it is vital for survival. These environments are well known to promote neuroplasticity, and in turn to help improve multilingual language competency; indeed, the more we practice using languages and switching between them, the easier it will be to communicate in a multilingual environment. Interestingly, similar outcomes have been suggested for individuals speaking two *versions* of the same language, i.e. the standard version and a regional dialect, also known as bidialectals.[5] To the extent that these individuals need to manage the use of their two language versions in ways similar to those applying to multilinguals, it is very possible that such environments can also promote neuroplasticity, but also improve the communication abilities of bidialectals.[6] But what is perhaps even more interesting is that we will not only improve in communication but also in other thinking abilities which do not have much to do with language.

Research shows that people who speak multiple languages can have improved attention, the ability to resolve conflict, retain a thought longer[7] and, last but not least, are more creative.[8] To

---

[4] Korenar, Treffers-Daller, & Pliatsikas, 2023.
[5] Alrwaita, Houston-Price, & Pliatsikas, 2022.
[6] Ibid.
[7] Korenar, Treffers-Daller, & Pliatsikas, 2023.
[8] Fürst & Grin, 2018.

understand why this is so, let's think back to our analogy with doing push-ups. When we diligently stick to our New Year's resolution and achieve having strong arms thanks to the regular push-up training, it does not mean that we will be able to use the new strength only for doing push-ups. We will be able to throw with more force, we will not tire as much when we carry heavy shopping bags and, thanks to movement, we will also strengthen our overall physical condition, which, for example, can prevent the development of heart diseases. This reflects the fact that our body is an interconnected, well-functioning system that uses all its parts efficiently. Our brain works in a very similar way. The brain can put the experiences and skills gained during speaking of multiple languages to use for other mental activities. And how does this transferable multilingual training actually manifest itself?

Code-switching—a specific mental training

Although the training in controlling two languages can likely also benefit other thinking processes, the way multilinguals use their languages still matters. If we use our push-up metaphor, it is probably true that doing push-ups will have positive effects on your overall physical condition, but it is also logical that you will see the most striking results of your sporting endeavors on your arms. Arms are simply the single most used part of your body when it comes to push-ups. Likely, the same applies to multilingualism: the way we communicate tends to reinforce the cognitive processes necessary to manage the various languages in our minds.

Multilingual speakers, especially those who live abroad, very often find themselves in situations when all the participants of the conversation know the same set of languages. This means that both languages multilinguals know can be used in such situations.[9] Imagine that you are a Ukrainian speaker who moves to England together with your family to work there as a nuclear engineer. After several years living and working there, you and your family are proficient users of English. The language of the country you live in is widely spoken at your work. Two of your colleagues are also

---

[9] Treffers-Daller, 2009.

Ukrainian speakers and every now and then, when you are alone with them, you switch to Ukrainian because you know that everybody will understand this language. On the other hand, your thoughts are wired to the expectation that in the working environment, you use English most of the time. That is also a reason why you mostly know the terminology from nuclear engineering in English but not so in Ukrainian. As a result, you use English words when you speak with your Ukrainian colleagues about your work, as in (2) below, where most of the technical terms (steam generator, loop) are in English. All Ukrainian words are given in italics.

(2) *Zavtra vstanovlyuyemo novyy* steam generator *na druhiy* loop.

Tomorrow we will install new steam generator on second loop.

"Tomorrow we will install the new steam generator on the second loop."

Such language mixing comes very handy in situations when you are not able to find the right word but know that your communication partners will understand you if you use a word from a different language. In this vein, one might think that mixing languages is just a sign of a poor mastery of one of the languages. Others might even go as far as calling code-switchers lazy for not trying to find the right word in the language of the conversation at that moment. However, to be able to decide which words and with whom you can say in a different language is not trivial. Your brain needs to assess the language knowledge of your communication partner and whether the social setting would allow it.[10] Only then can the brain decide to fish for words from both languages and explore all the opportunities which come with being multilingual: for example, to use some English words in an otherwise Ukrainian sentence.

Also, as you already know, our brains must suppress other languages if we want to use only one of them. But in sentences like (2), the brain likely cannot just decide to shut all the other

---

[10] Blanco-Elorrieta & Pylkkänen, 2017.

languages. Instead, it needs to selectively allow the speaker's English to be activated only for a very short amount of time, long enough to find the right word and use it.[11] This trains the "brain muscle" of a multilingual's attention and ability to selectively suppress unwanted information. In our research we asked people to indicate how often they hear multilingual conversations around them, in which people switch their languages between sentences.[12] Furthermore, we asked the same question about sentences where people switch within one sentence and say one or two words in a different language. Afterwards, we measured the size of people's brain using magnetic resonance imaging. The results showed that people who often engage in switching between sentences or say longer stretches of text in one language and then in the other one, have larger volumes of the thalamus. The thalamus is a small region roughly in the middle of our brain, which is responsible for our attention, especially if things get hard. Also, people who engage in code-switching of whatever kind had larger caudate nucleus. Caudate nucleus can also be found in the middle of our brain. This evolutionary old part of our brain makes it possible to do one activity, stop it and concentrate on another activity. In other words: it is responsible for switching, in the broad sense of that word.

What do these results mean? These results likely show that mixing languages in general is demanding and that the part of our brain which helps us with switching gets trained and grows in people who mix languages often. It also likely matters how people mix their languages. Switching language between sentences means that the brain needs to exert effort to suppress the other languages for longer than to suppress a single word. Such a language use likely also trains our attention and ability to suppress more intensely.[13]

We just learned that language mixing trains our brain in making the most of all the opportunities which can come in handy, and it also trains our attention and the ability to suppress unwanted pieces of information. You might ask yourself: Are these small changes

---

[11] Hofweber, Marinis, & Treffers-Daller, 2020.
[12] Korenar, Treffers-Daller, & Pliatsikas, 2022.
[13] van Hell & Witteman, 2009.

really meaningful? Can we use them in everyday life? What if we told you that people who code-switch are often more creative!

Code-switching and creativity

Creativity is not only the domain of artists. Every day, we unknowingly use creative solutions to the problems that arise. When you're cooking a lovely stew and you run out of marjoram, use oregano instead! Do you have a visitor and you don't have enough glasses? Serve tea in empty jam-jars! Did you find on your way out from your home that you have a run in your stockings and don't have time to change? Put on your high boots and no one will see it! These are only small examples of everyday creativity, i.e., the ability to come up with new and useful solutions to unexpected situations.[14] Creativity is considered one of the most important human abilities that drives the industrial and scientific development of our society. Without creativity, we would not develop new recipes, we would not see any technological development, such as the development of new medicines.

Indeed, scientists have recently come up with evidence that knowledge of multiple languages can influence even such a complex and seemingly elusive concept as creativity.[15] This is probably related to the way in which we use the languages we know. Look at (3), where Czech words are given in italics and English in regular type font:

(3) *Jsem* transporter and I'm *taky* a *dodávka* driver, *který* drive a van.

I'm a transporter and I'm also a van driver, who drives a van.

This is not a figment of our imagination, but a real conversation between two Czech students studying at the University of Reading. In this code-switch, compared to the previous examples, the words and grammatical structures of two languages intertwine. One might call this a creative act! It is a challenging thought process where speakers use all available means very effectively to successfully communicate their idea. English words are the oregano in the stew

---

[14] Beaty, Benedek, Silvia, & Schacter, 2016.
[15] Kim & Lee, 2019.

of Czech sentences, with which we replace Czech marjoram when we don't have it at hand during communication. People who are used to mixing the languages they speak thus adopt a mental strategy of using all available means and combining them to the effective achievement of their goals.

Kharkhurin and Wei measured creativity in laboratories using standardized psychological tests.[16] Participants in these tests make creative drawings or imagine that they could fly and list all the possible problems which would come together with this exciting skill. The researchers compared creativity scores of three different groups: monolinguals, multilinguals who do not mix their languages often, and habitual code-switchers. The results showed that it is multilingual "code-switchers" who usually achieve better results in these tests compared to the monolingual population, but also compared to other multilingual speakers.

So, if you sometimes can't remember a word, you don't have to be so strict with yourself, just cook your language stew with a word from another language! The good news for you is that you have just practiced creative thinking.

Code-switching in multilingual children

Parents are often worried about their children's code-switching. They think children are unable to speak either of their languages properly if they mix the two in one sentence. One Dutch-English bilingual family in Berlin therefore had a family language policy which included the rule: "one language per sentence." But children do not necessarily copy their parents' way of speaking and can come up with creative language forms that were not heard before in the speech community. A common phenomenon among young bilingual children is the use of function words such as articles (*the, a*) or negation (*not, no*) from one language in sentences that mainly consist of words from another language as in (4), where Tiffany (who is two years and five months old at that time) uses the French negation *pas* "not" in an English sentence:[17]

---

[16] Kharkhurin & Wei, 2015.
[17] Jisa, 2000.

(4) Tiffany: wan *pas*. wan *pas* 'gurt

want not, want not yoghurt.

"I don't want it, don't want yoghurt."

Tiffany probably did not hear such sentences from her parents, so this is an example of creative language used on her part. In the course of time, such mixes of function words disappear if this type of mixing is not common in the bilingual community where the children live. While separation of languages is valued in some communities, that is not always the case. The task for the children is therefore to find out when mixing languages is appropriate and when it is not in their speech community. They learn to follow the societal norms for code-switching in the course of time. So, parents don't need to worry about sentences such as (4). Instead, they can enjoy their children's creative language use, and laugh together at Spanish-English bilingual jokes such as (5)

(5) Why are cows lazy?

Because they are always on *vacaciones*.[18]

Conclusion

You learned in this chapter that multilinguals do not always use only one language at a time. When multilinguals who speak the same languages communicate with each other, they can mix the languages they know. This language mixing is called code-switching. Multilinguals can opportunistically use both languages to communicate more efficiently. Code-switching is not a sign of laziness but rather an act in which they must pay attention and assess that their communication partner will understand them.

Furthermore, multilinguals' brains need to work hard to suppress the language they do not want to use when switching from one language to the other. This constitutes brain training in suppression, attention, and optimal use of language resources. To support the view that code-switching can train our brains,

---

[18] *Vaca* means "cow" in Spanish, and *vacaciones* means "holiday."

researchers studied the brains of people who code-switch. The brain parts responsible for attention and switching are larger in people who code-switch.

Code-switching comes in many forms and can sometimes be very creative. The surprising and unconventional language use and the above-mentioned brain training are perhaps why code-switchers often perform well in creativity tests. Therefore, verbal salad, as code-switching is often called, is part of the linguistic reality of many multilinguals, and can be good for us.

Chapter 2. Is it only about language? Implications of multilingualism in other domains

Sofia Castro and Zofia Wodniecka

Did you know that multilingualism impacts the way you perceive the world? We would like to show you how the knowledge of more than one language has consequences in various domains of our lives. We will focus on the influence that multilingualism can have on different mental abilities and how multilingualism can help us maintain these mental abilities throughout our lifespan. In addition, we will also talk about how multilingualism impacts the way we process information about other people and how we understand their mental states.

Does multilingualism help our mental abilities? A large body of research within the field of multilingualism has focused on the consequences of multilingualism in a set of mental processes referred to as executive control.[19]

Metaphorically speaking, executive control is the "orchestra director" of our brain; it helps us regulate our behavior to achieve our goals. For example, let's consider the goal of driving your car to work. While driving, you receive a text message on your smartphone. The screen lights up, and you feel the urge to look at the message. At this moment, your executive control system is helping you contain the desire to unlock your screen. After successfully ignoring the text message, you continue the route through a crowded street and stop on a three-line road with several traffic lights. Thanks to your executive control, you can focus on your traffic light while ignoring all the other lights. Finally, you

---

[19] Other terms such as executive functions or cognitive control are frequently used.

arrive at your destination: your office. It is time to park! You notice a free parking spot in front of the entrance and decide to park there, using the side mirrors to measure the distance that separates your car from the others. Unfortunately, your parking skills are not on point today; you cannot park properly. Wait! Your executive control has not abandoned you yet! After a couple of failed parking attempts, your executive control helps you switch your attention, and you start looking through the rearview mirror. Congratulations, mission accomplished! Your vehicle is parked, and you have made it safely to work.

As we can see in the previous example, executive control is involved in many aspects of our lives. Interestingly, our executive control abilities do not stay the same for our entire life; they change while we grow up (and when we grow older!). In addition, different life experiences can work as a "personal trainer" for our executive control system. These experiences may include, for example, playing a musical instrument or doing physical exercise. Considering the topic of this book, we are sure you can guess another example of a life experience that can impact our executive control abilities. Exactly, multilingualism.

For the last decades, scientists have attempted to learn the possible influence of multilingualism on executive control. The initial studies started by comparing how good multilinguals and monolinguals were in tasks that required the exertion of executive control. A critical discovery propelled this research: multilinguals keep their languages active all the time and, as such, need a mechanism (possibly executive control) to effectively ignore the languages that are irrelevant at a given moment. If using more than one language "trains" our executive control, then multilinguals should do better than monolinguals in executive control tasks.

Crucially, executive control does not represent a single ability; it is considered an umbrella term for a variety of skills. Therefore, there is not a single task that can measure executive control as a whole. Instead, researchers have developed different procedures that can be used to assess various aspects of executive control. Although we do not attempt to present a detailed description of all the tasks typically used to measure different executive control aspects, we would like to provide two examples: the flanker task and the switching task.

The goal of the flanker task is to ignore irrelevant aspects of a stimulus presented to us. In the classic version of this task, the stimuli are a group of arrows. These arrows are displayed very fast on a computer screen. All arrows can point in the same direction (for example, →→→→→) or in different directions (for example, ←←→←←). What we have to do is to indicate the direction of the arrow that is located in the middle. As you probably noticed, it is easier to indicate the direction of the central arrow when all arrows point in the same direction compared to when they point in different directions.

A second task used to measure executive control is the switching task. The goal of the switching task is to efficiently change from one task to another or focus on a different aspect of the same task. In a classical switching task, different pictures are displayed on a computer screen, one by one. Our job is to categorize the images following two rules. For example, suppose we see red and green circles and triangles on the screen. In that case, we might have to categorize them according to their color (red versus green) or shape (triangle versus circle). We must always be alert during the task, as the categorization rule changes frequently and randomly. When the categorization rule changes (for example, to categorize by color after shape), the task is more challenging than when the categorization rule stays the same for some time (for example, to categorize by color after color). In addition to the flanker and switching tasks, other frequently used tasks are the Stroop task, the Simon task, the anti-saccade task, and the stop-signal task. If you are curious, you can find detailed descriptions of these tasks online (and you might want to try some of them yourself!)

Now that we are familiar with some of the tasks typically used to measure a few aspects of executive control, let's go back to our topic: multilingualism. *Do monolinguals and multilinguals differ in their executive control abilities?* Research has shown that, in general, multilinguals tend to perform better than monolinguals in tasks such as the flanker task or the switching task.[20] We can find an example of this difference in a study by Prior and MacWhinney (2010). In their experiment, a group of monolinguals and a group of bilinguals completed a switching task similar to the one described above. They found that bilinguals could switch between the categorization rules faster than monolinguals. In a different study, Costa, and collaborators (2008), used a variation of the flanker task. Among other things, they found that bilinguals were overall faster than monolinguals and had fewer difficulties in processing the arrows when they pointed in different directions (←←→←←), which is typically more challenging.

In addition to differences in task performance, some studies have also reported changes in the brain structure of multilinguals and monolinguals, as well as in the way their brain works.[21] Notably, the influence of multilingualism on executive control has also been found in children[22] and even in small infants.[23]

So far, the studies described above suggest that multilinguals and monolinguals differ in their executive control abilities. However, the research on this topic is controversial. The differences between multilinguals and monolinguals are not always observed[24] or are reported only in particular executive control abilities, such as task switching.[25]

The fact that not all studies find differences between multilinguals and monolinguals should not be taken as a surprise, as there is considerable heterogeneity among both multilinguals and monolinguals. Even defining the meaning of *monolingual* and *multilingual* is difficult because the linguistic experiences that monolinguals and multilinguals have may differ vastly. Let's do a short activity: try to picture two people from your environment that know only one language and are, in theory, monolingual. Their

---

[20] for a review, see Bialystok, 2017.
[21] you can find reviews on this topic in Bialystok, 2017; Bialystok et al., 2012.
[22] for a review, see Giovannoli et al., 2020.
[23] Kovács & Mehler, 2009.
[24] for a meta-analysis, see Lehtonen et al., 2018.
[25] Prior & MacWhinney, 2010.

lives are probably very different, as well as their experiences with foreign languages. For example, one might have learned a foreign language at school, whereas the other might not; one might have hobbies that involve foreign languages (for example, listening to music in a foreign language), whereas the other prefers non-linguistic activities such as painting or knitting. As you can see, they are both "monolinguals", but their experiences are not the same.

In addition, finding monolinguals with *zero* experience with foreign languages is becoming harder and harder, as language learning is part of the educational curriculum (how many people do you know that have *not* studied more than one language at school?). We are also exposed to multiple languages daily, for example, due to access to foreign-language media on different streaming platforms. Evidence of the presence of multiple languages in theoretically monolingual societies can be found in a recent study where we analyzed the linguistic experiences of a large group of monolinguals from the United Kingdom.[26] We found that more than 80% of individuals from the United Kingdom who identified as monolinguals had learned other languages at some point in their lives, and more than half of those who had learned other languages reported using them. The idea of comparing monolinguals and multilinguals rests on the assumption that monolinguals have no experience with other languages. Thus, the fact that multiple languages are often present in the lives of monolinguals makes the comparison harder. There is also growing evidence suggesting that even relatively short and limited exposure to a new language rewires our brain, even if we are monolingual.[27]

In the same way that two monolinguals are not identical in terms of their language experiences, multilingual people also differ vastly. For example, some multilinguals might use only one language despite knowing other languages; other multilingual people might use one of their languages sporadically with friends, and yet others might use all their languages constantly. If, as we mentioned at the beginning of the chapter, different life experiences affect executive

---

[26] Castro, Wodniecka et al., 2022.
[27] Bice & Kroll, 2019.

control, then the different linguistic experiences of monolinguals and multilinguals might influence executive control to various degrees. That is why, instead of assuming that all monolinguals and multilinguals will have the same linguistic experiences, researchers have started to explore which specific multilingual experiences may serve as training for executive control.

One of the experiences that have caught scientists' attention is language switching. Language switching is the act of changing the languages we use depending on the situation or the interlocutor (for example, using English with our parents and Spanish with our friends)[28]. The assumption would be that more frequent language switching would increase the demands on our executive control system, thus providing a more robust "training." One of the first studies analyzing the influence of language switching on executive control was conducted by Prior and Gollan (2011). They compared a group of monolinguals and two groups of bilinguals engaged in a switching task that required categorizing geometric forms by color or shape. One crucial difference between the two groups of bilinguals was the degree of language switching, that is, how frequently they switched between the languages they knew. The authors of the study found that the bilinguals who switched languages more often were better at switching between the color and the shape categorization rules, compared to the monolinguals and the other group of bilinguals who switched languages less often. In addition to language switching, aspects such as more frequent use of different languages, higher language proficiency in another language, or acquiring languages at a younger age have also been linked to enhanced executive control.

Nonetheless, similarly to the research comparing multilinguals and monolinguals, some studies found no support for the influence of multilinguals' language experiences on some aspects of executive

---

[28] You can find more information on language switching and mixing in Chapter 1 written by Michal Korenar, Jeanine Treffers-Daller & Christos Pliatsikas.

control.[29] So, *is multilingualism "better" for our mental abilities or not?* The answer to this question is complex. The available evidence suggests that multilingualism indeed trains our executive control. Still, more research needs to be done to understand how multilinguals and monolinguals differ in their executive control abilities and how the different experiences of multilingualism (for example, switching or not between languages) may influence the various facets of executive control.

To sum up, several studies have shown that multilingualism impacts executive control. However, multilingualism is a heterogeneous phenomenon. Thus, researchers must explore which aspects of multilingual experience are more closely related to differences in executive control abilities. Significantly, the benefits of multilingualism on executive control are not restricted to lifelong multilingual experiences (that is, they are not limited to multilinguals who have known more than one language since childhood), as some studies have found that even short language training can have positive effects.

The benefits of multilingualism for the elderly

As we mentioned before, our executive control abilities change with time. We develop them during childhood and adolescence, and they decline rapidly as we age. If multilingualism has a positive effect on our executive control during adulthood, *can multilingualism also have benefits for the mental abilities of the elderly? Should our grandparents enroll in a foreign language course to preserve their mental abilities?*

The results from several studies show that the symptoms of dementia appear later in multilingual older adults compared to monolinguals of the same age.[30] For example, Craik and collaborators (2010) compared a group of monolinguals and a group of multilinguals diagnosed with Alzheimer's disease. They

---

[29] for example, Kałamała et al., 2020.
[30] for a review on this topic, see Bialystok et al., 2007, 2012; for a meta-analysis, see Anderson et al., 2020.

found that the multilingual patients were diagnosed later than the monolingual ones and had a later onset of symptoms.

The difference between the physical status of our brain and the mental abilities that are preserved is called "cognitive reserve." Let's imagine two people: Peter and John. Both have been diagnosed with Alzheimer's disease and have the same degree of brain damage (that is, the physical status of their brain is identical). However, Peter's mental abilities are still preserved, whereas John is experiencing many difficulties. In this example, Peter's cognitive reserve is helping him to maintain his mental abilities (including executive control) for a more extended period. The results from the studies with older multilingual patients show that multilingualism can be a form of cognitive reserve, keeping our brains exercised and healthy for longer. In light of these findings, language training in older adults has started to be considered as a potential measure to delay the onset of dementia. To sum up, research shows that the knowledge and use of more than one language benefits our mental abilities, regardless of age. Thus, it is never late to start learning a new language!

Multilingualism and the perception of others

In the previous section, we argued that multilingualism could promote the development and maintenance of different mental abilities, such as executive control. *Does multilingualism also influence how we process our environment?* Multilingualism has also been associated with differences in how we process information about other people, including how we categorize others. Categorization is the mental operation by which we classify objects and events (for instance, we categorize a squirrel as an animal and a strawberry as a fruit). Categorization helps us understand the complexity of our world. One type of categorization, social categorization, allows us to classify people, for example, based on their age, ethnicity, or gender.

Researchers studying multilingualism have also attempted to understand whether being multilingual influences how we categorize others. Although there are not many studies exploring this possibility, Marzecová and collaborators (2013) analyzed the differences between bilinguals and monolinguals in a switching task where it was necessary to categorize faces of people by their sex (male vs. female) or by their age (old vs. young). They found that, in general, bilinguals performed the task better than monolinguals.

Importantly, despite helping us process complex environments, social categorization can also result in the development and expression of social biases, such as stereotypes and prejudice. Stereotypes refer to beliefs that we have about members of other groups, and prejudice refers to the evaluations (predominantly negative) that we make about other groups. Social biases can have negative consequences and lead to discriminatory behaviors. At the same time, research shows that individuals with enhanced executive functions are less likely to express social biases.[31] Considering the existing link between multilingualism and executive control, recent studies have explored the possibility of multilingualism being associated with fewer social biases. In a recent study from 2020, Singh and collaborators found that bilingual children expressed less race bias than monolingual children. In 2022, we found a similar pattern in adults.[32] We observed that multilingual adults expressed fewer social biases. More importantly, executive control seemed to be the underlying mechanism that connected multilingualism with these reduced social biases.

In addition to social categorization and social biases, another group of studies have analyzed whether multilinguals differ from monolinguals in how they make judgements about others. These studies explored the development of perspective-taking abilities and Theory of Mind in multilingual and monolingual children. Perspective taking is the ability to understand a situation from the point of view of another person, and Theory of Mind is the ability to comprehend that our knowledge, thoughts, feelings, or intentions might differ from those of other people.

---

[31] for example, Amodio et al., 2008.
[32] Castro, Bukowski et al., 2022.

The "Three Mountains Task" is the classic task to measure perspective-taking. In this task, a child is presented with a model of three mountains with different sizes and characteristics. An observer (a doll) is placed at various locations around the mountains. From a list of pictures, the child must select the ones that represent the doll's point of view with respect to the mountains. Using a variation of this task, Greenberg and collaborators (2013) found that bilingual children were better at determining the doll's perspective compared to monolinguals, especially when the doll was placed at the most challenging locations.

The "Sally-Anne task" is typically used to evaluate Theory of Mind development. In this task, children are presented with a story about two dolls, Sally and Anne. Sally has a basket and Anne has a box. Sally puts a marble in her basket and leaves the room for a walk. While Sally is away, Anne takes Sally's marble and hides it in her box. Then, Sally enters the room again. After this representation, children are asked to indicate where Sally will look for her marble. Children who have developed their Theory of Mind will answer that Sally will look for the marble in her basket, as this answer would align with Sally's knowledge. Overall, research has found that multilingual children perform better in Theory of Mind tasks such as the "Sally-Anne task" compared to monolingual children[33]. Studies on Theory of Mind are not restricted to children, and similar results have been found in adults, with multilinguals again outperforming monolinguals.[34] The linguistic experiences of multilinguals are also relevant when it comes to the Theory of Mind. In another recent study, Navarro and collaborators (2022) found that regularly using a second language, switching between languages, and having experienced multiple languages during childhood were all positively related to Theory of Mind abilities in adults.

---

[33] for a meta-analysis, see Schroeder, 2018.
[34] for example, Navarro & Conway, 2021.

Conclusion

In this chapter, we provided evidence that the consequences of multilingualism go beyond language competence itself, outlining some of the effects of multilingualism on our mental abilities. We have shown how multilingualism influences the development of executive control abilities and the onset of symptoms of age-related disorders, such as Alzheimer's disease. We also learned that being multilingual promotes a more flexible categorization of people into groups, can reduce social biases, and helps develop our perspective-taking and Theory of Mind abilities. Although these are not the only lines of research evaluating the impact of multilingualism in non-linguistic aspects of our lives, they represent some examples of the role that multilingualism can have in our mental development and how we perceive our world.

Chapter 3. Language and music: Are they so different? Preliminary insight from research on multilingualism

*Dávid György, Doug Saddy,
Antonella Sorace, and Julie Franck*

A popular belief holds that music and language are two completely separate faculties of the human brain, music being processed only by the right 'artsy' half of the brain and language only by the left 'logicky' half. Are the two systems really separate? Science tells us that despite their differences, language and music are highly interconnected, and rhythmic stimulation or training can even influence language performance.

Speaking languages and playing or just appreciating music are two very important qualities that make us humans a bit different from other animals. For a long time, psychologists and brain researchers believed that music and language were represented in two separate modules of the human brain. According to this so-called 'modular' view, music is dealt with in the right half of the brain (which we refer to as right *hemisphere*), while language is processed in the left hemisphere. While it is still a possible and relatively popular view that music and language are processed by different brain systems, the birth of modern neuroimaging techniques such as Functional Magnetic Resonance Imaging (fMRI, please refer to Chapter 5 by Pereira Soares et al. for a detailed discussion)[35] in the 20th century

---

[35] In an fMRI machine, a very powerful magnet is used to measure the oxygen level in the blood. This very expensive and complicated method is based on a very simple principle. If a lot of neurons (nerve cells) are working hard in a given brain region, they will need more oxygen to do their job than

has helped demonstrate that the question is a bit more complex than a simple right hemisphere—left hemisphere distinction. In short, it appears that language mostly activates the left and music mostly activates the right half of the brain, but some regions of the right hemisphere are also active in some language tasks and vice-versa for music.

Nevertheless, music and language still seem easy to imagine as two relatively different human functions. On the one hand, language can be used to convey incredibly precise meaning through the use of words, phrases (groups of words) and sentences. Even though music can communicate ideas or emotions, we must admit that it is a far cry from the complex concepts that can be expressed through language. On the other hand, music can be extremely pleasurable (or quite the opposite depending on your taste) to listen to. Individual sounds can be joined together through *harmony*, and very often musical rhythm is highly *periodic*, as sounds or groups of sounds appear and reappear at regular time intervals. Most documented languages cannot come anywhere close to regular and pleasurable structures such as these.[36] Besides these properties, some patient studies also provide important arguments for a language-music distinction: there have been a few documented cases of a music

---

when they are not doing any particular work. Therefore, if a particular region is involved in, say, grammar, neurons in that region of the brain will need more oxygen when a participant in an experiment has to decide if a sentence is grammatically correct than when the participant is at rest or is thinking about how beautiful that strong magnet is. As fMRI measures the amount of oxygen that neurons in a particular brain region need to sustain their activation rather than measuring the work of neurons themselves, it is an *indirect* measure of brain activation. This makes it a bit slower than other methods (low temporal resolution), but it is very precise in telling us exactly what regions are active (high spatial resolution).

[36] As long as we are talking about everyday language use. Poetry, rap, and several other genres can produce incredible rhythmicity using language.

patients[37] with no language problems and aphasic patients[38] who can perform musical tasks perfectly well. In scientific terms, this is called a double dissociation: it is evidence that either one of these systems can function more or less seamlessly if the other one is damaged or impaired. Therefore, neither system seems *necessary* for the other to keep working properly. Based on these arguments, we can say with confidence that music and language are not the same thing. However, the fact that neither system is necessary for the other to function properly does not rule out the possibility that the two systems *overlap*, sharing similarities that might be dealt with by similar systems or resources.[39] For example, it is plausible that systems like memory or attention are shared between language and music. But it may be more than that.

It is perhaps not so intuitive to say that music and language might actually be similar. But when you stop to think about it, the similarities become clear. Music and language are both sound signals that develop in time from a beginning to an end.[40] When you look a bit closer, you notice that both are built up of several different layers and can be described in tree-like structures in which smaller units combine into larger groups of units that go together.[41,42] Indeed, in music, a relatively regular rhythm allows us to extract a beat, which is the frequency you often tap to while you listen to music. This frequency is not necessarily there in the actual sound signal of the track. Then, we go even further up the tree and create a metrical structure by grouping beats together (such as 1-2-3-4 in a march as illustrated in **Figure 1b**). In language, we combine sounds into words, words into groups of words, then groups of words into sentences as illustrated in **Figure 1a**.

---

[37] Patients who are unable to recognize or reproduce musical tones, either from birth or as a result of brain damage

[38] Patients with a language disorder affecting expression or comprehension, caused by damage in a specific area of the brain.

[39] Patel, 2008.
[40] Kotz, Ravignani, Fitch, 2018.
[41] Fitch & Martins, 2014.
[42] Fiveash, Bedoin, Gordon, Tillmann, 2021.

Crucially, language and music both contain a certain level of rhythmicity. As we mentioned above, musical rhythm is far more regular than everyday language when it comes to rhythmic periodicity. Nevertheless, we have all probably heard at least some examples of rhythm in language. In some languages, such as English or Dutch, the amount of time that passes between strong syllables (/TA/ and /DRI/ in TAxi DRIver) is relatively stable.

Trees in language	Trees in musical rhythm

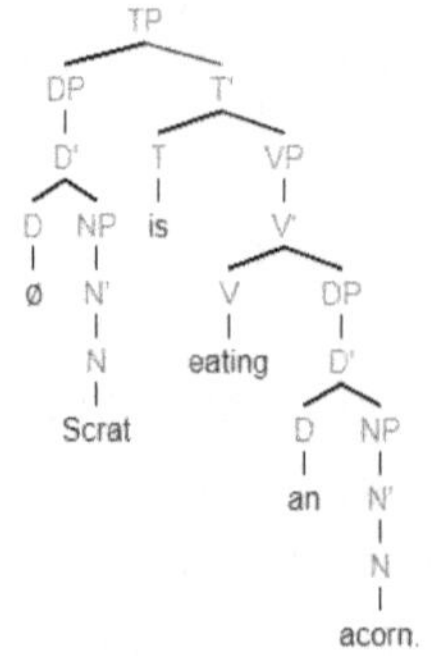

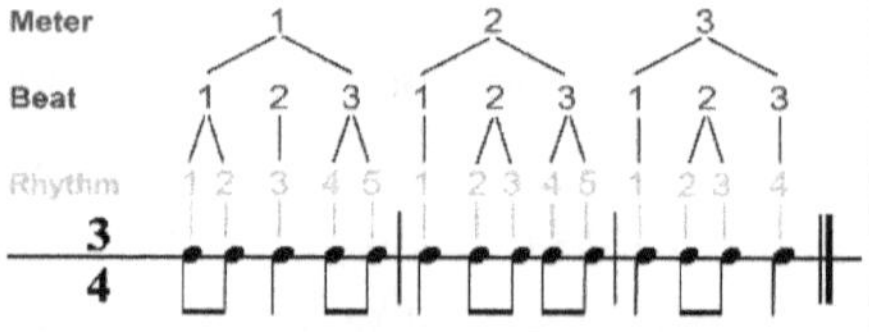

Figure 1a: Hierarchical representation of the sentence 'Scrat is eating an acorn.' In a syntactic tree, words combine into phrases (groups of words), which combine into clauses, which combine into sentences.

Figure 1b: Hierarchical representation of musical metrical structure. While listening to music, the brain extracts a beat (which we can also clap to) based on the distribution of sounds in time. These beats then combine to make up larger groups in a meter (for example, 1-2-3 in a waltz, figure adapted from Heard & Lee, 2020).

In French or Spanish, the duration of each syllable seems to be relatively comparable in everyday speech. In Japanese, the duration of each mora[43] is quite similar. What is more, it seems that the

---

[43] Much like a syllable for French and Spanish, a mora is a basic timing unit of some languages like Japanese.

alternation of phonemes[44] is semi-regular, albeit, again, nowhere near as periodic as what we could expect in music. Given all of these similarities (and a few others that would need more detail than we have in this chapter), some researchers believe that while systems responsible for doing music and language in the brain are not the same per se, they do rely on similar resources.[45,46,47,48] If both speech and music require processing of a signal that unfolds over time and that has similar structural regularities, why would the brain make use of two completely different systems rather than using the same resources differently, fine-tuned for either music or language?

In the paragraphs that follow, we skim through a series of scientific observations showing links between musical rhythm, language, and multilingualism. We have chosen rhythm because the work on musical rhythm is the closest to our own research and this is what we are most familiar with. We should stress that rhythm is not the only commonality between music and language.[49]

Links between musical rhythm and language

Numerous relationships have been found between musical abilities and language performance, supporting some level of overlap between music and language in the brain. Expert musicians are often better than non-musicians at several language tasks. In the domain of rhythm processing, two recent studies have found that comprehending sentences in noisy environments is related to rhythmic skills, but not related to other aspects of musical abilities, like melody. Additionally, it was shown that percussionists (who excel at rhythm) outdo both vocalists (who excel at melody) and non-musicians when it comes to understanding sentences in a noisy

---

[44] The smallest sounds in language that we can distinguish such as the consonants /t/ or /k/ in the word 'taxi.'
[45] Patel, 2008.
[46] Kotz, Ravignani, Fitch, 2018.
[47] Fitch & Martins, 2014.
[48] Fiveash, Bedoin, Gordon, Tillmann, 2021.
[49] For a more detailed discussion on music, language, and the brain, you can refer to *Music, Language and the Brain* by Aniruddh D. Patel.

environment.⁵⁰,⁵¹ At the brain level, a recent systematic review of a large number of articles found that a lot of grammar and musical rhythm tasks activated a number of similar brain regions, notably in left frontal and in motor areas, suggesting an overlap in brain regions activated by the two domains.⁵²

A few experiments have also found important rhythm-language links during language development. In one such study, 3-4-year-old children were asked to use their fingers to tap to a musical rhythm. Children who were better able to synchronize their tapping to the rhythm they heard also did better on several tasks that are commonly used to predict reading abilities in preschool children.⁵³ On the grammar front, two recent studies have found links between musical rhythmic abilities and language performance.

Both of these used a musical rhythm discrimination task in which a child hears two rhythms and has to decide whether they are the same or different. In one study,⁵⁴ children and adolescents between 7 and 17 years old had to answer 'Who-did-what-to-whom?' kind of questions on sentences like 'Boys that help girls are nice' and 'Boys that girls help are nice'. Children who did better in the rhythm discrimination task also scored higher in the comprehension questions when age, gender, musical training, the mother's level of education and working memory were controlled.⁵⁵

---

[50] Slater & Kraus. 2016.
[51] Yates, Moore, Amitay, Barry, 2019.
[52] Heard & Lee, 2020.
[53] Woodruff Carr, White-Schwoch, Tierney, Strait, Kraus, 2014.
[54] Lee, Ahn, Holt, Schellenberg, 2020.
[55] Controlling for a variable is a procedure that is used to make sure that the relationship we observe between two variables cannot be explained by a variable other than the ones we are trying to manipulate. Therefore, it indirectly increases the chances of our explanation being correct. For instance, if we hypothesized that a certain species of housecat likes wet food

In another experiment,[56] researchers used an elicited morphosyntax production task: a fancy term to say that the experimenter shows children an image and asks them a question that is designed to make the child produce a certain grammatical structure (say, the irregular past tense of a verb like 'went'). Interestingly, children with better rhythm discrimination ability also showed better production of the grammatical structures they were expected to produce.[57]

As far as atypical populations are concerned, it appears that children with developmental dyslexia and developmental language disorder are also weaker in several rhythmic tasks, pointing towards a possible link between their rhythm and language difficulties. Please refer to Chapter 14 by Taha and colleagues for a detailed discussion on developmental language disorder.

Musical rhythm can influence language performance

Another line of research took a different approach towards exploring the rhythm-language link. Some experiments investigated whether listening to musical rhythms just before performing a language task can actually influence how well people perform on the language task.

---

better than dry food, we would predict that they will eat wet rather than dry food if given the choice. Therefore, we could test this hypothesis by giving them equal portions of both kinds of food in similar containers. However, if dry food is served in boring grey bowls while wet food is served in bowls that have stickers of rainbows and unicorns on them, we may have a problem. If we observe that our cats eat more wet food than dry food, that might potentially be because they like rainbows and unicorns, not because of the food. Therefore, to make sure that the difference we find is due to the food and the food only, it is best to serve wet and dry food in the same kind of bowl, thus controlling for the variable 'container'.

[56] Gordon, Shivers, Wieland, Kotz, Yoder, Devin Mcauley, 2015.
[57] Even if non-verbal IQ, socioeconomic status, and musical education were controlled.

One line of studies used a *rhythmic priming* paradigm that manipulates the structural regularity of the musical rhythmic prime independently of the rhythmicity of the language task, while other studies used a *rhythmic cueing* paradigm which manipulates the mapping between musical rhythm and speech rhythm.

Rhythmic priming experiments[58,59,60,61] have found that participants can more accurately decide whether or not a sentence they hear is grammatically correct after listening to rhythmically regular music (regular prime) compared to rhythmically irregular music (irregular prime), noise or silence. Our own data show a very short-term version of this effect in typical adults hearing sentences in their first language. To give a rough idea of what researchers mean by regular and irregular, we need to remember that metrical structure is a tree-like structure that we can 'hear', but that is not necessarily in the actual sound signal. The authors define a regular prime as one that is composed to make it very easy to 'hear' a metrical structure, while an irregular prime makes it more difficult to 'hear' a metrical structure. One could say that a regular prime is more likely to make you want to clap your hands or tap your feet to the rhythm. Remarkably, after hearing a regular rhythm, people are better at judging the grammaticality of a sentence when compared to people who have been exposed to a preceding irregular rhythm, noise, or silence. This has been shown for speakers of French, English, and Hungarian. How could this be explained? Some studies have shown that if listeners can build the metrical structure in their head, their own attentional rhythms will oscillate at frequencies that are relevant to the music. To put it simply, attention is not constant over time.[62] When we listen to something, sometimes our attention is highly concentrated on a particular event, and other times it is not. Our attention oscillates between attentional peaks (where it is maximal) and lower attentional states. If the music you listen to contains a pattern of sounds that periodically returns every second, some of our

---

[58] Bedoin, Brisseau, Molinier, Roch, Tillmann, 2016.
[59] Chern, Tillmann, Vaughan, Gordon, 2018.
[60] Canette, Bedoin, Lalitte, Bigand, Tillmann, Bedoin et al. 2020.
[61] Ladányi, Lukács, Gervain, 2021.
[62] Large & Jones, 1999.

internal attentional rhythms will pick up on this periodicity and oscillate themselves such that the attentional oscillation is at its peak exactly when the periodic pattern returns. Music often contains multiple different regular oscillations that multiple different attentional rhythms can entrain to.[63] Once our attentional rhythms are in sync with the music, we can better predict when the next beat is supposed to come. Researchers believe that similar processes are needed to process and understand a sentence: our brain rhythms need to 'entrain' to the rhythmicity of the sentence, we build a structure of how we think the sentence is built up, and we constantly try to predict what the next word is based on grammar (after an article like 'the', we expect to hear a noun such as 'cat', but not a verb like 'decorate') and meaning (while grammatically correct, 'I like my coffee with socks' is not a sentence we would expect to hear). All of these processes involved in predicting what will come next based on the structure of the previous signal are thought to be active while we listen to music or language. A regular prime helps us build a structure and predict what comes next rhythmically and it would somehow also influence how we process language immediately after listening to it. If this explanation seems a bit vague to you, you are probably doing something right. The truth is, we still do not fully understand precisely how the rhythmic priming effect works. That being said, it seems to be clear that this is a short-term effect that is more or less specific to language: researchers have tested a few non-linguistic tasks, and so far, none of them seems to show improved performance after hearing a regular rhythm.

Rhythmic cueing studies[64,65] have asked whether the similarity or difference between musical and speech rhythms can influence speech processing. In these experiments, participants hear a short series of strong and weak beats (something like TAM-tam-TAM-tam, which

---

[63] Entrainment is the process by which two or more oscillators become synchronized in frequency, phase, or both. As such, it does not necessarily mean complete synchronization between two rhythms. We use the word synchronization in the text as it is easier to grasp.
[64] Cason, Hidalgo, Isoard, Roman, Schön, 2015.
[65] Cason, Astésano, Schön, 2015.

would be described as STRONG-weak-STRONG-weak). Then, they hear a few words or a short sentence which contains stressed (strong) and unstressed (weak) syllables that either match the pattern they heard (TA-xi-DRI-ver would be considered STRONG-weak-STRONG-weak) or mismatch it (YUM-my de-SSERT would be considered STRONG-weak-weak-STRONG). The task participants are asked to do in these studies is called 'phoneme detection'. A phoneme is the smallest sound unit our brain is able to distinguish in speech (e.g., the vowel /i/ or the consonant /t/ in the word taxi). In a phoneme detection task, participants are asked to press a response button as soon as they hear a given target phoneme. Interestingly, when the strong-weak pattern of the musical cue matches the syllabic rhythm of the target sentence or word, the target phoneme is usually identified faster than when there is a mismatch between the two. For instance, the vowel /ə/ will be detected faster if Taxi DRIver is preceded by the musical cue TAM-tam-TAM-tam than if it is preceded by tam-TAM-tam-TAM. The idea here is perhaps a bit more straightforward than in priming studies: once our brain rhythms sync up to a given rhythmic pattern like they do whenever we listen to music, processing a similar rhythmic pattern is easier than processing a different pattern using syllables instead of beats.

And what if we speak more than one language?

The studies presented so far explore the rhythm-language connection from two angles. Some experiments provide evidence that there is some kind of relationship between the two domains, but do not make claims as to the direction of the effect (are we good at language because we are good at rhythm or are we good at rhythm because we are good at language?). Rhythmic priming and cueing studies provide evidence for rhythm to language transfer effects: these experiments show that rhythmic stimulation or training can influence language performance. However, to our knowledge, the opposite direction is under-researched: only one published study has investigated whether exposure to multiple languages can lead to better musical rhythmic skills.[66] In this experiment, monolingual German speakers and

---

[66] Roncaglia-Denissen, Kotz, Dolscheid, Planck. 2013.

Turkish learners of German had to decide whether two musical rhythmic patterns are the same or different. Interestingly, the bilingual group showed significantly better rhythm discrimination accuracy than the monolingual group when the authors controlled for short-term memory, working memory, melodic abilities and how often participants listened to music. The researchers argue that exposure to languages of different rhythmic features (such as German and Turkish) might actually hone participants' sensitivity to rhythm in domains other than language.

Some preliminary results from our own work also point towards a link between multilingualism and musical rhythmic skills. Unlike the study above (and most conventional studies in multilingualism), we chose not to recruit two pre-determined groups of monolingual and multilingual participants, but rather used self-reported questionnaires to characterize the nature of our participants' profiles.[67] We are currently working on one or more indices that would help us precisely characterize our participants' multilingual profiles. The reason for this was two-fold. On the one hand, many multilingualism researchers suggest that as the multilingual experience differs greatly from person to person, we should look at multilingualism as a spectrum rather than just comparing participants who speak one language with those who know more than one. On the other hand, we are running these experiments in Geneva, where (very much like in most places around the world) it is extremely hard to find people who speak only one language. In our data, the rhythm task that shows a link with multilingualism was a metronome beat anticipation task called the Warning Imperative.[68] In this task, participants hear a metronome built up of two different tones: a standard (frequent) and a deviant (less frequent) tone. The deviant tones always come in pairs, such that an example stimulus would sound something like S-S-S-S-D-**D**-S-S-S-S-S-S-S-S-D-**D**-S-S-D-**D**-S-S-S.[69] Participants have to press a response button for the

---

[67] Marian, Blumenfeld, Kaushanskaya. (2007).
[68] Pagliarini, Scocchia, Granocchioa, Sarti, Stucchi, Guasti, 2020.
[69] Ds in bold represent an imperative beat, where the participant is expected to press a response button.

second and only the second deviant tone in each pair. The idea behind the task is deceptively simple: if the participant has managed to sync up to the periodicity of the metronome, then upon hearing the first (warning) deviant tone, they should be able to anticipate exactly when the second (imperative) tone comes (as they know that deviant tones always come in pairs, and they have learned how much time passes between any two metronome beats). Therefore, they should be able to press the button exactly on time or perhaps even slightly before the arrival of the second deviant if they manage to anticipate it, but definitely faster than a simple motor reaction with no anticipation would allow (which would be roughly 200ms). In short, the faster the participant presses the response button, the better their performance in this task. In our sample of roughly 90 adults, we found that people who speak more languages above a certain self-reported oral proficiency level tend to respond faster (anticipate more) than those who speak fewer languages or only one. Please note that this is very much work in progress, and the number of languages spoken is not the only potential difference between our participants. Nevertheless, taken together with the study above, our results motivate further targeted research on rhythmic skills in multilingual populations.

Clinical and educational applications of the music-language link: careful!

The convincing number of links between music, language, and other functions of the human mind has motivated several people to use music to improve language, relieve stress or increase brain functions. Sometimes, these ideas attract the right kinds of people: clinicians, teachers and researchers who realize that any educational, diagnostic, or therapeutic tool needs to be tested rigorously. Other times, they attract business people who realize how easy it is to sell the idea of learning or healing through music because it just sounds super cool and futuristic. We have to stress that as of writing this chapter, the observations we have discussed are currently under research and do not support the use of any commercially available educational, diagnostic, or therapeutic tool. In general, we would urge our readers to take caution and do their homework before believing what sounds too good to be true. Importantly, we do not mean to say that music is completely worthless as a diagnostic or therapeutic tool. There are already some well-documented methods based on solid evidence (such as Melodic Intonation Therapy for treating aphasia) and researchers are actively investigating whether the numerous scientific observations that we have seen in this chapter can be used for diagnostic or therapeutic purposes. However, there are also a number of very well marketed tools that are selling for sometimes very high prices with non-existent or extremely lackluster evidence backing them. Please always keep in mind that there is high variability in the human species. You should always look for evidence-based practices that have replicable results in various samples of participants, and that are supported by a series of studies and clinical trials. This way, you reduce your chances of running into negative (side-)effects caused by a poorly tested tool or spending your money on empty promises with no scientific backing.

Conclusion

In this chapter, we have aimed to present evidence on a very hot topic in current scientific research: in the human brain and mind, are music and language completely independent? Are they part of the same system or different systems using similar brain networks? The rather dated myth that music uses only the right half and language only the left half of the brain really seems to be just a myth. Numerous behavioral and brain-level studies show that the two systems are connected, and that rhythmic stimulation or training can influence language performance, with all results speaking for some level of rhythm-language link. However, exactly how the two systems are connected is still up for debate.

Part 2:
Myths on language learning and the brain

Chapter 4. Multilinguals reveal the brain's capacity for lifelong transformation

*Jia'en Yee, Ngee Thai Yap,
and Christos Pliatsikas*

Think the human brain stops transforming in adulthood? You might want to think again! Contrary to popular belief, the human brain continues to change throughout our lifetime in response to the various experiences that we acquire. One such experience is the use of more than one language—an activity many of us already engage in in our daily lives. Join us in this chapter as we debunk the misconception of a static adult brain and delve into the evidence of multilingualism-induced neuroplasticity.

A commonly held misconception is that the human brain is an organ that does not change once it reaches adulthood. This myth is even ingrained in a saying many of us have heard once too many: "you cannot teach an old dog new tricks." Unsurprisingly, even scientists had once thought that the adult brain becomes hard-wired and is unable to grow new neurons upon reaching maturity.[70] Sure, it is more challenging to change an established set of behaviors, break a bad habit, transform a mindset, or learn a new skill. After all, the minds of infants and typically developing children have immense potential for change and are far more malleable than the average adults. However, more recent studies have shown that modifications to the brain are not restricted to childhood and adolescence. Instead, the mature brain (i.e., post-adolescent ages; beyond 19 years of age) continues to grow new neurons,[71] and adapts by creating and pruning connections in response to new demands in our day-to-day

---

[70] Bonfanti, 2016.
[71] Boldrini et al., 2018.

experiences.[72] In other words, the brain exhibits plasticity, capable of changes in terms of activity, shape, and volume throughout our lifetimes.

Immersive experiences such as learning to read, road navigation, meditation, exercise, learning a musical instrument, and video-gaming have all been found to rewire the brain due to their reliance on specific cognitive resources.[73] The almost universal phenomenon of using more than one language (i.e., multilingualism) is a cognitively demanding experience that similarly influences changes in the human brain—both in function and in structure. Even mixing two languages in a single conversation or sentence can prompt variation in brain activity (read Chapter 1 for a discussion on code-switching). Multilingualism is therefore a good test case for neuroplasticity in the adult brain. While changes in brain function can be found in Chapter 5, this chapter will review some of the structural changes that occur in the mature brain through the use of more than one language, with the changes reflecting the intensity and frequency of language use.

Relevant brain regions and ways to study structural changes

Before we explore the structural changes that occur through multilingualism in adults, it is important to first have a broad understanding of what brain structure refers to as well as the methods that are used to study the changes occurring in them. The brain is largely divided into two kinds of tissue—grey matter and white matter. Grey matter is the site of information processing, while white matter is the site of information transmission. At a more granular level, the brain is made up of roughly 86 billion brain cells (i.e., neurons) with extensive interconnections, and they transmit information through electrical impulses and chemical signals. The "head" of the neuron consists of many branch-like structures called dendrites which is where information from other neurons is received (see Figure 1).

---

[72] Pliatsikas, 2020; Lövdén et al., 2013.
[73] Lövdén et al., 2013.

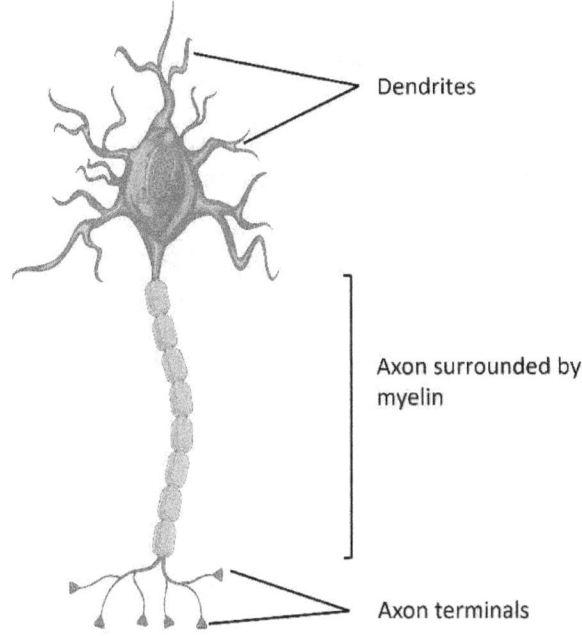

Figure 1. Figure modified to be desaturated in color and to include text, markings (lines), and annotation after adaptation of "Neuron" from Servier Medical Art by Servier, licensed under a Creative Commons Attribution 3.0 Unported License.

The information received at the dendrites travels down the axon or "tail" of the neuron towards another cluster of branch-like structures known as the axon terminals. The axon terminals are then responsible for transmitting the information to the next neuron. When billions of neurons are packed densely together, the two portions of the neuron that receive and transmit information make up the grey matter of the brain, while the axons make up the white matter. The axon is wrapped with a layer of fatty insulation called myelin which gives it its white color and enables the efficient transmission of electrical impulses along neurons.

Grey matter is primarily found across the surface of the brain, known as the cortex, whereas there are some grey matter regions set deep in the brain, referred to as subcortical regions. Like a mega factory where different departments have specific responsibilities to ensure the smooth production of various items, different parts of the brain perform unique roles and also cooperate to deliver different functions. Different regions have to communicate with each other, and this is undertaken by white matter tracts, which can be thought of as pathways connecting the different departments. There are different types of white matter tracts—some connect regions *between* the two hemispheres (e.g., corpus callosum), some connect the lobes of the cortex *within* hemispheres (e.g., arcuate fasciculus, inferior fronto-occipital fasciculus (IFOF)), others connect cortical and subcortical regions, while some are short-range connections that link up areas within the same lobe. When the demands for a given function increase, relevant grey matter regions of the brain can adapt in volume and density to better meet these demands—in the same way departments can increase manpower or upgrade employees' skillsets to support output. When certain regions are consistently activated in concert, the integrity of the white matter tracts connecting them can be enhanced to improve the efficiency of information transmission—in the same way additional lanes can be included on the pathway to facilitate traffic flow. In contrast, if damage occurs at white matter tracts, interference in signal transmission between cortical regions can happen, and this is believed to underpin a series of cognitive dysfunctions.

To study changes in grey and white matter structure, structural Magnetic Resonance Imaging (MRI) is typically employed. This technique creates highly detailed three-dimensional images of the brain that can be differentiated into different tissue types. This enables the observation of changes in shape, thickness, volume, integrity, and connectivity across the brain. Figure 2 illustrates a side profile and cross-section of the brain, where the regions in white depict white matter tracts, while the regions in grey represent grey matter. DTI is an MRI technique that allows for the tracking of neurological pathways by examining the flow of water molecules in the brain. Water molecules can move freely unless they encounter obstacles with reduced diffusivity, such as white matter tracts. In that case, their "flow" becomes directional (i.e., along but not across the track), and we can measure those differences in diffusivity. The differences in diffusivity can then be used as measures of white matter integrity, where lower diffusivity generally indicates increased myelination and consequently, more efficient structural connectivity. Now that we have a better understanding of the brain at a biological level, as well as the mechanisms of MRI, we can explore structural changes in the context of multilingualism.

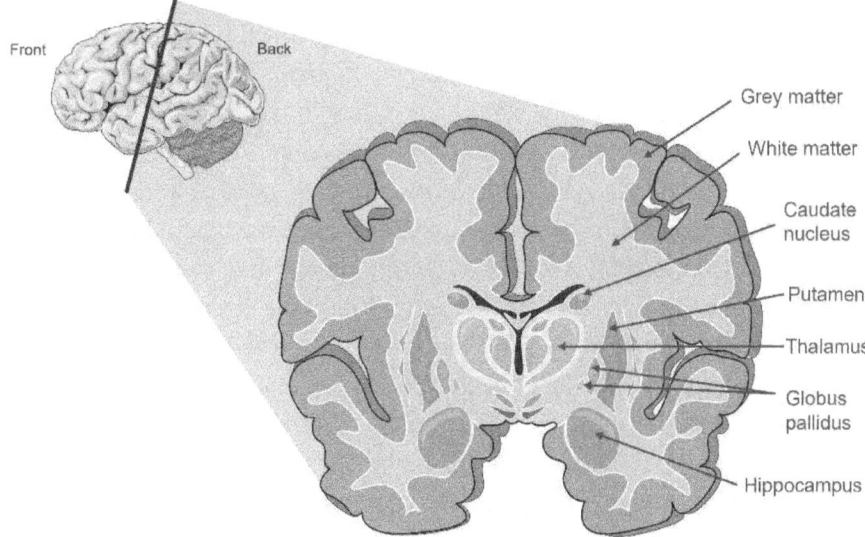

Figure 2. A labelled illustration of a cross-section (coronal plane) of the brain. Figure modified to be desaturated in color and to include text after adaptation of "Brain" from Servier Medical Art by Servier, licensed under a Creative Commons Attribution 3.0 Unported License.

A model developed to explain the plasticity of the brain through language experience is the Dynamic Restructuring Model (DRM)[74] which will be used to guide the review of the available evidence. The DRM is a three-stage model that frames the patterns of adaptations according to the level of language experience—from *initial exposure* (i.e., limited multilingual experiences) to *consolidation* and *peak efficiency* (i.e., capable of high intensity language-switching). Some of the studies that will be reviewed have used cross-sectional designs where populations with different language experiences (i.e., monolinguals, inexperienced bilinguals, immersed bilinguals, multilinguals) are compared with one another, while others have

---

[74] Pliatsikas, 2020.

used longitudinal designs where language learners are compared against themselves over time.

Plasticity through language training

Learning a second language in adulthood is akin to acquiring a complex skill, which exerts new demands on the brain in terms of language processing and cognitive control. When an individual knows more than one language, they have multiple languages activated concurrently at any point in time. This means having multiple linguistic systems to manage; rules to learn and apply, and multiple lexical alternatives to consider. The concurrent activation of two languages creates a state of competition where in choosing to use one language over the other, the multilingual brain has to suppress the unselected language(s). This is an incredible feat that relies on a set of cognitive skills collectively known as executive functions, which include attentional control, monitoring, and conflict resolution,[75] all of which seem to be accomplished unconsciously. The day-to-day experience of switching between languages acts as a form of training that enhances these general cognitive functions. Therefore, to correspond with changes in language experience, a network of regions in the brain that manages these functions adapts, leading to changes in grey and white matter.

Structural adaptations through additional language learning can be investigated by comparing second language learners with themselves over time. Some may have been immersed in multiple languages for decades of their lives, making them highly experienced, while others may have only just begun learning a foreign language. The latter thus consists of individuals who are considered to have the least language experience. At this initial exposure stage of multilingualism, individuals are newly exposed to an additional language system and must scramble to manage their fast-expanding vocabulary and the selection of lexical candidates for identical concepts. Research has revealed an increase in grey matter density in a network of regions which underlie higher-level cognitive abilities such as attention, decision-making and cognitive control (i.e., the

---

[75] Bialystok, 2007.

frontal cortex and anterior regions), as well as areas involved in language-specific functions such as the learning of novel speech sounds, vocabulary and semantics (i.e., temporal and parietal cortices: superior temporal gyrus, inferior parietal lobule).[76] Interestingly, the increase in density of these regions correlates with the proficiency of the language that the individual is trying to acquire.

Apart from cortical regions, subcortical regions such as the caudate nucleus and hippocampus also appeared to increase in volume through learning a second language in adulthood.[77] For example, a group of individuals from the Swedish Armed Forces Interpreter Academy underwent an intensive language training in either Arabic, Russian or Dari and demonstrated expansions in three cortical regions as well as the hippocampus.[78] Notably, the degree of growth in these regions correlated with better performance as well as how much effort these trainees invested in their language learning. On the other hand, the control group which did not go through the language training showed no volumetric differences before and after the same three-month period. In a different study, structural expansions of the cerebellum were also observed, accompanied by greater efficiency in processing second language grammatical rules.[79] The cerebellum is linked to essential areas of the language control network and is pertinent in speech production and comprehension.[80] It underlies the learning and processing of grammar which are functions particularly taxing in the early days of acquiring a new language. Highlighting the responsiveness of the adult brain, these findings thus suggest that as individuals acquire a new language, relevant brain regions grow in volume, which is thought to underlie their growing capacity to meet behavioral changes.

While white matter tract adaptations tend to be absent in populations with limited bilingual experience, intensive training in a new language can still influence white matter structure, particularly

---

[76] Mårtensson et al., 2012; Stein et al., 2012.
[77] Mårtensson et al., 2012; Bellander et al., 2016.
[78] Mårtensson et al., 2012.
[79] Pliatsikas et al., 2014.
[80] Calabria et al., 2018.

in tracts that bridge regions essential for language processing and control.[81] For example, white matter tracts that connect the frontal cortices with the caudate nucleus were shown to decrease in diffusivity, which reflects greater integrity and better communication among language control areas. Previously, changes in brain structure were thought to occur only after weeks or months of language training. However, a remarkable demonstration of neuroplasticity was found amongst young adults undergoing intensive word learning where microstructural grey and white matter changes were identified after less than an hour of training.[82] White matter tracts that exhibited greater diffusivity included the superior longitudinal fasciculus (SLF) which is a key link between the prefrontal cortex and regions underlying language processing functions such as reading and lexical access (i.e., inferior frontal gyrus, middle temporal gyrus, and inferior parietal lobule). Furthermore, in the same study, the diffusivity of the SLF was shown to correlate with the rate of learning new words, indicating that the brain restructures itself with increasing language experience. Interestingly, the structural changes induced by training decreased or disappeared in the months following the end of the training program.[83] This intriguing finding suggests that the brain is not a static entity; rather, it undergoes a streamlining process upon acquisition of a new skill.

Changes in brain structure can also be explored by comparing between populations that differ in their multilingual experiences. Known as cross-sectional studies, this kind of research is typically conducted with monolingual controls who serve as the baseline comparison for bilingual populations. The controls are matched based on factors like age, sex, and education level. Monolinguals serve as suitable controls since they do not experience the control demands of juggling two languages throughout their lives. Consequently, the adaptive changes that result from additional demands in language control, learning and processing are not expected to occur in the monolingual brain. In comparing

---

[81] Hosoda et al., 2013.
[82] Hofstetter et al., 2017.
[83] Hosoda et al., 2013.

monolinguals with bilinguals, many cross-sectional studies have produced overlapping findings with longitudinal studies. They have similarly observed changes in regions relating to language learning and processing, and the cognitive control system. For example, in bilinguals, regions such as the inferior parietal lobule and supramarginal gyrus which are essential for handling vocabulary, integrating semantics across languages, and phonological working memory have been observed to be larger than in their monolingual counterparts.[84] Additionally, regions that play a role in conflict monitoring (anterior cingulate cortex), helming cognitive and language control (caudate nucleus), attention, and decision-making (prefrontal cortices) also appear to be larger in bilinguals than monolinguals. Apart from the modification of structures tightly linked to language processing and control, learning a language with a different writing system (i.e., L1: alphabetic, L2: logographic) have also been found to correlate with changes in a region associated with the processing of visual input (medial occipitotemporal gyrus), particularly of letters.[85] The evidence from this segment thus not only highlights the additional demands involved in learning a new language, but also the agile responses of the adult brain in meeting these demands.

Plasticity through immersive/lifelong multilingualism

What we have read so far establishes the flexibility of the mature brain as it acquires an additional language, but what happens with extended language immersion or greater language experience? It appears that increasing language experience continues to exert plasticity on the mature brain, but the patterns of adaptations are not the same as that of multilinguals with relatively lesser experience. More specifically, as multilinguals become more immersed or experienced in managing more than one language, they could be said to move on to the *consolidation* stage of the DRM. This is a stage characterized by reductions in volumes of several regions that expanded in the *initial exposure* stage, as well as the emergence of subcortical and white matter adaptations. The reduction in volumes

---

[84] Della Rosa et al., 2013.
[85] Tu et al., 2022.

is posited to reflect cortical pruning that occurs upon successful acquisition of a skill. During the pruning process, the dendritic spines that grew in the beginning of language learning are streamlined to preserve only the most efficient connections. Individuals who are considered to have reached the *consolidation* stage include simultaneous multilinguals or multilinguals who have spent a significant amount of time in a country where their non-native language is spoken, providing them with extensive opportunities to utilize their languages. After optimizing the neural mechanisms that underlie lexical learning and control in the *initial exposure* stage, the next crucial step is to attend to and select between various alternatives in semantics, phonology, and grammar. These are functions undertaken by more deeply seated structures such as the basal ganglia and thalamus. Therefore, it would make sense that adaptations in these regions as well as the pathways that connect them would occur with greater language experience.

Indeed, subcortical structures like the globus pallidus, putamen and thalamus have been shown to exhibit expansions in simultaneous multilinguals in comparison to monolinguals.[86] The putamen and globus pallidus are involved in orchestrating motor programs and articulatory control, which are functions integral to multilingual speech production.[87] Furthermore, the globus pallidus plays a unique role in controlling lexical-semantic operations,[88] and the thalamus has been proposed to be involved in a host of multilingual functions - language selection, production, speech monitoring, and semantic processing.[89] The increased volumes in these subcortical structures reflect the additional recruitment of neural resources to meet the increased need in managing lexical and semantic selections as well as new demands in the control and coordination of motor programs. Even though there is largely a lack of expansion in cortical regions that were found in the *initial exposure* stage, the white matter tracts that connect those regions have been

---

[86] Burgaleta et al., 2016; Pliatsikas et al., 2017.
[87] Pliatsikas et al., 2017; Burgaleta et al., 2016.
[88] Whelan et al., 2004.
[89] Burgaleta et al., 2016; Pliatsikas et al., 2017.

observed to decrease in diffusivity. These tracts form wide-spread connections between frontal, temporal and parietal regions that link regions relevant to the language network.[90] In other words, a different pattern of structural adaptations in the brain emerges with increased language experience. This consists of subcortical and white matter adaptations instead of cortical effects, and it suggests that as language experience mounts, the brain adapts to meet the demands of language control rather than language learning.

Beyond the simultaneous use of languages, the use of more than one language across one's lifetime is undeniably a form of consistent and extensive language experience. A unique population to study neuroplasticity is thus older lifelong users of multiple languages. Mirroring the findings from the previous studies, evidence of better structural integrity and higher volume density has been found in lifelong multilinguals when compared to monolinguals.[91] Rather than an indication of structural growth in older multilinguals, these findings have been interpreted as the maintenance of structural integrity.[92] More specifically, these differences suggest that the strengthening of the brain through multi-language control and processing across the lifetime would make the aging or diseased brain more resistant against atrophy and neurodegeneration. This bears testament to the effect that lifelong multilingualism has in keeping neural mechanisms responsive to the constant need for learning and cognitive control.

Plasticity through extreme language control

Now that we have seen evidence of neuroplasticity in the form of expansions in cortical regions followed by expansions in subcortical regions as language experience increases, would relevant brain regions continue to expand indefinitely in response to even further language experiences? Examples of such experiences would include simultaneous interpretation as well as the use of even more languages; both of which demand extreme levels of language control.

---

[90] Hämäläinen et al., 2017; Pliatsikas et al., 2015.
[91] Pliatsikas, 2020.
[92] DeLuca and Voits, 2022.

Individuals with such experiences may arrive at the peak efficiency stage of the DRM. Instead of expansions as observed in the previous two stages, this stage predicts reduced subcortical volumes (i.e., renormalization), greater diffusivity of white matter tracts in frontal regions, and reduced white matter diffusivity in posterior and subcortical areas.

Simultaneous interpreters are individuals with the ability to switch between languages on the spot, much more frequently and at higher intensities than the average multilingual. This demanding task of language control has been found to facilitate adaptations in areas key in cognitive control. For example, the volume of the caudate nucleus decreased with increasing hours spent on simultaneous-interpreting.[93] In other words, the more they engaged with language switching, the smaller the volumes of the caudate nucleus were. Additionally, when simultaneous interpreters were compared with multilingual controls, they exhibited smaller volumes in the anterior cingulate gyrus and left SMG, both of which are important for cognitive control. In terms of white matter, simultaneous interpreters demonstrated greater structural connectivity between the executive frontal regions and the basal ganglia, as well as in the subnetwork consisting of the cerebellum and supplementary motor area—both of which support the production of speech in language switching.[94] The decreased volumes of subcortical structures and higher integrity of white matter tracts that deliver cognitive control suggest the optimization and efficiency of these mechanisms.

As a concluding review to this chapter, a recent study from our lab[95] explored the continual adaptation of the brain across the three stages of the DRM by comparing the volumes of several subcortical structures across monolinguals, immersed bilinguals, trilinguals and quadrilinguals. In line with the predictions, instead of continuous subcortical expansions from monolinguals to quadrilinguals, we found a non-linear pattern of adaptations in structures involved in cognitive control (caudate nucleus, nucleus accumbens) and

---

[93] Elmer et al., 2014.
[94] van de Putte et al., 2018.
[95] Yee et al., 2023.

articulatory programming (globus pallidus and putamen). In comparison to monolingual baseline volumes, immersed bilinguals had larger volumes in the nucleus accumbens, putamen, globus pallidus and thalamus. However, these differences in volumes were absent for the caudate nucleus when immersed bilinguals were compared with monolinguals. Additionally, the nucleus accumbens, putamen and globus pallidus showed patterns of renormalization in trilinguals and/or quadrilinguals where volumes in these groups did not differ from monolingual volumes. These structures did not appear to increase linearly in volume as we move across the continuum of individuals with increasing language experience. More specifically, the caudate nucleus and nucleus accumbens required lesser language experience to renormalize (i.e., expand and contract), while structures relating to executing language (i.e., globus pallidus and putamen) required more language experience before renormalizing to monolingual baseline volumes. Adding to the pool of neuroplasticity research, and like other studies with highly experienced multilinguals, the results showed that as language experience increases, reductions rather than expansions are found in subcortical structures.

Conclusions

In reviewing the evidence of the brain adapting with changing language experiences, we see that our brains have an extraordinary ability to modify itself functionally and structurally, even beyond childhood or the so-called "sensitive periods" in life. The use of more than one language is a cognitively challenging skill that influences the reorganization of the brain in many ways. Grey matter structures and white matter tracts adapt to meet changing demands in language learning, processing, and control. Furthermore, the adaptations that occur through different language experiences are responsive and dynamic; they progress and regress depending on the nature of the experiences.

Not only does the use of multiple languages bring about structural adaptations in the brain and make the learning of a subsequent language easier, but it also brings about cognitive and social benefits. Bilinguals and multilinguals have exhibited enhanced performance in various cognitive tasks, ranging from tasks of creativity, memory, to executive functioning.[96] A detailed review of the evidence on improved cognition can be found in Chapter 2. Socially, Multilingualism also confers benefits that are especially valuable in our globalized society. It enables us to form direct international and intercultural relations, and in turn hone intercultural communication skills. Through first-hand interactions, we can foster a greater appreciation and understanding of cross-cultural perspectives. On an individual level, being able to use multiple languages could improve our career opportunities and enrich our travelling experiences. Moreover, in directly interacting with others from different cultures, we are in a better position to derive insights that may be invisible to non-speakers. For example, Vladimir Skultety, a polyglot of 22 languages mentioned that speaking foreign languages well allowed him to form deeper connections with foreign cultures and opened his eyes to the nuances of a given culture.

Finally, a note to language learners: keep on practicing! Do not worry about sounding silly or making mistakes, connect with a native speaker, engage with the culture, and know your reason for learning which will be essential in keeping you motivated. Afterall, your brain is a formidable and dynamic machine that adapts to anything you give it.

---

[96] Kharkhurin et al., 2023; Bialystok, 2007.

Chapter 5. It's never too late for the brain! Evidence suggests neurological maturation cannot explain observable differences in non-native language

Sergio Miguel Pereira Soares, Tanja Kupisch, and Jason Rothman

According to the critical period hypothesis (CPH), a theory proposed by Lenneberg in 1967, there is an ideal time window—with a cut-off point around puberty—for the brain to acquire language, after which the nativelike mastery of new language becomes impossible. The core of the hypothesis is that the brain's natural capability to adapt to new environmental stimuli is drastically reduced over time (i.e., loss of brain plasticity). In the present chapter, we will first introduce the core aspects of the CPH. Next, we will showcase current scientific work from language studies using two different brain methodologies—Event Related Potentials (ERPs) and Magnetic Resonance Imaging (MRI)—pointing in the direction that brain plasticity carries on over the lifespan and that the same brain mechanisms underlie language processing in native speakers and late learner adults.

One of the major scientific questions in adult second language acquisition studies is whether adults, under the most favorable conditions, are able to learn additional languages to the same degree as would be expected of a child learning the same language as their first. Following up on this, it is important to find out to what extent people who have learned a language after puberty make use of the same language processing and brain mechanisms as those who have learned the same language from birth. If the same mechanisms underlie all instances of language processing, then what explains the common observation of differences in early and late acquired language skills? The idea that language learning in adulthood is fundamentally different is captured under the 'Critical Period Hypothesis' (CPH[97]), which assumes that the human brain progressively loses its ability—around the time of puberty—to adapt to new (environmental) conditions (plasticity[98]). This, in turn, leads to a gradual loss of those brain mechanisms that govern language acquisition in the first years of life. Even though there is no question that the language skills of adults who learned a language early and late differ, it is not at all clear that such observations entail fundamentally distinct language processes or brain mechanisms. The findings from contemporary cognitive neuroscience are clear: brain plasticity—the loss of which is assumed in the CPH—persists over the lifespan.[99] So why should the language skills between native speakers and adults who acquire a language later in life differ? In this chapter, we review behavioral work favoring the CPH, to then unpack what recent data based on brain techniques indicate to help us better understand current positions with respect to a sensitive period for language acquisition.

Setting the Stage: The Critical Period Hypothesis (CPH)

It should come as no surprise that adults usually struggle to learn a second language (L2 henceforth), and that significant interindividual variability can be observed. However, we all know people who have somehow attained such an outstanding overall level in their L2 that we can hardly believe they are not native speakers of that language. What makes them so special? On second thought, are they really that special after all? Perhaps in addition to having some particular talent or 'aptitude' for languages and extreme motivation, a good portion of their success can be attributed to particular opportunities to learn language not all have. For example, these so-called exceptional L2 learners might find themselves in highly favorable conditions for excelling as L2

---

[97] Lenneberg, 1967.
[98] Brain plasticity relates to all those changes in the brain (at the level of the structures, functions, and connections) driven by both internal and external stimuli.
[99] Deluca, Miller, Pliatsikas, & Rothman, 2019.

learners, such as living in a place where high-quality exposure to their L2 is constantly present. So, what is it that makes them special: their inner talent or external conditions that favor optimal language learning? As we will see below, this is a central question to better understand the CPH.

The CPH by Lenneberg assumes that there is a crucial window of time, or sensitive period, in development after which the underlying mental/neurological mechanisms responsible for language acquisition are no longer accessible in the same way. This is believed to happen around puberty. Under its original articulation, the CPH claimed that language learning becomes much more constrained and difficult as a result of brain lateralization. This means that regions of the brain 'crystalize' into specialized functions. Such crystallization would constrain the brain's ability to adapt and change over time. Lenneberg based his claims on observations made from patients suffering aphasia and/or some sort of language loss after brain injuries. He noticed that language recovery was faster and more successful if the brain injury happened in children before puberty as compared to when it occurred after it. This observation led him to hypothesize that there must be something inherent to the brain that differs depending on the person's age, differentially affecting language. In this context, it is important to note that Lenneberg's hypothesis was primarily concerned with the acquisition of the first language, which is to say he made no explicit claims regarding how critical periods would apply after a first grammar was fully[100] acquired. Lenneberg's claims were strongly supported by studies in the 70s through the early 90s, which examined either children who did not receive any (or very minimal) type of language exposure in childhood (like the famous cases of *Genie* and *Chelsea*[101,102] or deaf children, where exposure to a first language (L1) was severely delayed[103]). Crucially, all these studies dealt with either the recovery or failed acquisition

---

[100] 'fully' is often implicitly taken to mean 'akin to a native speaker who grew up speaking only one language'.
[101] Curtiss, 1977.
[102] Curtiss, 1988.
[103] Mayberry, 1993.

of an L1. Does it then mean that adults, who have already successfully learned and have had years of experience with a full native language system, will also have difficulties to acquire an L2 in the same way as those extreme cases of linguistic isolation in the early years? In other words, is it really the case that there is a hard age threshold after which brain maturation processes constrain native-like language learning no matter how much previous linguistic experience they had?

To start answering this question, we need to first examine if and what differences exist between child L1 and adult L2 acquisition. Generally speaking, the vast majority of monolingual children learn their L1 in an environment enriched by high quality and usually quantity of input from adults speaking their native language. Importantly, if the child is only exposed to one language, children do not have to deal with possible influence (*cross-linguistic influence/transfer* are the terms used by linguists) from previously acquired languages that might in one way, or another affect the trajectory of language development. On top of this, they have an inherent need to use language, i.e., to understand, communicate and interact with the world that surrounds them. Opposingly, when adults start learning an L2, they may have limited access to native speakers of that language, they may have much reduced opportunities to use the L2, they might need to somehow deal with positive and negative influences of their previous linguistic systems and they might have significantly lower motivation to learn a new language, since they already have a language to communicate and exist as social beings via their L1 experience. As a last non-trivial point, they will likely receive a significant amount of L2 input—in many cases, the vast majority of it—from non-native speakers with low language proficiency, so the input they receive may be of low quality. Keeping these points in mind, two different scenarios emerge. First, it might simply be the case that children have better language acquisition abilities and processing than adults,[104] and/or that more successful adult L2 learners have higher abilities to learn patterns and structures allowing them to use their L1 as a positive

---

[104] Clahsen, & Muyske, 1989.

resource in the learning of the L2, and/or these adults have higher metalinguistic[105] knowledge. Second, it might be the case that variability in the environmental factors mentioned above are at least in part responsible for the differences between adults who learned a language from birth and those who learned it later on (and not some sort of critical period 'brain maturation' effect).[106,107] This second scenario is strongly supported by recent literature in neuroscience.[108] In fact, the rate at which brain plasticity decreases over the lifespan is minimal until the last years of elderly life and varies across individuals; some people show faster or slower declines than others. It is, thus, rather a by-product of typical biological aging mechanisms.

In the two subsections that follow, we will showcase evidence that bears on claims of the CPH from two lines of adult L2 research, which employ different methodologies well-known in neurosciences—electroencephalography/event-related potentials (EEG/ERPs) and functional magnetic resonance spectroscopy ((f)MRI). Before presenting the evidence, we will briefly introduce these methodologies.

ERP evidence for similar mechanisms in native speakers and second language learners

EEG is an extremely accurate, fast, and non-invasive method used in research to analyze the way the human brain processes information. This methodology is primarily used in clinical settings for the diagnosis of brain diseases like epilepsy or brain inflammation. EEG takes advantage of the electrical activity generated by neurons, the brain's cells. A patient (or participant in an experiment) is fitted with what looks very similar to a swimming cap with electrodes fixed throughout, which measure the electrical activity of the brain that propagates on the scalp. The electrodes on the cap capture the brain's

---

[105] Metalinguistic knowledge (or awareness) refers to the conscious ability to reflect about and perceive language. This skill varies highly in its degree from one person to the next.
[106] Rothman, 2008.
[107] Friederici, Steinhauer, & Pfeifer, 2002.
[108] Fuchs, & Flügge, 2014.

current, which is then amplified and sometimes filtered, rending brain waves visible in real time on a computer screen (see Figure 1).

The participant sits in front of the computer where the stimuli are presented. Electrical activity is captured by the electrodes placed on the cap. This brain signal goes through an amplifier (and sometimes filters) that magnifies it, which would otherwise be very small and impossible to analyze. This signal provided by each electrode is then sent to the recording computer (bottom picture). The event codes (also called triggers) can also be seen on the recording computer, therefore allowing researchers to know exactly when a particular stimulus appeared on the presentation computer. Thus, the exact temporal coupling of the event codes with the EEG signal allows the researchers to analyze the data.

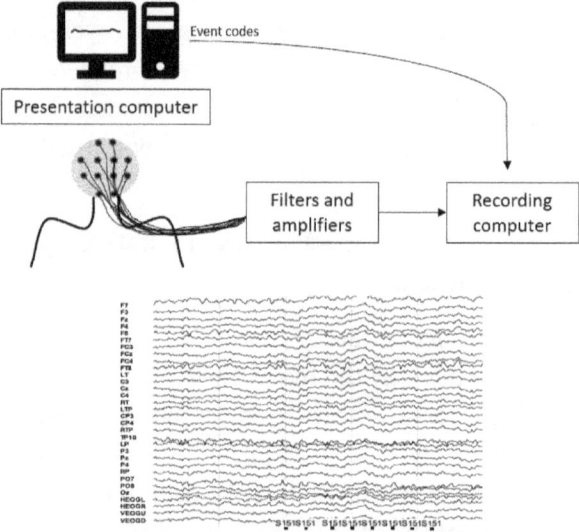

Figure 1. Schematic representation of a typical EEG set up in the lab.

Although there are several techniques to look at the EEG data, we will only discuss the one most commonly used in language research, event-related potentials (ERPs). ERPs represent the averaged brain activity over many events (or trials) that are produced at the millisecond level in response to all sorts of higher cognitive/sensory functions, such as memory, attention, and language processing. In other words, we can measure the instantaneous brain response to language stimuli that can be presented visually on a computer or auditorily through headphones.

ERPs are always measured via the comparison between a so-called 'baseline' stimulus, usually grammatically correct (e.g., *He sits*) and a so-called 'violation', introducing some sort of ungrammaticality (**He sit*). A crucial characteristic of ERPs is that different types of linguistic violations give rise to different brain reactions called 'components' (see Chapter 6 for illustrations of ERP components). These components emerge when sentence structure is violated, but also when these violations are present at the level of sentence meaning or at the level of the sounds of the language. Two of the most prominent and well-studied ERP components in language sciences are the N400 and the P600. The N400 is thought to index surprising continuations at the level of sentence meaning, as in *I like cake when it is **sweet*** (baseline) vs **I like cake when it is **crucial*** (meaning violation). It presents itself as a negative ongoing wave (negative with respect to the baseline condition) around 400 milliseconds after the violation (hence its name N400). In contrast, violations at the level of sentence structure like the one mentioned earlier (**he **hit***) typically lead to a positive wave around 600 milliseconds after the violation, therefore referred to as the P600.

Coming back to the central question of this chapter: if we observed similar (or the same) ERP responses to linguistic stimuli in L2 learning adults and native L1 speakers, this would support the claim that the two groups are using the same brain mechanisms. By contrast, if the two groups' ERP responses differ, it would suggest that their language processing is qualitatively different.[109] What do studies comparing the N400 and the P600 in adult L2 learners and adult L1 monolinguals show?

In recent years more and more ERP work has shown that under very controlled (laboratory) conditions, with informed matching of subjects across comparison groups and/or measuring and regressing out individual difference variables (in an effort to

---

[109] Steinhauer, White, & Drury, 2009.

minimize confounding variables), L2 learners can process information in the newly acquired language in the same way as native speakers.[110] Even more impressively, this was found to be true in many different scenarios: when the linguistic property tested is similar between the L1 and the L2, but also when this is not the case, for example when investigating grammatical gender (which exists in the Romance languages but not in English), and even in the learning of artificial grammars/languages where participants are taught a non-existing/non-natural language.[111]

Let's examine more in detail two concrete exemplar studies. The first one[112] tested native English speakers who were learning Spanish as an L2 at three proficiency levels (beginners, intermediate and advanced). The authors measured the ERPs generated in their brains by grammatical violations in Spanish gender (e.g., *el casa*, the house, which should be *la casa* because the noun is feminine) and in number (**las casa*, which should be *la casa* because the noun is singular). At low levels of Spanish L2 proficiency, they observed only very subtle P600 effects for both linguistic domains, which means that participants were barely sensitive to the violations. The intermediate learners showed an advantage in number over gender; since English has number but not gender, this suggests that the participants' brains could use this similarity advantageously. Nevertheless, the overall brain reactivity was similar to those of native speakers. Finally, the advanced group patterned completely with the native speakers in terms of brain reactivity in the form of a P600 for both grammatical gender and number. These results show that advanced L2 learners especially appear to be using similar processing mechanisms as native speakers. Interpreting these findings in the context of the CPH, there seems to be a shift in the way the brain of adult language learners perceives, and processes later acquired languages as a function of increased proficiency over their developmental trajectory. Thus, something at the level of the brain is changing over time, pointing to plasticity, and this speaks

---

[110] Kotz, 2009.
[111] Morgan-Short, 2020.
[112] Gabriele, Fiorentino, & Bañón, 2013.

against a language/brain maturational cut, as the CPH puts forward.

Perhaps an even more illustrative way to test ERP brain responses development in nonnative speakers is to follow the same L2 learners longitudinally, along their acquisitional path. To do so, some authors[113] repeatedly tested L2 learners progressing through their first year of French instruction on agreement violations between the subject and the verb (*je parle* (I speak) vs **je parles*—which is a morphosyntactic linguistic domain, thus we would expect a P600 brain response). They observed that the brain responses shifted from an initial N400 to a P600 as learning and proficiency in the L2 increased. Interestingly, this gradual change in the brain responses to language violations did not happen at the same time for all participants, demonstrating a degree of variability in the individual trajectories of L2 learning. Unfortunately, the researchers could not disentangle what properties (e.g., intrinsic differences versus environmental differences) distinguished slow from fast learners.

In summary, the two reviewed studies represent just two of many examples of clever ways language scientists exploit ERP measures to investigate L2 learning. There is now a substantial amount of data in the literature providing evidence that the mechanisms by which highly proficient adult learners process a second language do not fundamentally differ from native speakers, contrary to what the CPH predicts. Such evidence seems to go against the pessimistic claim of a sensitive period for language acquisition beyond which learning a new language and speak 'like a native' becomes impossible (see Chapter 6 for further examples).

(f)MRI evidence of language-related brain plasticity in adulthood

Magnetic resonance spectroscopy (MRI) is another neuroimaging method that originated from clinical settings as a tool to diagnose all sorts of dysfunctions and disorders in the human body. MRI research has seen an upsurge in its use starting from the mid-late 90s, including research related to language sciences. This non-

---

[113] Osterhout et al., 2008.

invasive technique takes advantage of strong magnetic fields and radio pulses to create very accurate pictures/images of (soft tissue) structures and functioning inside the body. Given that we are focusing on language, we will primarily discuss brain MRI (Figure 2).

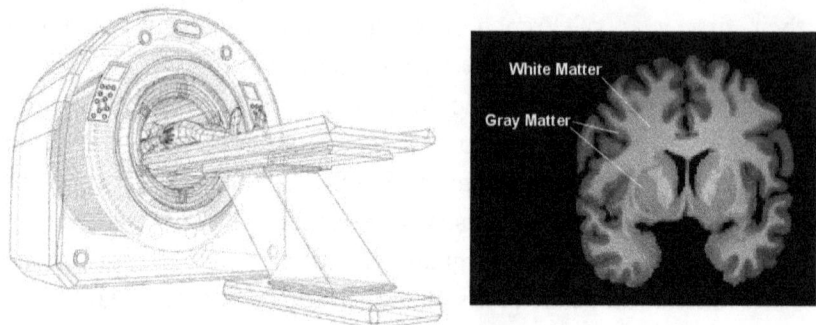

Figure 2. Schematic representation of an MRI machine and a structural picture of the brain. (Left) The participant is transported via a mobile bed into the MRI machine. The tube contains a series of large magnets and coils which work together to take detailed scans (pictures) of the brain. (Right) White (internal part of the brain) and grey (external part of the brain) matter can be observed in this structural brain scan. Pictures adopted form istockphoto.com (left) and the University of Missouri-Columbia website (right).

While many ways have been developed over the decades to analyze and look at MRI data, we will focus herein on two methodologies: structural scans, which allow us to localize brain changes in structures and areas, and functional (fMRI) scans, which allow us to study the activation of different brain regions as a response to a particular task being performed. Space does not permit us to go into details with regard to the precise brain areas that show adaptations in relation to language learning, but we refer the reader to an excellent review on the topic.[114] Instead, we will try to understand if and how there are brain changes in structures and activations in response to L2 learning and processing. This will then be related to the CPH. However, before discussing the relevant literature, we need to consider the conditions under which Lenneberg in 1967 developed the core ideas of the CPH: as explained further

---

[114] Abutalebi & Green, 2016.

above, he conceptualized his claims based on observations of behavioral language recovery patterns after brain injury in children versus adults. MRI, which was not developed until the 1970s, now gives us the advantageous opportunity to peak under the hood of the human brain, allowing us to (dis)confirm Lenneberg's predictions more directly about any brain maturational sensitive period for language learning.

Several complementary strains of literature have looked at structural and functional MRI brain changes as participants learn a new language, be it natural or artificial. Longitudinal studies examine the same participants over time. In contrast, cross-sectional studies involve groups of people who share particular variables/traits compared to each other. Most of these studies follow similar designs: brain scans are taken at a first time point and then compared between groups (in cross-sectional studies) or at a later point after language training (in longitudinal studies). Additional language measures are collected (e.g., proficiency, age of acquisition, length of exposure), as well as data from behavioral tests (where participants' skills are measured). Comparison between scans at the structural and functional levels and correlations of those scans with language and behavioral measures allow researchers to draw conclusions about language processing and brain regions. In general, findings converge on pointing to brain adaptations when a new language is being learned at all possible levels: in so-called grey matter areas and also in the pathways connecting brain areas, so-called white matter tracts (see Figure 2). These two types of structures could be one to one compared to the urban network in a country: whereas the grey matter areas function as cities—creating, processing, and deploying information—the white matter tracks mirror highways, allowing information to flow between grey matter brain areas.

We now review some studies in greater detail to better illustrate how this literature informs the CPH. In a Swedish study, young adults were tested who were pursuing an intense language training to become interpreters.[115] The training lasted for a period of three

---

[115] Mårtensson, Eriksson, Bodammer, Lindgren, Johansson, Nyberg, & Lövdén, 2012.

months. Brain scans were taken prior and at the end of the intense training period. The authors showed that several brain areas known to be involved in language had increased in volume/size for the interpreters in comparison to a control group of people who did not follow the training. Interestingly, those learners who achieved higher foreign language skills also showed the most substantial brain increases. Comparable results were found regarding white matter tracks. For example, another study[116] tested monolingual English adults versus late English–Spanish bilinguals living in the USA and found white matter adaptations in bilinguals across almost all tracks in the brain. These results too point to a certain degree of adaptability of the brain in adults who are exposed to new language input. Both studies show that skills in the new language are proportional to the amount of brain adaptations.

An interesting question for the present chapter is whether adult L2 learners are able to learn a language (or complex linguistic structures in a foreign language) to the level of native speakers and, in particular, if activation in selected brain areas in L2 learners and native speakers is comparable. To investigate this question, native and highly proficient non-native English learners were tested in the processing of past tense morphology in regular and irregular English verb pairs (*played-play/kept-keep*).[117] The study did not find any differences in brain activity between the two groups. What is more, the same authors showed in a later, similar study that the L2 learners' cerebellum[118] —an area located just above the brain stem in the back of the head, implicated in verbal fluency and expressive/receptive grammar processing—changed in response to the learning of grammatical rules, which again indicates brain plasticity in adulthood. Finally, brain adaptations were examined in young Dutch adults in the process of learning an artificial language.[119] As little as five weeks of language training were enough to observe differences in activation in specific language-related brain areas when

---

[116] Kuhl, Stevenson, Corrigan, Van Bosch, Can, & Richards, 2016.
[117] Pliatsikas, Johnstone, & Marinis, 2014.
[118] Distinct part of the brain in the posterior part of the head that is mainly responsible for fine movement and muscular activity control.
[119] Petersson, Folia, & Hagoort, 2012.

ungrammatical sentences were presented, illustrating fast brain adaptation.

Taken together, recent MRI findings clearly show that brain adaptations take place in adult L2 learning. Furthermore, the same brain regions activate and engage in language comprehension in native and non-native speakers. These two observations constitute a substantial challenge to the original assumptions of the CPH.

Conclusion

It is undeniable that adults show great variability with respect to their competencies in learning a new language. However, this does not mean that language processing and brain mechanisms that underlie it are quantitatively or qualitatively different in adults who learn a language later compared to those who learned it from birth. In this chapter, we attempted to revisit one of the core presuppositions of the CPH: that brain plasticity drastically diminishes at some point around puberty and that, linked to this, there is a disadvantage in learning a language later in life compared to learning it early. We provided convincing evidence from studies in neuroscience that challenge the idea that brain maturation prevents adults from learning new languages and processing them akin to adults who have learned them during the first years of life. All in all, the existing evidence suggests that the brain mechanisms required to process early and late acquired language(s) can be the same. Nevertheless, for the vast majority of adults, it is more difficult to learn a new language compared to children. Since the neurological mechanisms underlying language processing can remain the same across the lifespan, variables other than brain plasticity must be responsible for the frequently observed native versus non-native differences. Present and future research is set to understand what these variables are and how they influence the brain mechanisms underlying adult novel language learning.

Chapter 6. Can we learn and master a new language as adults? Absolutely!

*Sarah von Grebmer zu Wolfsthurn,
Leticia Pablos-Robles, and Niels O. Schiller*

Many of us believe that it is impossible to learn a new language as adults. But is this really true? Fascinating studies of our brains show that adults are actually very much capable of learning a new language well enough to perfectly function in that new language, and to simultaneously resemble a native speaker—even when the language was learnt later in life.

Flicking through the science section of a magazine or a newspaper, you may have come across articles describing why mastering a new language as an adult is "impossible" and destined to fail. This popular belief has dominated our way of thinking for many years and has prevented swaths of people from learning a new language. In this chapter, we will refer to this belief as a *rumor* because our main goal here is to challenge its truth value. We even go as far as (spoiler-alert) scientifically deconstructing the rumor altogether: the rumor is inaccurate because we are perfectly capable of operating as well as communicating in a new language. What is even more important is that in doing so, some speakers bear a striking resemblance to native speakers. Impressive, right? By the end of this chapter, you will know what we mean by all of this and why this can be the case.

"Acquiring" our native language

Before we get into dismantling the rumor, we need to provide some context on how the native language is acquired and how it compares to learning a new language later in life. "Learning" how to use your native language is something that simply *happens* to most of us during early childhood. When examining the age-old question about how babies acquire a language, scientists have come up with a fairly elaborate answer. At birth, new-borns can already discriminate between their native language and a language with a different rhythm. At two months, they start developing more specific knowledge of their own native language and can discriminate it from other foreign languages they have never heard before. At around four months of age, infants have developed preferences for different properties of language, for example, specific tones or sounds of the language they are exposed to. At around six months of age, infants show an understanding of the meaning of some words (although we cannot be sure whether the meaning is the same as that for adults). It is also around that age that infants attempt to combine sounds in their language to "produce" language for the first time—they start babbling, like *dadada* (or produce repetitive syllables, in more scientific terms). At the age of eight months, infants know that certain syllables co-occur together more often compared to other syllables. In turn, this helps them to discover words and their boundaries. The production of the first real words comes shortly after around the age of ten to twelve months. Between seventeen and twenty months of age, those same infants start putting together words to form simple sentences. Amazingly, at only three years of age, most children can produce relatively complicated sentences with the words in the correct order. At around six years of age, children have accumulated an awe-inspiring 8,000 words.[120]

Another notable fact is that children acquire their native language without really needing explicit instructions: parents do not typically sit down with their new-borns and explain the grammatical rules of a language. When parents correct their children on something they said, for example, the classic "swimmed" instead of "swam", research has shown that these corrections do not actually have a big impact on the development of language in children. In other words,

---

[120] For more information about the development of the native language or a new language in children and adults, please see the book by Maria Teresa Guasti entitled *"Language Acquisition: The Growth of Grammar."* MIT Press, 2017; and the book by Albert Costa entitled *"The Bilingual Brain and what it tells us about the science of language."* Penguin UK, 2017.

children do not necessarily take feedback from their parents on board. Instead, children use what is called *positive evidence* to develop their native language: they simply use the language they hear in their immediate environment to extract words and grammatical rules. This ability to pick up on specific linguistic patterns emerges early during development and perseveres all the way through to adulthood. All in all, acquiring and developing the native language typically happens quite automatically throughout early childhood and is very remarkable. What makes native language development even more special is the fact that the timeline is not unique to a specific language. In fact, most children follow a similar timeline, regardless of the native language they are exposed to in their environment. Therefore, think about what children across the world have typically been able to achieve at six years old—quite extraordinary, right? However, let us remember that language development is not yet complete at the age of six. There is still much more to learn, for example, how to read, how to put sounds into writing, how to use language efficiently in dialogues, how to form passive sentences ("The apple was eaten by the boy") and—a very handy skill—how to use sarcasm and irony to confuse others in conversations, among others.

You may also know some children who *happen* to learn two languages from birth. For example, this might be because their parents or guardians speak two different languages around the house. These children are often called *simultaneous bilinguals*. Growing up, they typically have a comparable command of both languages and can easily engage in one language or the other without being explicitly aware of this. In other words, in these cases understanding and speaking both languages rely on largely automatic and subconscious processes.

Learning a new language: the case of late language learners

Now, what about those who learn a new language not as babies, but as older children or adults? They belong to a different group of learners, namely *late language learners*. In particular, adult late language learners are our main interest in this chapter. What is the difference between the simultaneous bilinguals we described above and late language learners, and how is it connected to our ability to learn a new language? As mentioned before, simultaneous bilinguals are exposed to two or more languages *from birth*. This often results in overall quite high proficiency levels in the languages they speak from an early age. In contrast, late language learners typically acquire a new language *after* they have already learnt their native language (this is also known as *sequential* bilingualism). Looking at data on how many people in the European Union speak an additional language (either from birth or learnt later), we know that more than two thirds of working-aged adults between 25 and 64 years of age speak one or more additional language.[121] In Sweden, Denmark, Latvia, Estonia, and Malta this number climbs to almost 100%, meaning that in those countries essentially everyone speaks at least one additional language. Therefore, most of the population in Europe has learnt how to speak multiple languages, making it even more important to get all the facts right since it concerns so many people.

Late language learners are a particularly fascinating group because they are actually in an optimal position to learn a new language. For starters, most of them do not have to worry about learning how to read and write anymore. Next, they are typically extremely motivated to learn a new language as it is often a matter of explicit choice (or sometimes necessity). There are probably hundreds of different, very valid reasons to learn a new language as adults and to effectively become adult late language learners: taking language classes for a job in a new country, learning the language of a partner or of friends, being able to chat with the new neighbors or locals, talking to the cat we know has Italian owners and which seems to love the little bench on our balcony, or simply to take up a new personal challenge. Most importantly, late language learners are *already* equipped with a fully developed language system, namely that of their native language. Therefore, they already have a good idea of the words in another language (*vocabulary*), their meaning (*semantics*), their pronunciation (*phonology*), the grammatical rules that govern it (*syntax*), the way that words and sentences are written (*orthography*) and on how to use all of the above in an appropriate communicative and social context with other speakers (*pragmatics*). In other words,

---

[121] Eurostat, 2019

they have *been* through the entire process of learning a language, while probably being blissfully unaware of this happening at all. Therefore, when late language learners get started on, well, a new language, they can rely on their experience and understanding of their native language to facilitate the learning process. This is less the case for simultaneous bilinguals, who essentially learn two languages in parallel and therefore cannot draw from a fully-formed language just yet. To illustrate this, have you ever talked to an adult taking language classes and heard them say that they find a particular aspect of a new language "easy because it is similar to their native language"? Such remarks indicate that late language learners make both conscious and unconscious links between their native language and the new language to be learnt. This meta-linguistic insight into both their native language and the new language is worth gold and shows that late language learners are well-equipped for learning a new language.

All of these skills are even more impressive when we consider that learning a new language is by no means a piece of cake. For example, it can sometimes be difficult for some late language learners to learn the grammatical rules or the sounds of the new language (yes, especially those—think about how often you have had friends complain about finding it difficult to improve their accent). Depending on the learner and the circumstances under which the new language is learnt, there can be low proficient and high proficient late language learners. While learning and mastering a new language as adults can be challenging, scientific evidence suggests that some late language learners can actually reach proficiency levels that are close to native speakers. What we mean by this is that late language learners can achieve language levels in the new language considered to be extremely *similar* to native speakers of that language, against the wide-spread rumor that this is impossible. The important distinction here is between being highly similar to native speakers (which this chapter is all about) vs. being identical to native speakers. So, how can this be happening?

To get everyone onto the same page, what does it really mean for late language learners to *master* a new language to begin with? First, we have the *learning* aspect, for example, expanding your vocabulary, learning phonology and grammar and so on. Second, we have the *processing* aspect, namely the ability to use, understand and produce sentences and to have a functional command of the new language. More importantly, looking at how people use or process the new language can give us a good idea about how *successful* (or not) the learning process has been and what the similarities with native speakers are. This will be exactly the type of evidence that we are discussing below.

Into the thick of it: dismantling the rumor

At the core of the rumor that learning and mastering a new language as adults is impossible is the notion that the *age of acquisition* of the new language plays a significant role. In other words, people commonly believe that languages can *only* be successfully learnt by children up to a certain age. There are numerous studies which have investigated the role of age of acquisition in adult language learning in great detail. If age of acquisition was truly *the* (only) determining factor, then we would expect at least two things: first, that child late language learners (i.e., those children who learnt a new language later during late childhood rather than from birth *after* they had already acquired their native language) would still make different errors compared to adult late language learners. However, studies have consistently found that child late language learners and adult late language learners make surprisingly similar types of errors when communicating in a newly learnt language. For example, adult late language learners behave similarly to those children with respect to the grammar of the new language. Second, if age of acquisition was really the only determining factor, it would also mean that we would never expect any late language learner to reach proficiency levels similar to native speakers in any linguistic domain. Yet, studies found that both child and adult late language learners can become highly functional in more than one language and reach high proficiency levels in multiple languages. More importantly, research overwhelmingly suggests that late language learners can in fact be remarkably similar to native speakers in domains such as grammar, vocabulary, or in the use of language in a particular context, as we will discuss in more detail below.

In other words, contrary to the wide-spread rumor, reaching levels similar to native speakers is perfectly achievable in many domains even if the language acquisition process started during adulthood. Note that we are not arguing here that the age of acquisition plays *no* role at all in mastering a new language. However, if late language learners can still achieve extremely high functionality in the new language in some domains, then the age of acquisition must be less of an important factor, in contrast to what people think. With this, the foundations of the rumor are beginning to slowly crumble since it is looking like perhaps learning a new language as adults may well be possible, after all.

Now, let us zoom into research which has specifically investigated the question whether achieving a high command of grammar similar to native speakers is possible for adult late language learners. One way to answer this question would be to, for example, compare the ability of late language learners and native speakers to detect grammatical errors. Consider hearing a sentence such as "The girl *ride* to school on her bike." where there is a grammatical error on the verb (*ride* instead of *rides*). The fundamental question here is whether late language learners' brains will behave similarly to native speakers when they apply or process grammatical rules in the new language. But how could we know if the brains of different speakers behave similarly to each other?

One very effective approach is to compare the *neural activity patterns* in the brains of late language learners and native speakers to examine their sensitivity to detect grammatical errors. If we were to find similar neural activity patterns for processing grammatical errors in at least some of the late language learners and native speakers, this would suggest that the mastery of grammatical rules in the new language reached a level which resembles that of native speakers. In other words, similar neural activity patterns would mean that achieving a high command of grammar similar to native speakers is possible, even if the new language was learnt later in life.

A popular technique used to investigate the neural activity patterns connected to grammatical errors is *electroencephalography* (EEG). EEG measures the electrophysiological state of the brain and allows researchers to track so-called *event-related brain potentials* (ERPs). Fundamentally, it is a non-invasive technique to connect changes in the brain's neural activity to a specific event, for example, detecting a grammatical error in a sentence. ERPs have featured in studies on language for many years because they provide an incredibly precise window into the brain's neural activity and also the timing of the underlying processing mechanisms compared to simply pressing a button to respond. Therefore, studying the neural activity connected to language processing can shine light onto the ongoing brain mechanisms in real time.[122]

The ERP most commonly linked to the detection of grammatical errors is the so-called *P600 component*. Generally speaking, the P600 component is a positive-going wave with a voltage (yes, voltage!) peak around 600 milliseconds after the event,[123] e.g., the grammatical error. The *P600 effect* refers to higher voltage amplitudes for sentences containing a grammatical error compared to sentences without, for example. In other words, the P600 effect shows that there is a measurable difference in the way that the brain adapts its neural activity in response to an ungrammatical sentence compared to a grammatical sentence. More concretely, the P600 effect indicates that the brain has detected grammatical errors and is rapidly performing repairs on the sentence in order to construct a grammatically sound one.

Early studies on this topic claimed that late language learners were nothing like native speakers when detecting grammatical errors such as in the sentence above.[124] For example, some ERP studies looking at the processing of grammatical errors in native speakers vs. late language learners failed to provide evidence for a P600 effect in adult late language learners.[125] In turn, this implied that adult late language learners, in particular those with lower

---

[122] If you are interested in gaining an even broader insight into how the brain deals with learning languages in adulthood, read Chapter 5 by Pereira Soares et al. in this same book.
[123] Steinhauer, White, & Drury, 2009.
[124] Clahsen, & Felser, 2006.
[125] Rossi & Prystauka, 2020.

proficiency levels, may not be sensitive to grammatical errors to begin with and could therefore never resemble native speakers.

However, much more recent research using ERPs consistently reports highly comparable P600 effects for adult late language learners and native speakers. For example, one study directly compared the P600 effect between low and high proficient late language learners of German, lower and highly proficient late language learners of Italian as well as native speakers of German and native speakers of Italian.[126] Results showed that the P600 effect was remarkably similar across the highly proficient late language speakers of German and Italian and the native speakers. The less proficient late language learners also showed a P600 effect, although slightly delayed compared to the native speakers. Therefore, both lower and highly proficient adult late language learners showed a sensitivity to grammatical errors. This result is in direct contrast with studies suggesting that the P600 effect may be absent in late language learners and subsequently, that they are less sensitive to grammatical errors or not at all.[127] More importantly, the highly proficient late learners displayed similar ERP patterns compared to native speakers in the detection of grammatical errors. This shows that at least some late language learners can develop grammatical processing abilities in the new language[128] which resemble native speakers.[129]

Extending on those findings, another study dug even deeper into the ERP signal connected to grammatical errors.[130] Fundamentally, the ERP signal is composed of waves of different frequencies, which are measured in Hertz (Hz). Since the early twentieth century, we know that specific frequencies are linked to specific cognitive processes (e.g., detecting grammatical errors vs. listening to music). In other words, the composition of frequencies in our brains

---

[126] Rossi, Gugler, Friederici, & Hahne, 2006.
[127] Rossi, Kroll, & Dussias, 2014.
[128] Gillon-Dowens, Vergara, Barber, & Carreiras, 2010; and Van Hell & Tokowicz, 2010.
[129] Sabourin, Stowe, & De Haan, 2006.
[130] Rossi, & Prystauka, 2020.

constantly changes depending on the task we are performing. The frequencies present in an ERP signal are typically grouped into so-called *frequency bands*.[131] Researchers can quantify the amount, or *power* of a specific frequency band present in the ERP signal and connect it to a cognitive process. For example, the frequency range between 4 Hz and 8 Hz is also known as the *theta* frequency band.[132] Studies examining the processing of grammatical errors found an *increase* in theta frequency power in the ERP signal for grammatical errors compared to correct sentences in native speakers of Dutch.[133] With respect to the ERP signal characteristics of late language learners and native speakers, one study directly compared the composition and frequency band power of the ERP signal in late language learners and native speakers of Spanish.[134] The results showed that both the composition of the ERP signal and the frequency band power were remarkably similar across both groups. From studies such as these, it becomes clear that late language learners not only show comparable ERP patterns to native speakers when processing grammatical errors, but also a similar composition of the frequencies within the ERP signal as in native speakers. In turn, this again suggests that some language learners process grammatical errors remarkably similarly to native speakers. Subsequently, this represents evidence in favor of the ability of adults to learn and master a new language: in order to succeed at these tasks and for the ERP signal to be similar to native speakers, learning of the grammar must have been extremely successful in at least some late language learners. Now, the rumor about this actually being completely impossible is sounding less and less plausible, right…?

In addition to having a firm grasp on grammar, a second critical aspect of learning and mastering a new language is to be able to understand the incoming auditory input. Unlike in reading, there is no equivalent for the blank spaces between words and the

---

[131] Bastiaansen, Oostenveld, Jensen, & Hagoort, 2008.
[132] Güntekin, & Basar, 2007.
[133] Bastiaansen, Van Berkum, & Hagoort, 2002.
[134] Rossi, & Prystauka, 2020.

possibility to go back and reread a word during a normal face-to-face conversation. Instead, when we are having a conversation with someone, there is a rapid and constant flow of acoustic and linguistic input that we need to process to understand what is being said. During this process, our brain takes on the role as a sort of fortune teller that tries to predict *upcoming* information based on the incoming linguistic input.[135] Take the example of hearing the sentence "I drink my coffee with milk and *sugar*." We know from research that our brain tries to *predict* the final word *before* we even hear the full sentence. In this example, our brain will have predicted the word "sugar" as the final word of the sentence by the time we get to "and." For this, our brain uses the information from the first part of the sentence to make a reasonable prediction of what could come next in the sentence. In this, it determines that "sugar" is the most fitting word in this context. However, when we hear a sentence such as "I drink my coffee with milk and *dog*," it will make our brain raise an eyebrow or two: while this sentence is technically grammatically correct, the word "*dog*" does not fit with what our brain had predicted (because people do not typically put dogs into their coffee, or at least, we hope not). In those cases where predictions are violated and there is a mismatch with the auditory input, i.e., the word "dog" instead of the word "sugar", another event-related (ERP) brain potential is produced, namely the *N400 component*.

The N400 component is one of the most-researched ERP components in the field of language sciences, with the first studies dating back to the 1980s. The N400 component is a negative-going wave with a voltage amplitude peak around 400 milliseconds after a specific event. Taking the example sentence of "I drink my coffee with milk and X," N400 voltage amplitudes are larger if the word "*dog*" is presented compared to when the word "*sugar*" is presented. The resulting *N400 effect* therefore indexes this mismatch between what the listener was expecting and what they effectively heard. Subsequently, the N400 component is seen as a biological marker for embedding words within their appropriate context. Just like the

---

[135] Ito, Martin, & Nieuwland, 2017.

P600 component, the N400 component is another excellent tool to examine the claim that adult late language learners can master a new language at a level that resembles native speakers. The reasoning here is the following: if late language learners are able to resemble native speakers in predicting incoming auditory input, then we would expect the N400 effect in late language learners to look similar to the one in native speakers. Subsequently, this would mean that late language learners are comparable to native speakers in their ability to predict upcoming linguistic input. There are some studies which suggest that the act of prediction may be less effective in late language learners because reading and comprehension are more effortful for late language learners.[136] Subsequently, it was proposed that prediction mechanisms are widely different in native speakers compared to late language learners and that the corresponding neural patterns differ drastically between the two groups,[137] meaning that a resemblance is virtually impossible.

However, other studies using EEG and ERPs have examined more systematically whether late language learners can show N400 patterns that are similar to native speakers. Those studies, which included sentences like our example from before, report highly similar N400 effects in late language learners compared to native speakers. This shows that at least some late language learners do engage in predicting the upcoming word in a sentence similarly to native speakers, although possibly not in the exact same way. In other words, these results show that just like in native speakers, the brains of late language learners also act as fortune tellers and are surprised when their predictions do not match the incoming auditory input. Therefore, in line with our discussion around the P600 component, the ERP signal composition and frequency power, we present evidence from the N400 component that the neural signatures for language prediction can be extremely similar in late language learners and native speakers. In turn, this is evidence that it is indeed very well possible to virtually resemble

---

[136] Clahsen & Felser, 2006.
[137] Martin, Thierry, Kuipers, Boutonnet, Foucart, & Costa, 2013.

native speakers in a new language, even as an adult language learner.

Conclusion

The rumor that learning and mastering a new language as adults is impossible has dominated our way of thinking for many years. Yet, examining the current scientific evidence, the emerging picture is quite different: overall, striking similarities are found between the neural activity patterns observed in some adult late language learners, particularly with high proficiency levels, and native speakers. This shows that adult language learners can reach high proficiency levels resembling native speakers, even if this new language was learnt later in life. While it may not be possible for *all* late language learners, the answer to our original question of whether adults can learn and master a new language is a resounding *yes*. There are many, many late language learners among us who are the living proof for this. Therefore, as a message to anyone who is doubting whether or not to pick up a new language—the evidence is strongly in your favor, so *go for it*!

Part 3: Myths on multilingualism and language acquisition

Chapter 7. "I hear, I hear, with my little ear": Multilingual and monolingual children perceive speech sounds differently

Theresa Bloder, Tanja Rinker, and Valerie Shafer

Before the 1960s, multilingualism was vastly considered a handicap that slowed down a child's development by forcing them to spend too much time and effort on trying to distinguish between their languages. This misconception was mainly fueled by the widespread belief that, in each of their languages, multilingual children ought to develop in line with monolinguals. However, over thirty years of experimental research on the acquisition of speech sounds in multilingual and monolingual children has shown that the almost century-old myth, that multilinguals must behave like two monolinguals in one, is wrong. Rather, everyone's multilingual experience is different, and each multilingual person is unique in the profiles of their different languages.

For a long time, it was thought that multilinguals are essentially multiple monolinguals in one. Almost a century ago, Leonard Bloomfield, for instance, defined bilingualism as the "native-like control of two languages."[138] Many people firmly believed—and some still do today—that children who acquire two or more languages from birth (so-called *simultaneous multilingual* children) will develop all of their language skills similarly to monolingual children in each language and should, thus, have equally strong language abilities in all of their languages. This view will likely lead to unrealistic expectations regarding the developmental trajectory and timeline of multilingual language acquisition. In response, parents and professionals may mistakenly think that a multilingual child's

---

[138] See Bloomfield, 1933.

language development is deficient or even disordered if it is not the same as a monolingual child's development. At worst, this may lead to a child being misdiagnosed as having language impairment, which clinicians call developmental language disorder (shortened to DLD). (Monolingual) Children with DLD often show poor speech perception skills (for example, misperceiving "rid" as "red", indicating poor speech sound discrimination between the vowel /ɪ/ as in "rid" and the vowel /ɛ/ as in "red"). Multilingual typically developing children may also show speech sound misperceptions when first acquiring a new language. Thus, even when the multilingual child is not diagnosed as having DLD, the child may still be thought to have poor language skills. This incorrect evaluation of a child's language abilities can affect educational choices (for example, seeking out less demanding schools, less demanding classes, or, in the case of misdiagnosis, placing the child in special education). Research has shown that around 7% of all children have DLD, independent of whether or not they are raised multilingually. However, the high percentage of multilingual children in speech therapy or special classes indicates that many of these children are likely to have been misdiagnosed.[139] For more information regarding language impairment in the context of multilingual language development refer to Eikerling & Lorusso, Chapter 13 in this volume.

In 1989, Swiss linguist Francois Grosjean wrote the article "Neurolinguists, Beware! The Bilingual Is Not Two Monolinguals in One Person."[140] He argued that multilinguals develop their individual linguistic profile according to their individual situation in life. Let's take a look at two examples that illustrate this statement.

Matilda is a three-year-old girl who grows up being exposed to German and Spanish in the north of Germany. While Matilda's German mother is speaking exclusively German to her daughter, the Chilean father is speaking only Spanish to the child. Both parents are self-employed and work from home most of the time, thus interacting

---

[139] For current clinical approaches towards multilingualism across Speech and Language Pathologists in Europe see Bloder, Eikerling, Rinker, & Lorusso, 2021.
[140] Grosjean, 1989.

very frequently with the child. Matilda attends a German-speaking kindergarten and all friends, neighbors, and family members on the mother's side speak German to her. Due to the distance to Chile, visits from extended Spanish-speaking family members are rare. Which language is Matilda's strongest language? Yes, of course: German. While she is able to easily speak and understand complex and grammatically correct German, her ability to speak and understand complex Spanish is much weaker. She understands most of what she hears in Spanish, but she is only able to speak a few words and simple sentences. Matilda has the advantage that she is strong in the societal language that will eventually become her main language of schooling. But if tested in Spanish (her heritage language), she is likely to show weaker skills because she makes less use of Spanish.

Another case is Aida, who is an 8-year-old girl who grows up in Munich, Germany, with Turkish-speaking parents. She speaks Turkish to her parents at home and lives in a community where there are many other Turkish speakers, but she attends a German-speaking school. When first entering kindergarten, her skills were stronger in Turkish. But after three years in a German school, interacting with her German-speaking teachers and other children, and learning to read and write in German, she has good skills in German. Nevertheless, she still speaks Turkish well. By 11 years of age, she shifts to dominance in German but retains strong skills in Turkish for only a few areas in the home and community. The concern for Aida is that she might be misidentified as having language impairment when assessed in German in the years that she is just developing her German skills, that is specifically around her entry into the German school system. Unfortunately, children like Aida are not always tested in their other language (in this case Turkish) when it is not a societal language.

These examples illustrate Grosjean's point. The language abilities of Matilda and Aida are a direct reflection of their language "input" and "output" for each language in different contexts. Input refers to all the language a child hears (listens to), whereas output is what they produce (speak). For children under 5 years of age, typically, the parents and direct caregivers (such as grandparents, childcare minders) are the most important people to provide language to them.

Speaking with the child during activities such as meals, bathroom routines, playing games, and story reading will provide input in the languages of the home. As the child begins to spend more time outside the home, for example, when going shopping or to playgrounds, increased input will come from people living in the community. When the child enters school, additional input in the societal language(s) will be provided by teachers and schoolmates, both in spoken and written forms. Subsequently, children will begin speaking in the societal language in these situations. Moreover, they will also receive input from media, including the TV and internet, and, as they get older, from written conversations with friends via social media. Their written output is likely to be in the societal language. They will also have input from their older siblings, who may have already shifted to favoring the societal language and will, thus also shift to speaking in the societal language with them.

The amount of each language used in children's everyday situations is crucial to evaluate the effect of their language input and output on their skills in the home versus societal language(s). Measuring language input and output can be done using questionnaires or interviews with the main caregivers. Usually, the caregivers are asked about their children's daily routines and the language(s) used for each of their activities. This information can help provide insight into each child's individual pattern of everyday, multi-language use, and can provide a measure of children's "relative language exposure." This measure assesses the waking hours of a child and divides them up according to the relative amount of time the child is interacting with each language. A German or Spanish monolingual child would be exposed 100% to their one language, whereas the caregiver of a multilingual child such as Matilda might report that 70% of the language that she hears in any given week is German and only 30% is Spanish. Multilingual children may have a lot of input, but less output in a language. For example, a girl like Aida, who at home receives more input in Turkish might nevertheless choose to speak mostly in German.

Not surprisingly, research shows that vocabularies size increases and pronunciation improves for multilingual children as input and/or output increase for a particular language. For example, one study showed that for five-year-old multilingual Spanish-English children, the proportion of use of each language was strongly related to pronunciation accuracy of both vowels and consonants in English and Spanish.[141]

In this chapter, we look closely at how the perception and production of speech sounds develop in multilinguals in accordance with their language input and output. As noted above, some previous studies have shown poor speech sound discrimination in monolingual children with language disorders. We wanted to better understand the timeline for developing two different phonological systems for bilingual Italian-German children to gain insight on how they differ from monolingual peers of German or Italian. Understanding these differences will allow us to avoid making mistakes in the diagnosis of DLD and will further illustrate that multilingual children should not be judged by looking at only one of their languages.

Speech sound perception in children

The earliest and most basic building blocks of a language are speech sounds. In order to comprehend spoken language, listeners not only need to be able to hear the acoustic signal that is speech, but they also need to process the acoustic information appropriately to identify the words in the nearly continuous speech and to identify the meaning of each word. The complexity of this task is more obvious when we try to pick out the sounds and words of a foreign language. Speech sounds (referred to as *phonemes* in linguistics) are the smallest building blocks of spoken language and changing one phoneme will change word meaning. Compare, for instance, the two English words "bear" (the wild carnivorous mammal) and "pear" (the greenish sweet fruit) that only differ with respect to their word-initial phoneme: /b/ and /p/ (the slashes indicate that we are talking about phonemes). The importance of discriminating between these two phonemes and thus correctly perceiving /b/ and /p/ can be illustrated by the following example: Imagine being out on a hike and suddenly hearing someone shout "Look, a pear!" In a situation like this, you should not be

---

[141] Ruiz-Felter, Cooperson, Bedore, & Peña, 2016.

having to think twice about whether you have correctly perceived the word "pear" or actually "bear" as it would surely affect your reaction. Therefore, you more than ever rely on your ability to discriminate between these two sounds: accurate perception has the potential to save your life! German and English speakers perceive "bear" when the same pronunciation for an Italian or Spanish speaker would be perceived as "pear." The decision of whether to run away or look forward to a tasty piece of fruit depends on the listener's language background.

Taken together, the speech sounds of all the world's languages total about 600 possible consonants and 200 possible vowels. Individual languages, however, not only make use of a much smaller and unique subset of speech sounds, but they can also differ in how individual phonemes are produced. These subtle differences are referred to as *phonetic detail* in linguistics. For example, [pʰ] describes a sound where the lips shut off the air by complete closure and then after opening, release a puff of air, called aspiration. The word "pear" in English is produced with [pʰ]. Languages like Italian and Spanish do not use aspiration following the phoneme /p/ and for this reason, an Italian or Spanish speaker's pronunciation of "pear" will often sound like "bear" to a German or English listener.

Research has shown that children are born as "universal listeners." This means that babies are born with the ability to acoustically discriminate between almost all of the speech sounds of any language of the world. This contrasts with adults' capabilities in this area. Adults often struggle to discriminate between speech sounds of a new language that are not part of their native language. This is because by the end of their first year of life, babies become attuned to the speech sounds that are specific to their native language and stop paying attention to phonetic details that are not relevant. As they become older and reach adulthood, they perceive all other languages through the filter of their first language speech sounds. For example, English and German speakers ignore whether a /d/ is produced with the tongue tip on the back of the teeth or just behind the alveolar ridge (in English and German, the tongue is usually placed on the ridge when saying "d"). But for a Hindi speaker, this difference in placement changes word meaning. Likewise, for a

Japanese listener, English /l/ and /r/ are perceived as the same sound because in Japanese the change in pronunciation does not lead to a change in word meaning. In other words, the first language sounds interfere with perceiving new speech sounds in a new language. This is likely because listeners become highly automatic and skilled in quickly perceiving the speech sounds of the first language and it is difficult to overcome these "overlearned" skills. A fascinating question is how children who acquire more than one language manage to develop the skills to decide which language sound system is in use; clearly, choosing the wrong system could have consequences, as in interpreting [p] as "bear" using English phonemes, but as "pear" for Spanish phonemes. We do not know enough yet about how children who simultaneously acquire two or more languages attune to the speech sounds of their different languages. What we do know is that lack of this understanding can lead to differences in their language skills being treated as impairment rather than as the natural pattern of multilingual language development.

Simultaneous multilingual children are exposed to more than one language from birth and have to acquire two or more phonological systems. These systems will overlap partially. Particularly when there is overlap but with subtle differences, as it is the case for /b/ and /p/ in German/English versus Italian/Spanish, that we need to better understand multilingual development. Two crucial questions are: (1) How will a multilingual child's development of each language's phonology differ from the monolingual pattern? (2) How will the amount of exposure to each of a multilingual child's languages affect pronunciation and perception of speech sounds.

How do we study speech sound perception in children?

How do we study what speakers and listeners are doing when they pronounce and perceive speech sounds? In adult studies, it is common to ask the adult to read a list of words or sentences (for pronunciation), and to listen to speech sounds in isolation or in pairs (for perception). For example, some studies ask the adult to decide whether a pair of words presented over headphones, such as "lake" and "rake", are the same or different. For studying children, the methods are modified to be more child-friendly. In other words, the tasks used with children are less complex and less cognitively demanding. For example, children can be asked to name a picture in a speech production task. In a speech perception task, they can be shown two pictures that differ by one phoneme, such as "bear" and "pear," and asked to "Look at the bear" or "Look at the pear." The researcher can then observe whether the child looks longer at the correct picture than at the competitor.

A third method, that we often use, is to measure the brain responses recorded from electrodes placed on the scalp. This is a safe method that can reveal whether the child discriminates between two sounds. This method is particularly useful for populations that are unable to perform a task, such as pushing a button, or who are unable to speak. The method records the electroencephalogram (EEG), which are our brain waves, in relation to speech sounds that the child is listening to. As will be shown below, the researcher can identify points in the timeline of an EEG waveform that indicate discrimination of speech sounds. The waveforms to speech differ for the different electrode sites and we use this information (topographic distribution) to figure out which part of the brain is processing the sound (for more details and a graphic overview see Chapter 5 in this volume, Pereira Soares et al.).

For studying speech sound discrimination in the brain using the EEG, we employ a method called 'Mismatch Negativity' (MMN, for short). In this method, the listener hears two different speech sounds. The 'standard' speech sound is presented frequently while the 'deviant' sound is presented rarely. For example, [pa] [pa] [pa] **[ba]** [pa] [pa] [pa] **[ba]** [pa] and so on, until at least 100 deviant sounds are presented. The EEG waveforms that correspond to each sound are averaged to isolate the brain activity generated to the sound. The brainwave response to the deviant and to the standard sounds can be compared. An easy way to examine the difference is to subtract them. If the brain response is the same to the speech sounds, then there will be no difference (that is, the subtraction will be zero). When a listener can discriminate between the speech sounds the brain response to the deviant is more negative than to the standard, and this is called the MMN. The negativity usually begins about 1/10th of a second after detection of the difference and can continue for 2/10th of a second. In addition, easy discriminations (for example, for very distinct contrasts) will show a larger and earlier MMN than difficult discriminations (for very subtle contrasts). In adults, discriminating between our native-language phonemes is automatic and does not need us to pay attention. For babies and young children, some sounds are very difficult to discriminate, unless they are paying attention. Over time, as the child receives more language input, speech sound discrimination becomes more automatic. This more automatic processing means that the MMN will occur whether the child is paying attention or not.

Speech sound perception in multilingual children

Very few studies asked whether multilingual children perceive the speech sounds in their languages with similar automaticity to monolingual speech perception. Using the MMN method, one study found evidence that 5-year-old Turkish-German children do not show brain responses indicating automatic discrimination of German vowel phonemes compared to their monolingual peers. These children began acquiring German after Turkish, and most had around three years of exposure to German (they were attending a German kindergarten). They did, however, show automatic discrimination of phonemes that exist in both Turkish and German.[142]

In a recent experiment, we looked at another multilingual group in Germany: children growing up with Italian and German. Even though Italian, similar to Turkish, is a heritage language in Germany, the language input situation is quite different. The Italian-speaking communities are much smaller than the Turkish ones and the pressure to use German is much stronger. In addition, it is more common for the Italian-German child to come from a household where one parent is a native German speaker and the other is a native Italian or multilingual Italian-German speaker compared to the Turkish-German child. The Italian-German children examined in

---

[142] Rinker, Alku, Brosch, & Kiefer, 2010.

our study all attended multilingual Italian-German kindergartens, thus ensuring that they were all getting some consistent input in Italian. We tested whether the amount of input in German and Italian would influence discrimination of /pa/ and /ba/ using the MMN method. As we described above, /p/ and /b/ are produced differently in Italian and German. When German speakers pronounce /pa/ they aspirate the sound, when at the beginning of a word. In addition, the time lag between when the lips are released (called the burst) and when the vowel begins is much longer than for German /b/. The vowel is produced by vibrations of the vocal folds (you can put your finger on your throat to feel if your vocal cords are vibrating when you say "a"). We say that German /p/ is produced with long lag and aspiration before the onset of the vowel in a word like "Pizza." When German speakers pronounce /ba/, there is a very short lag (less than 1/100th of a second) or no lag before the vowel begins. Thus, German /b/ is described as short-lag voice onset. In contrast, when Italian speakers produce /ba/, the vocal cords start vibrating before the /b/. We call this "voicing lead" or "prevoicing", whereas in Italian /pa/ is produced with short lag. So, across both German and Italian, there are actually three different phonetic sounds: voicing lead [b], short lag [p], and long lag [p^h]. These differences in the timing between when the vocal folds vibrate and when the closure release occurs are called Voice Onset Time (or VOT). As listeners we are attuned to perceive speech sounds through the filter of our native language, and thus, the Italian [p] and [b] are typically both heard as "b" by German listeners who do not speak Italian, and conversely, the German [p^h] and [p] are typically both heard as "p" by Italian speakers who do not speak German. In addition, listeners hear these non-native pronunciations as "accent" even when they are not quite sure why the pronunciation is not quite native-like.

We were particularly interested in whether multilingual children, who grow up speaking Italian and German, would show differences in how they discriminated the German "b" vs "p" (short lag [p] versus long-lag aspirated [p^h] VOT) and the Italian "b" vs "p" (prevoiced [b] versus short lag [p] VOT) and how the amount of experience in Italian and German affected discrimination.

To answer this question, we recorded the EEG of 4- to 6-year-old multilingual Italian-German and monolingual German children while they listened to [ba], [pa], and [pʰa] using the MMN method.[143] We wanted to test automatic processing, so we had the children watch a muted cartoon while listening to the speech sounds. The monolingual German children showed robust brain discrimination (that is, MMN) of German-specific /ba/ and /pa/ (phonetically [pa] and [pʰa]), but the Italian-German children did not. This finding shows a difference between typically-developing monolingual children and multilingual children who are still in the process of acquiring their languages. A similar finding was observed for Spanish-English 4- to 6-year-old children in New York City; they did not show brain discrimination of the vowel difference in "bed" and "bid."[144] These vowels are typically difficult to perceive for Spanish monolinguals because Spanish does not have words with the vowel in "bid." However, by 8- to 10-years of age, Spanish-English children from the New York City population showed robust discrimination of the vowels.[145] These older children had been exposed to English for at least five years (they all had begun their schooling by age five years in New York City). We also are finding in these studies that the brain responses to speech sounds look different in multilinguals compared to monolinguals and suggest that this is because multilinguals need to pay some attention to the speech sounds to decide which language system is being used.

Taking an even closer look at the language exposure of the Italian-German speaking children who participated in our study (which was assessed via a parental questionnaire), we saw that their exposure was not balanced between German and Italian. Despite attending a bilingual Italian-German kindergarten, the children received most of their input in German (on average, 56% German vs 44% in Italian). Their language output was even more oriented towards German (on average, 63% German vs 37% Italian). Even so, these young children showed differences in discriminating the German speech sounds.

---

[143] Bloder, Rinker, & Shafer (submitted).
[144] Vidal, 2016.
[145] Datta, Hestvik, Vidal, Tessel, Hisagi, Wróblewski, & Shafer, 2019.

We did find that multilingual children receiving the most German input showed stronger brain discrimination than children receiving less German input, but their discrimination was still not as robust as seen for children receiving only German input. Other studies have also shown a similar finding with even younger children.[146] In addition, children receiving the least Italian input were less stable in producing Italian-like /b/ and /p/.

Conclusion

Our study, as well as many others, shows how important it is to investigate multilinguals with a greater focus on individual experience in their languages. Furthermore, professionals in Speech-Language Therapy and Education need to be aware that the amount of input and output in a multilingual child's languages will influence how quickly they acquire the various languages, as well as leading to differences from monolingual children that should be understood as patterns of typical development.

Future studies will need to track how speech sound perception, as well as production, changes over time in relation to experience with the various languages of a multilingual child. A critical issue is that multilingual children often show the greatest difference from monolingual children on speech sound perception at the age when they are first entering school. Mis-classifying these children as disordered, rather than as multilingual speakers, can have negative consequences that extend into adulthood.

Finally, we want to end this chapter with a word of caution and reiterate that "different" or even "weaker" language abilities do not indicate "deficiency" in a multilingual child. It remains important to identify those children who do have DLD; over- identification is as much a concern as under-identification of a child with a language impairment. Unfortunately, there are no clear-cut criteria for when a "weakness" should be considered deficient in multilingual children. Clinicians, teachers, and parents need to be aware that multilingual children's language attainment must be assessed in relation to

---

[146] For instance, see Garcia-Sierra, Ramírez-Esparza, & Kuhl, 2016.

children with similar language input and output experience. We acknowledge that this issue is complex because multilingual language performance exists on a continuum and is constantly in flux. As a result, a multilingual child's language skills will change in ways that cannot be predicted from monolingual patterns. To make the most accurate decision when assessing a multilingual child's language skills, we urge clinicians to consider the relevance of language input by taking a detailed case history of each child's language background to allow evaluations of language performance in terms of language exposure and use. An important task of future research is to develop improved measures to assess multilingual children's language development. In addition, existing diagnostic tools can be improved by obtaining multilingual norms.

Multilinguals should not be viewed as being multiple monolinguals in one person. We support a more synergistic view of multilingualism in which the coexistence of two languages in one speaker generates a unique linguistic profile. Therefore, it should never be expected that multilingual children's language skills develop according to monolingual standards. Thus, linguistic skills of multilingual children should not be measured against those of monolingual peers. Moreover, multilingual abilities add considerable value to a child's life. Specifically, these skills give access to different cultures, more diverse social experiences, as well as access to their heritage by allowing the child to speak with older generations (such as grandparents) who may not have skills in the societal language.

Chapter 8. Bilingualism and vocabulary: Why speaking two languages doesn't mean fewer words

Daniela S. Avila-Varela, Gonzalo Garcia-Castro, and Nuria Sebastian-Galles

Families of bilingual kids sometimes are worried about their children's linguistic development being delayed compared to their monolingual pairs. This study shows that monolingual and bilingual kids understand a similar number of words, so being bilingual does not mean they will have a hard time learning language.

A classic tool used to study vocabulary development is the MacArthur Communicative Development Inventory,[147] aimed at quantifying the infant's lexicon through parents' reports. The CDIs include a list of approximately 600 words, and for each one, caregivers indicate whether the child knows (passively comprehends) or says (voluntarily produces) them. As an output, the child's total receptive and productive vocabulary size is estimated. *Receptive vocabulary size* refers to the number of words someone understands. Previous studies have shown that children start to comprehend frequent words such as "cookie" or "hand" between 6-9 months of age.[148] *Productive vocabulary size* refers to the number of words someone says. Previous research has found that many children start to say their first words by the end of the first year of life, and by the time they are 30 months old, the words they say increase to 500-600 words.[149]

The CDIs have been widely used worldwide due to several factors, including their low cost and the high correlation between the

---

[147] CDIs, Fenson et al., 1994.
[148] Bergelson & Swingley, 2015.
[149] Bates & Goodman, 1997; Fenson et al., 1994.

results of the CDIs and those obtained from naturalistic observations. Several studies have investigated the reliability and validity of the CDIs and found that they are a valid and efficient tool for assessing young children's language development. For example, a study by Fenson and collaborators (1994) compared the results of the CDIs with those obtained from standardized vocabulary tests and direct observations and found that the CDIs were highly correlated with these measures.

In terms of the cost-effectiveness of the CDIs, the low cost of the inventories has been a contributing factor to their widespread use, as it makes them accessible to a large number of researchers and practitioners. Thus, the CDI has been translated and adapted to other languages and cultures. For example, the Fragebogen zur frühkindlichen Sprachentwicklung[150] is its German adaptation. More recently, inventories to measure bilingual children's vocabulary have been developed, for example, United Kingdom Bilingual Toddler Assessment Tool,[151] and the English–Spanish Vocabulary Inventory.[152]

The CDIs provide a convenient and efficient way to assess young children's language development, and the results obtained are considered reliable and valid. However, it is important to note that the reliability and validity of the CDIs are dependent on the quality of the administration and scoring of the assessments. Therefore, it is crucial to follow the recommended administration procedures and to receive proper training on the use of the CDIs to ensure accurate and consistent results. In addition, studies utilizing parent-reported vocabulary assessments have revealed that both mothers and fathers are equally accurate in their evaluation of their child's vocabulary and concur with evaluations provided by their child's teacher.[153]

In terms of comparison with the Language Environment Analysis (LENA), LENA is a tool that uses digital recording to measure the amount and type of language children receive in their environment.

---

[150] FRAKIS; Szagun et al., 2009.
[151] UKBTAT, Floccia et al., 2018.
[152] ESVI, De Anda et al., 2022.
[153] Stolarova et al., 2014.

Although the LENA and CDI measure different aspects of language development, both are frequently used in research on children's linguistic development and complement each other. For example, LENA can provide information about the quantity and quality of linguistic stimulation a child receives, while the CDI focuses on concrete linguistic skills a child has acquired. In a replication study,[154] contrasted the results obtained from LENA between North American English-speaking infants and toddlers, children who were learning the dialect of English spoken in the United Kingdom, and older children who were raised in a different linguistic and socio-cultural environment (Tsimane learners in rural Bolivia). They discovered minimal variation in precision based on the child's age, dialect, or socio-cultural background on the measures provided by LENA. Indicating the broad applicability of the LENA system to assess the linguistic input and output of different populations.

Children's vocabulary size is linked to how accurately and fast they recognize words, so the more extensive a child's vocabulary is, the faster and more accurately they will identify words' referents.[155] Previous studies have shown that toddlers, the same way as adults, are influenced by the words previously heard (we are faster at identifying the word "doctor" if we have heard "nurse" before, or we are faster to recognize "banana" if we have just heard "ball").[156] In addition, longitudinal studies have shown that children with large vocabularies show better academic performance later on.[157]

Several factors are known to influence vocabulary sizes, such as age, gender, or the family's socio-economic status. Girls tend to have larger vocabulary sizes than boys of the same age.[158] This effect has been associated with the type of social interactions that young children receive. That is, young girls are more often talked to, and young boys tend to receive social interactions involving physical

---

[154] Cristia et al., 2021.
[155] Fernald & Marchman, 2012; Lany et al., 2018.
[156] Arias-Trejo et al., 2022; Avila-Varela et al., 2021; Chow et al., 2017.
[157] Bleses et al., 2016; Duff et al., 2015; Marchman & Fernald, 2008; Morgan et al., 2015.
[158] Andersson et al., 2011; Toivainen et al., 2017.

actions (such as playing with toys).[159] Children growing up in families with limited access to educational and economic resources tend to have a smaller vocabulary size than children growing up in families without such limitations.[160] This effect has been associated with several factors linked to low income.

Studies have shown that several variables are associated with higher vocabulary in young children. One crucial factor is the amount of language input children receive from their environment. Research indicates that children exposed to more diverse and rich language experiences tend to have larger vocabularies.[161] Children's temperament has also been found to affect their vocabulary development. For example, results from empirical studies suggest that children with higher expressive and receptive vocabularies, when compared to those with weaker vocabularies, exhibit greater adaptability, more positive moods, less emotionality, greater stability, and longer attention spans.[162] These findings highlight the importance of both environmental and individual factors in shaping children's language development and the need for interventions to support young children's vocabulary growth.

One factor that has been linked to children's low vocabulary is multilingualism. Some studies have concluded that monolingual children have larger vocabulary sizes than their multilingual counterparts.[163] Such studies, however, only measured monolinguals' and bilinguals' knowledge of the shared language (often English). But multilingual children also know words in their other languages. When multilingual children total vocabulary has been measured (for example, considering words in English and Spanish), the results have shown that their vocabulary size is similar to or larger than monolinguals'.[164] Another way to compare monolinguals' and multilinguals' vocabulary sizes is by considering the number of

---

[159] Lindsey & Mize, 2001.
[160] De Anda et al., 2016; Fernald et al., 2013.
[161] Hart & Risley, 2003.
[162] Dixon & Hull, 2000; Morales et al., 2000.
[163] for example, Bialystok et al., 2010.
[164] Bosch & Ramon-Casas, 2014; Core et al., 2013; De Houwer et al., 2014

objects (or concepts) for which children know at least one word (if a Spanish-German bilingual knows the word *unicornio* [Spanish], or *Einhorn* [German], or both, it would be counted as one concept. Studies comparing monolinguals' and bilinguals' "conceptual" vocabulary in this way have not found differences between the two populations.[165]

Research has found that the processes in monolingual and bilingual linguistic development are the same, such as the dependence of language growth on the quantity and quality of language exposure and the relation between children's language use and language growth. However, monolingual and bilingual language development differs in terms of the outcomes. That is, they differ in the rate of language development and the profiles of expressive and receptive vocabulary. This is because of the immediate environments and larger sociocultural contexts in which bilinguals and monolinguals grow.[166] It is important to note that infants exposed to multiple languages vary in their linguistic exposure type, amount, and context. The amount of language a child receives is crucial for language acquisition, especially for children's vocabulary size. Bilingual children, while navigating switches in language inherent to bilingual environments, still face the same challenge of learning two languages simultaneously.[167] Language input patterns change dynamically over time, and as infants grow, their input and speech output contribute to their language development.[168]

Many children are exposed to multiple languages and learn words in each. How does the number of known languages impact the vocabulary development of multilingual individuals? In a study by Côté and collaborators (2020), the authors compared the vocabulary abilities of bilingual and trilingual toddlers raised in a bilingual community where French and English are spoken. They predicted that due to the reduction of French and English input caused by the time spent hearing their third language, trilinguals would have

---

[165] Mancilla-Martinez & Vagh, 2013.
[166] Hoff, 2017.
[167] Byers-Heinlein, 2020.
[168] Surrain & Luk, 2019.

smaller French-English vocabulary sizes than bilinguals. However, the difference was insignificant due to high levels of variability. Further analysis showed a correlation between the amount of input and vocabulary size. These results suggest that similar factors influence vocabulary development in toddlers regardless of the number of languages they are acquiring. Therefore, it has been suggested that policies that support frequent exposure to high-quality experiences in each of a child's languages are needed to promote successful bilingual development.[169]

Numerous studies have investigated the similarities and differences between monolingual and bilingual vocabulary development. Research has consistently shown that bilingual children can acquire vocabulary at a similar pace as monolingual children, although there may be some differences in the way that bilingual children learn words in their two languages. For example, a study by Bialystok and her team (2010) found that bilingual children tend to have smaller vocabularies in each of their languages compared to monolingual children, but they also have a larger overall vocabulary size due to their exposure to two languages. Overall, the research suggests that bilingual children are able to develop strong vocabulary skills in both of their languages, but the ways in which they learn words may be different from monolingual children. In a recent study, Floccia and collaborators (2018) discovered that bilingual infants who are learning languages that are closely related have larger vocabularies than those who are learning languages that are more distantly related. These results suggest that bilingual exposure can have an impact on the size and composition of children's vocabulary but that bilingual children are able to successfully acquire vocabulary in multiple languages. To fully understand the similarities and differences between monolingual and bilingual vocabulary development, more research is needed.

A study by Legacy and team (2018) explored the connection between lexical processing and vocabulary size in bilingual children. The study followed the lexical development of French-English

---

[169] Fibla et al., 2022.

bilingual toddlers over six months and found that all toddlers increased their understanding and use of words. The study revealed a connection between language exposure, vocabulary size, and processing speed, with the proportion of language exposure impacting vocabulary size.

To support bilingual children in developing their vocabulary, families can take several evidence-based approaches. One effective strategy is to provide bilingual children with a rich and diverse language environment, which has been shown to enhance children's vocabulary development in both their first and second languages.[170] This can be achieved through activities such as reading books, telling stories, and engaging in conversations in both languages. Additionally, it is important to support children's language learning by providing them with opportunities to use their language skills in real-life situations, such as visiting a store, park, or other location where they can interact with other speakers. Families can also encourage bilingual children to use their second language by finding opportunities for them to interact with native speakers or by enrolling them in language classes. These approaches will help bilingual children to expand their vocabulary in both languages and develop the ability to understand and use language in meaningful ways.

Although the difference between monolingual and bilingual children may seem trivial, the fact is that in multilingual communities, it is not uncommon for children growing up in monolingual environments to overhear the other languages. In what follows, we will present the results comparing monolingual and bilingual toddlers' total receptive vocabulary size. Wait! Monolinguals, by definition, only know and speak one language, right? Despite the many ways a monolingual can be defined, it is not easy to be a true monolingual, especially for adults who learn and use words from other languages.[171] This is the situation in Barcelona, where the study we are about to report took place. Multilingual environments are not uncommon; consider, for instance, the case of a child born in the US in an English monolingual household but

---

[170] Smithson et al., 2014.
[171] Castro, S., Wodniecka, Z., & Timmer, K., 2022.

growing up in a Latino borough in the US. One novelty of the present study is the fact that although we identify children as monolinguals and bilinguals, we have measured their knowledge in the two languages they may have been exposed to.

As just said, the present investigation took place in the great Barcelona area. There are two Romance languages spoken in Barcelona: Catalan and Spanish, to give a rough estimate about how different the two languages are, they are as similar (or different) as Italian and Spanish or as Dutch and German. Catalan and Spanish are co-official languages, and they are very well represented at all levels. Students are expected to have equivalent knowledge of the two languages at the end of the schooling system, and virtually everybody understands the two languages. Here we analyzed the total vocabulary size of Catalan monolinguals, Spanish monolinguals, and Catalan-Spanish bilingual children from the Barcelona Metropolitan Area. Following standard practice,[172] we considered 80% exposure to a single language the threshold to consider a child as growing up monolingual.

When comparing monolinguals and bilinguals, we took special care to match every monolingual participant with a bilingual participant of similar age and gender and raised by parents with equivalent educational levels. We included parental educational level as it is commonly used in infancy research to estimate socioeconomic status.[173]

We report data from 136 children. Sixty-eight children were monolinguals (35 females, 33 males), with an average age of 20.35 months (age range = 11-34 months). Fifty-three children were Catalan monolinguals (exposed to Catalan 97% of the time on average), and 15 were Spanish monolinguals (exposed to Spanish 95% of the time on average). Sixty-eight participants were bilinguals (females = 35, males = 33) with a mean age of 20.37 months (age range = 11-34 months). Forty-two bilinguals were predominantly exposed to Catalan (at least 70% of the time on average), 14

---

[172] Byers-Heinlein et al., 2021.
[173] Fung et al., 2019.

bilinguals were mainly exposed to Spanish (at least 70% of the time on average), and 12 were balanced bilinguals (meaning they were exposed half of the time to Catalan and half to Spanish). As said, the caregivers of the monolinguals and bilinguals had similar educational levels (at least one parent with a college degree: monolinguals = 57, bilinguals = 58). The process of sample selection is shown in Figure 1.

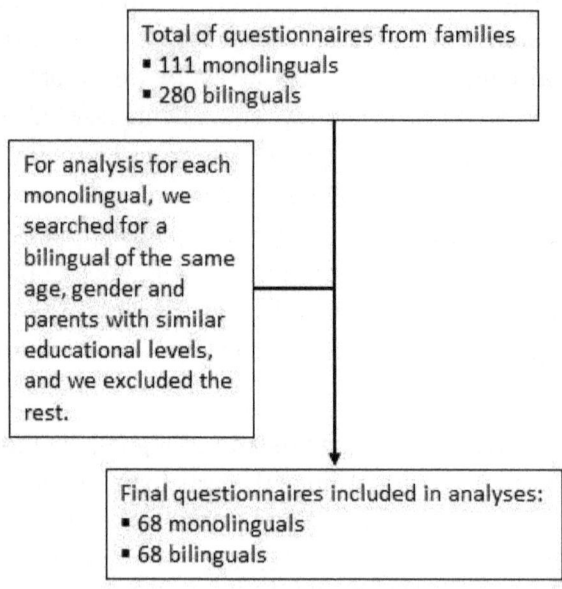

Figure 1. Final sample selection.

To estimate children's vocabulary size, we sent families an online vocabulary questionnaire by email: the Barcelona Vocabulary Questionnaire (BVQ).[174] The questionnaire included a list of words in Spanish and Catalan, for which parents had to specify whether the child understood or said that word. Here we report the total receptive vocabulary size, that is, the words understood in Spanish and those understood in Catalan. Monolinguals had a mean total receptive vocabulary size of 253 words (range = 6-631), and bilinguals knew around 295 words (range = 13-652). See Figure 2 for a graph of the

---

[174] Garcia-Castro et al., 2023.

total vocabulary size of monolinguals and bilinguals. The results showed no differences between the two groups.

We analyzed the data using binomial logistic regression. This statistical test determines whether the total vocabulary size will predict the child's linguistic profile (monolingual or bilingual). Results show that adding total vocabulary size to the model did not significantly improve predicting whether participants were monolingual or bilingual [$\chi2(1) = 2.59$, $p = .107$]. Therefore, there is no way to predict whether a child is bilingual, or monolingual based on the number of words they know.

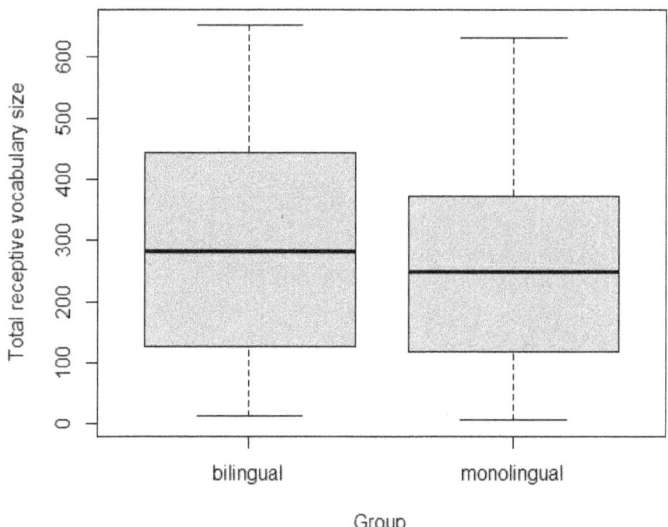

Figure 2. Total receptive vocabulary size of the participants, 68 monolinguals and 68 matched bilinguals in gender and parents' educational level.

The results of our study clearly show that bilingualism does not necessarily hinder the acquisition of vocabulary. They parallel recent research that has not found reduced total vocabulary size of bilinguals compared to monolinguals (Bosch & Ramon-Casas, 2014; Core et al., 2013; De Houwer et al., 2014). Our results indicate that provided enough environmental support (here, in the form of a bilingual society), bilinguals may develop equivalent vocabulary sizes in their languages. Words are learned because children hear them, so any factor influencing the amount of exposure to a certain language will have an impact on the vocabulary the child acquires.

Finally, we want to mention the existence of "confirmation bias" in some caregivers' perception: because caregivers of multilingual children may expect such children to be delayed, they only pay attention and interpret information that confirms such potential delay (like, for instance, comparing the multilingual child with another child with exceptional vocabulary, instead of comparing her with the average of the population).

Conclusion

Even though many families may be concerned about their children growing up using two or more languages, this study and others do not suggest that multilingual children have a reduced vocabulary compared to monolingual children.

Chapter 9. When learning two languages from birth is *not* confusing

Grazia Di Pisa and Theodoros Marinis

Will speaking two languages or more cause confusion or even delay my child's language development? Isn't it harder to acquire two languages than just one? Well, if any of this sounds familiar and you are concerned about your bilingual child's language development, then keep reading because you will find some answers to these common questions and some tips on how to raise your child bilingual.

In studies with multilinguals, testing sessions usually end with lots of questions from the participants on how to improve their language skills as well as with personal conversations on how they learned their languages. In a recent study on how people with Italian as a minority language who grew up in Germany acquire grammatical gender, one participant really struck us, not only because his performance was really good but mainly because he told us that he was going to be a father soon and he timidly admitted that he was not sure whether he wanted to talk with his daughter in Italian from the very beginning or if he should talk with her only in German. He said that maybe he should start talking with her in Italian when she is older. The main reasons were that he felt insecure about his level of Italian and that he was afraid of confusing her or that speaking to her using two languages would have been too much for his little girl. This was the starting point for a conversation that uncovered how a lot of misinformation is still surrounding bi-/multilingualism and raising children with more than one language. What made the conversation even more interesting to us was that he himself was raised bilingually and although he was not using Italian on a regular basis, his performance was stunning. We couldn't believe it—or maybe the researcher in us was a bit disappointed to hear that—bilingualism is still viewed by many people in a negative way even by those who have been raised bilingually themselves. So, this made us wonder where this misleading conception or idea about bilingualism—and being raised bilingually—is coming from and what we—researchers—can do to shake off this misconception.

Our study was done within the European context where bi-/multilingualism is a cornerstone of the European Union (EU) and nowadays being multilingual in Europe is becoming more prevalent and important. There are various examples of people speaking different languages in their daily lives: they use one language with their parents and another language with the people they live, work, or study with. For example, on a daily basis, we both speak three languages, Italian/Greek with our family and friends back in Italy/Greece, English with colleagues at work, and Dutch/English with our partners and Dutch/German with the people around us because we live in the Netherlands/Germany. *Do you know that one of the objectives of the EU's language policy is for every EU citizen to master two other languages in addition to their mother tongue?* Indeed, language learning has been designated as an important priority by the European Commission and every year a lot of programs and projects in this area are funded in order to promote mobility and intercultural understanding.[175] Furthermore, recently in its resolution of December 2020,[176] the EU Parliament expressed its support for protecting linguistic minorities and promoting language learning and linguistic diversity across the EU.

Contrary to the idea that two languages confuse children, research has consistently proven that well-developed bilingualism actually has a positive impact on the brain and cognitive development[177,178] as well as helping to prevent dementia in old age.[179] For example, bilinguals

---

[175] Retrieved from the European Education Area website / Focus topics / Improving quality / Multilingualism / Linguistic diversity.
[176] European Parliament resolution of 17 December 2020 on the European Citizens' Initiative Minority SafePack
[177] Bialystok, Craik, Luk, 2012.
[178] Kroll, Dussias, Bogulski, Kroff, 2012.
[179] Voits, Pliatsikas, Robson, Rothman, 2020.

tend to have better executive functions, which are skills that enable us to plan, focus attention, remember instructions, and juggle multiple tasks successfully (e.g., to keep the focus on a task despite distractions around us or to switch back and forth between different tasks).[180] Bilinguals have also been demonstrated to have a better working memory, which is the ability to keep something in memory while doing another task.[181] Furthermore, these advantages help them to multitask better and have more developed problem-solving abilities and creative thinking than monolinguals (see Chapter 1 in this volume). Finally, bilinguals have also been shown to have better metalinguistic awareness, which is being aware of the regularities and patterns of a language.[182,183] If you already know more than one language, you understand that every language has different ways to express an idea and sometimes it is difficult to translate an idea from language A to language B because language B doesn't have a specific word or it does have a word that is very similar to language A, but that word has a slightly different or a completely different meaning, which can be confusing. If you already know more than one language, you also understand that every language has a different grammar, and you actively look for the grammar of a new language. For example, if you speak English and Italian, you know that these languages have definite and indefinite articles (English: *the, a*; Italian: *il/la, un/una*) and Italian has different forms of articles for nouns with masculine versus feminine gender, but English doesn't. When learning a new language, for example, Dutch, you will look at whether Dutch is like English or Italian or whether it may also have a completely different system. If you already know more than one language, you have also developed some language-learning strategies that help you learn new languages. This better metalinguistic awareness and learning strategies together with better executive functions and working memory make bilinguals better at learning new languages than monolinguals.

---

[180] Bialystok, 2011.
[181] Blom, Küntay, Messer, Verhagen, Leseman, 2014.
[182] Bialystok, 1986.
[183] Bialystok & Barac 2012.

These are important advantages of bi-/multilingualism. It is true however that bilingual children usually have a smaller vocabulary[184] in each language than children who grew up with only one language. However, when we measure the vocabulary of both languages, they have the same or larger vocabulary compared to monolingual children[185] (see Chapter 8 in this volume). They also sometimes 'mix' the two languages and *some* children might temporarily lag behind their monolingual peers.[186] It is important to stress that *some* children might have a temporary lag while other children will not show any lag at all. This is because there is considerable variability within bilingual children and it depends on so many factors, such as how much exposure to the two languages the children get at home and from the society surrounding them or with how many people the child interacts in the two languages.[187, 188] Even though a temporary lag in bilingual children has been reported, possibly due to the fact that the brain has to accommodate two language systems, research has found that raising a child bilingually does not cause language learning difficulties and usually these children presenting a lag in speaking will catch up with their peers very soon (see Chapter 13 in this volume). Moreover, if we calculate the bilingual children's vocabulary in both languages they speak, then their vocabulary is as large or even larger than the vocabulary of monolingual children of the same age. So, it is not true that they know fewer words, they know the same number of words or even more words than their monolingual peers, but these words are distributed across two or more languages.

It is quite interesting—and shocking at the same time—that regardless of how commonplace bi-/multilingualism has become, so many myths and misconceptions still exist that learning two or more languages can have a negative effect on children despite the overwhelming research proving evidence otherwise.[189] As a

---

[184] Bialystok, E., Luk, G., Peets, K. F., & Sujin, Y. A. N. G. (2010).
[185] Bialystok, 2009.
[186] Bialystok, 2001.
[187] Unsworth, 2016.
[188] Altinkamis & Simon, 2020.
[189] Bialystok, 2009a.

consequence, many parents still get discouraged, and grow fearful of raising their children with more than one language because they are worried that this might affect their children's language development negatively. One of the myths about bilingualism that needs to be debunked as soon as possible is that "Exposing children to multiple languages may cause delays in speech development." Well, let's get this straight: bilingualism DOES NOT cause language delays in children.[190] Language development is different in all children and while some children will start talking earlier than others—which is also the case with some monolingual children—some bilingual children may start speaking fluently later than their monolingual peers. This is because they are learning a word in two languages, so they actually develop two vocabularies. However, this doesn't mean that their actual language is delayed, also because if a child has a language disorder, this will be visible in both languages. Another common misbelief is "Learning two languages will confuse my child" and this might come from the fact that bilingual children sometimes may use words from multiple languages in the same sentence or mix up grammar rules,[191] but this does not mean they are confused. Some of my participants who are parents and are raising their children bilingual (Italian-German), often asked me what is and isn't typical or expected, or how their child will differ from those children who are learning a single language. For example, two participants asked me if it was normal that their children said sentences like this: "Mama, Ich mag *gelato*." 'Mummy, I like ice-cream' or "Mama, wo ist *der Ball rote*?" 'Mummy, where is the red ball?'. *Gelato* means 'ice cream' in Italian and for *der Ball rote* while in German the attributive adjective always comes before the noun, in Italian, it is usually the other way around. So, what these children are doing is actually mixing vocabulary and grammar rules from German and Italian. Mixing languages or *code-switching* is completely normal and it is a natural part of bilingual language development.[192] Also, proficient adult bilinguals often code-switch when they converse with other bilinguals. We actually do it ourselves when we

---

[190] Genesee, 2001.
[191] Muysken, 2000.
[192] Pearson, 2008.

speak with our partners, sometimes we throw a word from different languages together. Parents raising bilingual children sometimes worry that this mixing is a negative consequence of learning two languages simultaneously, making them wonder if they did something wrong or even worse, they get discouraged and drop one of the languages.

We recently studied the acquisition of grammatical gender in bilingual Italian-German adults. These were second-generation Italians who were born, grew up, and lived in Germany, so-called 'heritage' speakers of Italian. Gender—masculine (*il libro* 'the book') vs. feminine (*la casa* 'the house')—is usually acquired early and easily by Italian monolingual children because the Italian gender system has a high degree of transparency, that is, the endings -a and -o of the noun indicate of the noun is feminine (-a) or masculine (-o). In German, gender is less transparent compared to Italian because there are no clear endings that indicate if a noun has a masculine, feminine, or neuter gender. Furthermore, some words that have one gender in Italian may have a different gender in German; for example, *il pane* 'the bread' in Italian is masculine, while in German *das Brot* is neuter. So, there could be some confusion about the gender of some nouns, especially when the nouns in the two languages have a different gender. Grammatical gender in many languages manifests itself also on adjectives, (una$_{FEM}$ torre$_{FEM}$ antica$_{FEM}$ 'a tower old'), a phenomenon called gender agreement. Previous studies have shown that second language learners have difficulties with grammatical gender, especially if the first language of the learner doesn't have gender.[193] It is unclear if the same holds for heritage speakers, this is why our study investigated whether heritage speakers of Italian are as good as monolingual Italians in acquiring the Italian grammatical gender. We compared how Italian-German bilingual and Italian monolingual adults processed Italian sentences that had correct gender agreement between the noun and the adjective (*una$_{FEM}$ torre$_{FEM}$ antica$_{FEM}$* 'a tower old') and sentences that had incorrect gender

---

[193] Dussias, Kroff, Tamargo & Gerfen, 2013.

agreement between the noun and the adjective (*una*$_{FEM}$ *torre*$_{FEM}$ **antico*$_{MASC}$ 'a tower old').

Our study included three different tasks designed to assess the participants' mastery of Italian gender. The first task was a self-paced reading task where participants were asked to silently read the sentences for comprehension. The task is called 'self-paced reading' because participants had to press a button on their keyboard to make each new word of the sentence appear and thus read the sentence word-by-word at their own pace. The computer registered the button presses which allowed us to find out how long it took to read each word in a sentence. Participants typically slow down if there is a grammatical error. Hence, if participants process gender agreement, they are expected to slow down when they read the adjective with the incorrect gender agreement. The second task was a 'judgment' task where participants needed to read the same sentences and decide whether they were grammatically correct or incorrect. The third task was an oral production task where we asked our participants to create a correct sentence with gender agreement by looking at some pictures and verbal stimuli (see example in Figure 1 for masculine nouns). Participants saw the beginning of a sentence and the noun and adjective they had to use to complete it. What they saw is called the 'probe'. Then they had to produce a sentence, the 'target'. We used three different tasks because we wanted to have a complete picture of how good they are not only in reading but also in judging and producing gender agreement.

The results from the reading task and the judgment task showed that overall heritage speakers of Italian were reading the sentences at a slower rate than monolinguals and were also less accurate in judging the correctness of sentences. However, both groups were faster in reading sentences and also more accurate in detecting errors when the sentences contained a masculine noun compared to sentences containing a feminine noun. This means despite reading slower and making more errors, the heritage speakers were processing gender errors in a similar way as monolingual Italians.

Figure 1. Example of an oral production task.

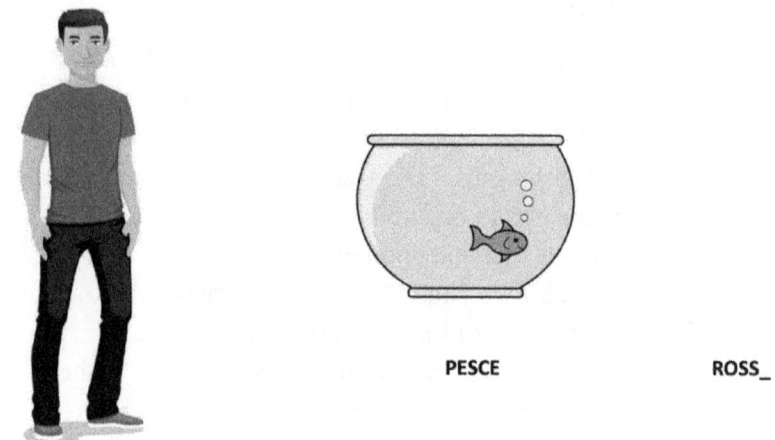

MARCO HA COMPRATO...

Probe: Marco ha comprato ___ pesce ross_.

Marco bought ___ fish red.

'Marco bought ...... red fish.'

Target: Marco ha comprato il/un$_{MASC}$ pesce$_{MASC}$ rosso$_{MASC}$.

Marco bought the/a fish red.

'Marco bought the/a red fish.'

The fact that our participants' performance was better with masculine nouns is consistent with the proposal that in Italian masculine is considered the 'default' gender and feminine the marked one. The default gender is usually more frequent in the language compared to the marked gender. In Italian, masculine nouns by far outnumber feminine ones: 60% of the nouns are masculine and 40% are feminine. Thus, there are more masculine words in Italian, and this could explain why our participants were better with sentences containing masculine nouns. Regarding the production task, our heritage speakers were better at creating sentences when the noun was masculine—again the default gender theory applies—furthermore, we found that bilinguals had more difficulties in assigning the correct gender to the noun than doing the correct agreement with the adjective.[194] This means that they know the grammatical rule about how to make the adjective agree with the noun but they actually struggle with knowing the gender of the noun. In addition, proficiency, and the amount of exposure at home to the minority language were the two factors that played an important role and were related to our heritage bilinguals' performance (see Chapter 5).

These results are important for language instructors and parents but also for researchers in language acquisition. For teachers and parents, the results from our study suggest that in the classroom or at home it would be better to invest more time and do more exercises with feminine compared to masculine nouns because masculine gender is the default gender and learners will learn it easier than feminine gender which is the marked gender. These exercises should focus not only on the articles but also on the gender agreement between the noun and the adjective and should draw the attention of the learners to the gender cues of the nouns (for example, in Italian a- for feminine). Knowledge of these cues can help the learners develop their metalinguistic awareness and exercises can help them internalize the rules.

In terms of language development, our results show that bilinguals who learned a minority language at home mainly from their parents and in a context where this minority language is not the language spoken in the society may make some errors in their production and when they judge the grammaticality of a sentence, but they process grammatical gender in the same way as monolinguals and their errors are related to their level of proficiency in Italian. Furthermore, the more bilinguals are exposed to the minority language in the home, the better they know the gender of the noun, the better they are at processing gender agreement, and the faster they become at reading in Italian. This suggests that more exposure to the heritage language in the home is beneficial for acquiring and maintaining gender agreement. Increasing your child's exposure to the minority language in the home could be easily done by providing your child with diverse

---

[194] Kupisch, Akpınar, & Stöhr, 2013.

original materials, for example, books and movies in the original language. Raising a bilingual child could be challenging, especially when the language you are trying to transmit to your child is not the language of society and not the language at school. So, in the remainder of this chapter, we would like to give some tips for parents who raise bilingual children in a society where the language in the home and school is not the language of the society.

First, we would like to emphasize the importance of making learning a language fun, natural, and consistent because this increases the children's motivation and quality of input.[195] It is also very important to make the child understand that the language they are learning serves a functional purpose. This is important because if the child does not need to use this language or sees no opportunities to use the language, then they will probably refuse or stop using it. So, the best advice would be to consistently give the child the opportunity to use the language in different scenarios and situations and ideally with a variety of speakers because this will expose them to different vocabulary, sentence types, and accents, which is beneficial for language learning.[196] Providing your child with many opportunities to hear, speak, play, and interact with the home language will increase the child's curiosity and interest in the language. For example, a good starting point would be to find playgroups where there are other children who speak the same language. Having face-time conversations or WhatsApp groups with the family back in the country of origin to interact with them orally or by text—especially for the older kids. Furthermore, in many countries, it is now becoming increasingly common to find Saturday courses specifically designed for minority languages at different levels of proficiency organized by your local municipality; so, another good tip would be to enroll your child in these courses. This will not only give them the opportunity to learn the language in a school environment and to learn how to read and write, which is crucial for language learning and maintenance[197] but it will also give them the

---

[195] Dornyei, 2019.
[196] Cohen, Bauer, & Minniear, 2021.
[197] Bialystok, 2002.

opportunity to make new friends they could speak with in the home language.

Reading is of course one of the best ways to bring a second language into your home. For example, you can establish a daily or weekly bedtime story routine where you will read aloud to your child in your home language(s). Picture books and storybooks are the best way to learn new vocabulary and new speech sounds while associating a specific word with a picture.[198] Movies and songs are also the perfect way to expose your child to new words and new sounds.[199,200] Nowadays you can find every kind of movie, cartoon, educational show and of course, a lot of songs for children and nursery rhymes in different languages, and also, so like for reading, listen with your child to the Italian version of 'Whisky il ragnetto' or in German 'Itze Bitze Spinne' and then why not, try to sing it together with your child, because it is fun, and children love to sing.

Of course, there are also plenty of child-friendly apps for learning languages because, let's be honest, children are surrounded by technology nowadays and we should also appreciate the benefits of these new media. Tablets and dedicated apps for learning languages could be a really easy and entertaining way to learn a language by playing.[201] Needless to say, these resources should be considered as an add-on to the rest because learning a language also means interaction, so the best way would be to integrate some learning apps once in a while especially for building up the vocabulary and for games. And of course, always keep an eye on screen time.

Conclusion

To sum up, we have seen that it is possible to acquire and master grammatical gender in bilinguals and that there are plenty of ways to increase the quantity but also the quality of exposure to a language at home. However, raising a child bilingually is a long journey that requires a lot of patience and dedication, especially when you are

---

[198] Logan, Justice, Yumus, & Chaparro-Moreno, 2019.
[199] Salcedo, 2010.
[200] Aliyev, & Albay, 2016.
[201] Loewen, Isbell & Sporn, 2020.

transmitting to your child a language that is not the language spoken in the society you and your child live in.

Part 4:
Myths on multilingualism and education

Chapter 10. Fostering multilingualism to support children's school success

Jasmijn E. Bosch and Francesca Foppolo

There seems to be a persistent myth that the use of the native language at school negatively affects the academic outcomes of multilingual children. However, evidence from a wide range of educational settings, including linguistically diverse classrooms in mainstream education, bilingual programs, and so-called 'submersion' contexts, suggests the exact opposite. Rather than seeing multilingualism as an obstacle, we therefore argue that it should be viewed as an opportunity to ensure inclusive education and equal opportunities for all.

Most parents, teachers and policy makers will agree that learning different languages is an important part of children's education, but not all languages are equally valued. When it comes to high-prestige European languages such as English or French, multilingualism is seen as an enrichment. Yet, the multilingualism that is brought into the classroom by students with a migration background is often seen as an obstacle rather than an opportunity. It is widely believed that academic performance of multilingual students can be improved by maximizing the amount of input in the school language and by rejecting the use of native languages at school. In some cases, teachers even encourage parents to use the majority language of the country in which they live rather than their native language.

However, current research shows that supporting native language development and multilingual literacy can have various positive effects on children's school success. In this chapter, we will review findings from very different educational contexts around the world, including linguistically diverse classrooms in monolingual mainstream education, bilingual education programs, and so called 'submersion' contexts in which students are fully taught in their second language. We will discuss the benefits of involving students' native languages in education, focusing on the positive effects on learning outcomes.

Linguistically diverse classrooms in monolingual education

In an increasingly globalizing world, schools are becoming more and more multilingual. For instance, in 2018, almost 15% of the students enrolled in European secondary schools spoke another language within their family.[202] In some schools, mostly in urban areas in countries that have attracted a lot of immigration during the last decades, it might even be difficult to find any monolingual native speakers of the majority language of the country. This means that multilingualism is the reality, even in monolingual schools.

There are many benefits to growing up with more than one language. Firstly, multilingual children may have an advantage when learning foreign languages because they are more sensitive to the sounds and structures of different languages. Secondly, some research suggests that their experience with managing and monitoring two languages in everyday life may have positive cognitive effects that extend beyond language. For example, multilingual children might be better at switching between tasks and at focusing on a specific task while filtering out irrelevant information.[203] And last but not least, speaking more than one language allows children to communicate with family members, it grants them access to another culture and it allows them to fully develop their own multicultural identity.

However, the multilingualism of immigrant students enrolled in schools is often problematized. International comparative research shows that on average 15-year-old students with a migration background tend to underperform in reading, mathematics, and science in comparison with their monolingual peers, a fact which is often ascribed to insufficient proficiency in the school language. Many countries have therefore developed educational language

---

[202] OECD, 2019.
[203] Bialystok & Barac, 2012.

policies that emphasize the importance of gaining a high proficiency in the language of instruction as early as possible.

Several studies have shown that teachers in different countries are concerned about the language development and school performance of students who speak another language at home. For example, in a study conducted in Italy, Austria and Great Britain, researchers found that even though primary school teachers show some awareness of the cognitive benefits of multilingualism, many of them still believe that the frequent use of the native language will hinder the learning of the school language, and that switching between languages will cause children to be confused. Because of this, a significant proportion of teachers indicated that they do not allow children to use their native language in class, and that they never make reference to the cultural or linguistic background of the students while teaching.[204] Similar results were found in other countries: while some teachers have up-to-date knowledge and positive views towards multilingualism, there are still many teachers across Europe with negative attitudes and monolingual mindsets.[205] Teachers' attitudes towards multilingualism matter, not only to create a more inclusive school environment, but also because they are related to teachers' expectations and trust in the academic engagement of their multilingual students. This is crucial, since students tend to perform better when their teachers have high expectations of them,[206] perhaps due to increased efforts on the teachers' part as well as improved self-confidence and motivation in students. This means that to ensure equal opportunities for multilingual students within a monolingual education system, teachers should be provided with effective training on issues related to linguistic and cultural diversity, including second language learning and the importance of native language maintenance.

Even if a teacher does not speak the native languages of the students, there are several ways in which multilingual approaches can be implemented in linguistically diverse classrooms. First, it is

---

[204] De Angelis, 2011.
[205] Bosch et al., submitted.
[206] Rosenthal & Jacobson, 1968.

important to acknowledge and appreciate the home languages of students, for example by learning how to greet each other or by singing songs in different native languages. Teachers can also build on students' knowledge in their native language, by allowing them to conduct group work with students who speak the same language or to look up information from sources in different languages. Moreover, multilingualism may be a resource during language teaching. For example, explicitly asking students how a certain grammatical structure works in their native language will improve their understanding of the language that is being taught, as well as their metalinguistic awareness about how language systems work in general. In Chapter 11 of this volume, Santarelli and Faloppa will discuss in more detail how teachers can implement multilingual pedagogy in their teaching, even if they do not speak the languages of their students themselves. In Chapter 12, Olioumtsevits, Franck and Papadopoulou will elaborate on how teachers can make use of students' prior linguistic knowledge to improve second language learning.

Recently, several research projects have shown positive effects of multilingual approaches in education. An interesting example is the *3M* project that was conducted in primary schools in the bilingual province of Friesland in the Netherlands; in which Frisian is spoken as a local minority language in addition to Dutch. In this project, the researchers developed, implemented and tested innovative multilingual teaching materials suitable for different ages. The goal of this project was not only to integrate Dutch, Frisian and English as languages of instruction, but also to increase appreciation of native languages of immigrant children by actively using them within the teaching program.[207] Similarly, positive results were found by the *L'AltRoparlante* project in the center and north of Italy, in which particular attention was paid to the physical presence of other languages in and around the classroom, as well as collaborative group work using different languages and multilingual storytelling with the help of parents.[208] This type of approach builds on the

---

[207] Duarte, & Günther-van der Meij, 2020.
[208] Carbonara & Scibetta, 2022.

linguistic resources of students by giving all languages a meaningful role in education.

In the next section, we will present findings from bilingual education, in which multilingualism is seen as a goal rather than a challenge to be dealt with. This specific educational context may provide valuable insights on how to improve learning outcomes of multilingual students.

Lessons from bilingual education

In a bilingual school, the goal is to teach the curriculum through two languages, so that students will obtain high proficiency and literacy in both of them. Some of the first bilingual programs were implemented in the 1960s in Quebec, a French-English bilingual region in Canada, in order to promote bilingualism among the English-speaking population. These schools were also referred to as 'language immersion' schools, because English-speaking children were immersed in their second language, French. The goal was to create an environment in which children could learn their second language in a natural and implicit way, by being exposed to a language in a meaningful social setting, quite similar to the way in which children acquire their first language. These schools made use of content- and language-integrated learning, in which second language learning and content learning of the subject matter take place simultaneously. Research shows that this type of approach can be very successful: students in French immersion programs typically show similar performance as comparable students in monolingual English programs, while they reach high levels of proficiency in French as a second language.[209]

Bilingual education is also quite common in the US, particularly in areas in which there are large communities of Spanish speakers. The large majority of these are transitional bilingual education programs that aim to prepare children for a monolingual English education system. This means that children are taught partly in Spanish during the first years of schooling (in early-exit programs) or

---

[209] Genesee, 2013.

during primary school (in late-exit programs). The disadvantage of such a program is that it does not support bi- or multilingualism since the aim is to replace the native language as soon as possible. In contrast, so-called 'dual language programs', which are gaining popularity during recent years, aim to provide Spanish-English bilingual education in which both languages are valued equally, by giving key importance to native language maintenance and literacy development. Research has shown many advantages of dual language education as compared to transitional bilingual programs and monolingual education. Not only does it lead to higher proficiency and stronger literacy skills in Spanish, but in some cases, children in dual language programs also perform better in other school subjects, such as science and mathematics, and even English.[210] In some cases, dual language schools make use of 'two-way immersion', in which Spanish-English bilingual children and monolingual children from English-speaking families are put together in the same bilingual program, so that they can learn with and from each other. This way, English-speaking children have the opportunity to learn Spanish, while bilingual children can fully develop their native language in addition to English.[211]

During the last decades, bilingual education has become more popular all over the world, not only in bilingual regions and border areas, but also as a way for children from monolingual families to become bilingual. The most common second language of instruction, besides the majority language of the country, is English. There seems to be a worldwide trend to use more and more English at different levels of education, as it tends to be regarded as a language of economic progress and international opportunities. As a result, many children in non-Anglophone countries are immersed in English at school, in addition to their native language. As long as the native language is not neglected, the effects of these programs seem to be positive. For example, researchers in Italy found that children in English-Italian bilingual schools reached high second language proficiency and strong reading skills in English by the end of primary

---

[210] Collier, & Thomas, 2004.
[211] Gándara, & Escamilla, 2017.

school, while their performance in Italian was at the same level as that of children with a similar type of background in monolingual Italian schools. Moreover, reading abilities across the two languages were strongly correlated, suggesting that bilingual literacy skills develop simultaneously.[212]

Other bilingual education programs use a local minority language in addition to the majority language. Aiming to investigate the effect of bilingual education on cognitive abilities, one study compared the linguistic and non-linguistic reasoning skills of bilingual and monolingual children living either in Scotland or in Sardinia in Italy. Bilingual children in Scotland were enrolled in a bilingual program where they learned to read and write in Gaelic (the minority language) and English (the majority language), while Sardinian children only spoke Sardinian (the minority language) within the family environment as they attended a monolingual Italian school. The results show that bilingual children in Scotland outperformed monolingual Scottish children and Sardinian children on nonverbal problem-solving skills, (meta-)linguistic abilities and mathematics. This suggests that bilingual programs in which children develop high proficiency in both languages may boost the cognitive benefits of bilingualism.[213]

Language immersion programs differ in the time that is devoted to each language within the curriculum, which may depend on the aims of the school and the background of the learners. Most bilingual schools make use of a partial immersion program, in which children receive instruction in each language for 50% of the time, or in which they are taught in one language for at least 20% of the time while the other language is used for up to 80% of the time.

Finally, there are education programs in which children are fully immersed in a second language 100% of the time. This is generally not considered to be bilingual education, as there is no attention to the maintenance and further development of the native language. The following section will deal with this type of education, which is

---

[212] Costa, Guasti, & Sharley, 2020.
[213] Lauchlan, Parisi, & Fadda, 2013.

referred to as 'submersion' or the 'sink-or-swim' approach, analogous with throwing someone in the water without teaching them how to swim.

The sink-or-swim approach

In many non-European countries that have experienced European colonialism, the language of the former colonizer—often English or French, is used as the medium of instruction in schools, even in cases in which this language is not spoken by the local population. This means that children are taught in a language they don't speak yet, often by teachers who are non-native speakers themselves. This type of submersion education has been heavily criticized because it threatens linguistic and cultural diversity, as well as human rights. The UN declaration of the Rights of the Child stipulates that every child has the right to education, and many argue that this implies education in a native language. When a foreign language is used as the only medium of instruction, this may limit access to education, and it impedes children's chances to succeed at school.

An interesting example of English-medium instruction in a non-Anglophone country can be found in the Maldives, which became independent from Great-Britain in 1965. The official language of the Maldives is Dhivehi, which is used for everyday spoken and written communication, on television and in politics. Dhivehi also used to be the language of instruction in education, but since the 1980s an increasing number of schools switched to English-medium instruction, and by the end of the century English was virtually the only language used in primary and secondary education. This development was driven by the increasing importance of tourism as a source of income, as well as by the implementation of international examinations. While parents and policy makers tend to have a strong preference for English, as it tends to be seen as the gateway for economic and academic progress, teachers have expressed their concerns about the effectiveness of English-medium instruction for the quality of education.[214] To examine the learning outcomes of Maldivian children more closely, a recent study tested the English

---

[214] Mohamed, 2013.

language proficiency, reading abilities in English and mathematics skills of a group of children attending the highest grades of a primary school on a small island. The results showed relatively poor performance across the board, which did not match children's high scores on a non-verbal intelligence test. While some children were able to read a text very rapidly (that is, they could spell out the words), almost all children had severe problems with reading comprehension. Moreover, children's reading accuracy was correlated with their vocabulary knowledge in English, reflecting the interrelatedness between spoken language and reading development. As for mathematics, many children were able to calculate simple subtractions, but they were not able to solve language-based mathematical problems that were presented as a story.[215]

The observations of this case study are supported by the findings of a large-scale research project conducted in India, where many different languages are spoken. In the MultiLiLa project, researchers investigated language and literacy development as well as mathematics skills of multilingual children that attended either English-medium schools or schools that provided education in a regional language (Hindi or Telugu). They found an advantage for children who were taught in their native language in reading acquisition in the regional language and in non-linguistic learning outcomes, while children in English-medium schools showed oral proficiency levels that were insufficient to understand the content of the textbooks that were used. Like in the study conducted in the Maldives, children showed great difficulties in reading comprehension, even if they were able to read aloud without any problems.[216] The advantage of education in the native language over second language submersion programs has been confirmed in many other contexts. For example, a study conducted in Ethiopia showed that children in regional-language programs perform better than children in English-medium programs in all subjects, including English.[217]

---

[215] Bosch, Tsimpli, & Guasti, 2022.
[216] Tsimpli et al., 2020.
[217] Heugh, Benson, Bogale, & Yohannes, 2007.

The main problem with these English-medium submersion programs is the 'sink-or-swim' approach: children are taught in a language that they don't know yet, with very little attention to their native language or to the fact that they are still learning the language of instruction. Although there may be important differences in terms of resources, teachers' qualifications, and cultural contexts, this is quite comparable to the situation in which many immigrant children in American or European schools find themselves. While many countries offer reception classes and second language support, these are not always available. In some cases, children still receive little to no language support, under the assumption that their 'sponge-like' capacity will be enough for them to pick up any language they are surrounded with. However, multilingual children need about three to five years of exposure to the school language to reach full proficiency in listening and speaking, and four to seven years to reach a level of reading and writing that is comparable to that of monolingual children.[218] Studies focusing on students with a migration background in Western contexts in fact mirror some of the findings reported by the literature on submersion programs. Most importantly, reading comprehension is also particularly challenging for immigrant children who are learning the school language as an additional language. As a result, they often have difficulties with language-based math problems, as well.[219]

In what follows, we will summarize the benefits of involving children's native language in education, drawing from evidence from linguistically diverse classrooms in monolingual education as well as bilingual education and language submersion programs.

The benefits of using children's native language in education

First of all, using children's native language in education is beneficial for content learning. It may seem quite obvious, but hearing or reading an explanation in a language that you speak very well improves your comprehension of the subject matter. This is one of the reasons why children in submersion programs often fail to

---

[218] Hakuta, Butler, & Witt, 2000.
[219] Trakulphadetkrai et al., 2017.

understand the lesson, and why they struggle with reading comprehension. The same holds for newly arrived immigrant students, who need to be given time to learn the language of instruction. This does not mean that it is impossible to teach different subjects in a new language before it is fully acquired; we know from bilingual education that content and language-integrated learning can work very well. However, it is crucial to take into account children's current level of proficiency, and to realize that they may already have knowledge of a subject even if they are not yet able to express themselves in the language of instruction. By encouraging children to complete an assignment in their native language, a teacher acknowledges their previously acquired skills, allowing them to build on this knowledge.

Secondly, involving the native language supports linguistic development. Native language development continues into adolescence, and children need rich input in order to fully develop their lexicon and to acquire complex grammar. For instance, when multilingual students are allowed to read books in their native language at school, they are not only given the opportunity to develop a high competence in that specific language, but they may also build a stronger linguistic foundation that will support second language learning. Certain linguistic abilities may transfer from one language to the other, a process which can be facilitated by explicitly comparing the different languages, as to improve children's metalinguistic awareness.[220]

A third reason to make use of children's native languages in primary education is that it supports early literacy acquisition.[221] Understanding that specific symbols correspond to certain sounds and meanings is more straight-forward in a native language, in which the phonemic categories and lexical meanings are more precisely defined and more strongly established. Reading development is also strongly related to oral language proficiency, and specifically vocabulary knowledge, which tends to be stronger in the dominant

---

[220] Cummins, 1979.
[221] Benson, 2004.

language of multilingual children. Learning to read and write may therefore be easier in one's native language, and as mentioned above, non-language specific skills such as letter-sound decoding or text comprehension strategies may transfer from one language to the other when children learn to read and write in two languages simultaneously. Thus, multilingual literacy is something that should be encouraged, for example by offering additional lessons in the native language at school, by involving the parents when children learn to read, or by using written examples of different languages and scripts in class.

Finally, taking a multilingual approach may enhance the sense of belonging, self-confidence, and motivation of multilingual students, all of which are crucial for learning. By acknowledging and appreciating the different linguistic and cultural backgrounds of students, a teacher can create a more inclusive environment in which children can fully develop their multicultural identities. Moreover, a teacher may boost students' self-confidence by letting them be the expert, for example by asking them how a certain grammatical structure works in their language or by asking them to explain something about their family's country of origin. For such a multilingual approach to be successful, it is crucial that teachers also adopt positive attitudes themselves, by valuing linguistic and cultural diversity and by trusting the potential of their multilingual students.

Conclusion

The available research suggests that a multilingual approach that uses all the linguistic resources of students is beneficial for their linguistic development, literacy acquisition and non-linguistic learning outcomes, and that valuing the different heritage languages and encouraging multilingualism may positively influence motivation and self-confidence. While these insights come from very different educational settings, which are not directly comparable due to obvious socioeconomic and cultural differences, they all point towards the benefits of fostering multilingualism for educational outcomes. In other words, regardless of whether it concerns Indian children being taught in English, Spanish-speaking immigrants in the US, or children attending Dutch-Frisian bilingual programs, we should not forget about their native language. Importantly, the benefits of growing up with more than one language hold for all children, including those who speak less prestigious languages, such as dialects or languages spoken by immigrant communities. Multilingualism is the reality, and rather than seeing it as an obstacle, it should be viewed as an opportunity to ensure inclusive education and equal opportunities for all.

Chapter 11. A vademecum on multilingual pedagogy for skeptical teachers

Solange Ariel Andrea Santarelli and Federico Faloppa

All too often, teachers refuse to believe that multilingual teaching practices can be used because they do not speak the language of the students present in the classroom, or because there are too many languages present in the class environment. Although the task can be challenging, in this contribution we argue that the problem can be solved by lowering expectations, in part by not demanding that teachers master all the languages present in the classroom. In this chapter we provide examples of how to make the most of students' languages and analyze the reasons behind teachers' centrality in fostering and promoting students' multilingualism.

Imagine being a teacher in Italy in a fourth-grade class with 22 students, 12 of whom are native Italian speakers while the remaining 10 speak 6 different languages and are learning Italian as a new language. You are not at your first experience with this typology of students. As a teacher you care about your students' progress and you have tried to enhance your teaching methods, taking account of this specific category of students. You are highly motivated and have participated in several specific training courses; in some of them, you came across multilingual pedagogy[222] but you are nevertheless unsure if this approach might truly be effective, also because you are concerned that you speak only Italian and some English, and you

---

[222] Ofelia García (2012) defines "multilingual pedagogies" those teaching approaches that meaningfully include learners and let them actively utilize their language practices.

have no knowledge of your students' native languages. You also know that although you are passionate about your job, you do not have the time to learn their languages—which in any case are clearly too many to be acquired even if the time was available. You have good will, but you feel overwhelmed. What do you do, then? Should not you simply ignore the problem, i.e., the multilingual nature of your class, and stick to the program, whose goal is to teach your students Italian? This could be the least problematic option... but would it be also the most effective one? In this chapter we will outline some of the reasons why it is not essential for a teacher to master all the languages spoken in the classroom and, more importantly, why it is always worth the effort to try and include these languages while teaching, rather than ignoring them.

Multilingualism in the classroom? I'd rather not...

Let's be honest: teaching is a demanding profession and teaching in a multilingual classroom is exceptionally challenging. When there are multiple languages present in the classroom with which teachers are not familiar it can be demotivating to try and follow the path of multilingual pedagogy; sometimes it might seem much easier to teachers to simply avoid acknowledging and taking into consideration students' native languages,[223] or indeed any other language that they might speak. This may have practical explanations (i.e., they do not feel they have the time and the competence to deal with this matter, especially if they are not language teachers) but also bias-motivated or ideological reasons, such as:

> in general, speakers are accustomed to labelling languages according to their cultural and social prestige, and to discriminating between high-prestige languages and low-prestige languages (including 'dialects'). Academic studies have demonstrated that teachers, too, make such distinctions,[224] with the result that they see the use of certain languages in the classroom as more acceptable than others. Indeed, there is this

---

[223] Hornberger & Cassels, 2007.
[224] Yiakoumetti, 2007.

strong belief that language skills in English, French, German or Spanish (the most taught languages in many European countries) are synonymous with multilingual competences and ability, while proficiency in Wolof, Bengali or Twi are deemed irrelevant. When multilingual learners speak both high-prestige and low-prestige languages (such as adult learners with a migration background speaking a high prestige language of instruction due to colonial legacies and one or more local language), teachers tend to foster the use of the high-prestige ones in the classroom while neglecting the others. For example, if a student from Mali speaks both Bambara and French, why should a teacher try and introduce Bambara in class rather than French, also given the fact that the latter is much more similar to the European language the student is learning?

Many people—and teachers among them—grow up with the idea that languages have different rankings according to how useful in the job market or widely spoken they are. When deciding on a new language to learn, it is quite normal that we ask ourselves one of the following questions: given that I already know English, what language should I learn now, French, or Spanish? Which of these is more widely spoken? Which one is more marketable? Which one might be more useful for me in the future? According to studies conducted in Germany,[225] native languages of students with a migration background are generally perceived as unappealing for the job market, and for this reason they should neither be preserved nor promoted.

Teachers may be biased towards multilingualism in the classroom, as they not only do not value the diverse cultural background of students, their families, their communities, and therefore are not inclined to advocate for the students' multilingual development, but also believe that multilingualism can be detrimental to achieve their didactic goals and should be strongly discouraged.[226]

---

[225] Bredthauer & Engfer, 2016.
[226] Midobuche, Benavides, & de Guyenne, 2010.

Even if teachers are not biased towards multilingualism or 'low prestige' languages, they do not usually feel responsible for the maintenance of the native language(s) of their students,[227] often underestimating or ignoring the pedagogical and social role of the L1. Indeed, a widely held belief is that the family, or the community of origin more generally, is the main social actor responsible for passing knowledge of the heritage language on to the young generations, with no intervention required from the teachers themselves.

Several empirical studies on language teaching at primary and secondary school level in Germany and Austria have also demonstrated that even when teachers are aware of the pedagogical and societal benefits of multilingualism, a "monolinguistic ideology"[228] nevertheless reigns in the classroom, including when multilingual students are present. Teachers therefore may be aware of the importance of multilingual pedagogy, but they cannot shift from understanding it in theory to turning it into practice, as they do not have any support in terms of policies and teaching strategies/material. Multilingual pedagogy is acknowledged, but for many contextual and circumstantial reasons still looks somehow utopian.

Debunking false myths about multilingualism

To what extent are these reasons justified and justifiable, though? From a linguistic point of view, it does not make any sense to distinguish between 'low prestige' and 'high prestige' languages. Prestige, i.e., the level of regard given to a specific language or variety according to socio-linguistic variables, does not have anything to do with the linguistic structure or functionality of a language, and should be looked at critically in education, also because it may trigger or reproduce social inequalities.[229] Furthermore, and referring back to the example presented in 1), from the learner's point of view Bambara—not French—may be the language that better represents their linguistic and cultural identity, and looks potentially more

---

[227] Cunningham, 2019.
[228] Phillipson, 1992; Kramsch, 2014.
[229] Metz, 2018.

beneficial to their own personal development and positive self-image. If the student's native language is marginalized or neglected, the student may feel that his identity is marginalized or neglected. On the contrary, if solicited the students would be able to recognize the importance of maintaining and reinforcing their competence in Bambara as well as in the other languages they speak. The use of native languages like Bambara inside the classroom could also facilitate a process of decolonization, both for the teacher(s) and for the students, by stressing the equal prestige of all languages in the school environment rather than dividing them into high or low-prestige categories according to a rationale of language commodification,[230] which is also reflected in the marketisation of languages in the job field.

Teachers' biased perceptions and attitudes towards multilingualism could have detrimental effects not only in class, but also outside the class. Teachers are generally seen as mentors and have an influence on families too. Parents of younger multilingual students, in particularly those with a migration background,[231] often worry about their children's poor performance in the language of the host country and are eager to receive advice on if and how to maintain a multilingual repertoire at home. However, if prompted by teachers to see multilingualism as a source of confusion for their children, they would be inclined to prevent the maintenance of L1.[232] Teachers should be fully aware that they have an enormous responsibility towards the multilingual competence of their students, both for enhancing their learning experience and for helping them maintain their linguistic repertoire and develop their linguistic resources, and they should also know that seeing multilingualism purely as an obstacle could not only neglect an important source of linguistic and metalinguistic knowledge for multilingual students and more in general to all students, but also undermine the use of heritage languages, and even impede family and social relations.

---

[230] Heller, 2010; Macedo, 2019.
[231] Will, 2019.
[232] Guiberson, 2013.

With regard to this, two key factors should be taken into account to advocate for multilingual pedagogy: social justice and social practice. Providing visibility to all the native languages spoken by students communicates a message of equality to learners, potentially fostering motivation, and participation of multilingual students within the classroom and letting in intercultural education. Such a message would certainly be beneficial to students who may experience injustice and discrimination inside and outside the classroom, e.g., multilingual speakers with a migration background (especially if their native language is considered a low-prestige language); allowing the use of the native languages of multilingual students in the classroom would also imply an important message for any students labelling multilingual students speaking 'low-prestige' languages as 'different'. Even before being functional to the teaching of languages and curricular disciplines, multilingual pedagogy would thus contribute to reinforcing open-mindedness and spreading a positive approach to languages and cultures that are identified as 'minority.' Paying attention to social justice encourages students to build on their linguistic and cultural strengths and develop their intercultural awareness, which then consolidates multilingual awareness. As far social practices are concerned, multilingual pedagogy facilitates "qualitative" interactions and fosters collaboration and cooperative learning.[233] Group collaboration increases students' opportunities to hear and be exposed to more languages, increasing participation and interaction with each other.[234]

So, what can teachers actually do?

Surveys show that when asked about the challenges they face in multilingual classrooms, and their ways to embrace and respond to them, teachers often emphasize the urgent need for professional development, in terms of both specific training and resources. Lack of training and limited resources for staff development can prevent teachers from fully engaging with their students' multilingualism, ultimately perceived as a burden rather than as an opportunity.[235]

---

[233] García, 2012.
[234] Gibbon, 2002.
[235] Bredthauer & Engfer, 2016.

Additionally, teaching addressing multilingualism in multi-level classrooms, i.e., classes where students have different levels of literacy and competence in their native language and in the national language of the hosting country (like at CPIA Palermo), requires further training in tailoring didactic approaches and materials to the individual learners. First of all, then, teachers should be provided with opportunities to generally identify their students' needs and to be vocal about their own needs.

Teachers (and schools) should become better familiar with their students' educational backgrounds. Collecting and having access to prior information about students' linguistic and educational backgrounds can in fact prove to be of great assistance to educators, especially when dealing with multi-level classes. Research has shown that learning a new language is much easier if it is typologically similar to the learner's native tongue.[236] In order to assist students, it is then vital that the teachers know what languages they speak; even if the teachers cannot speak them, they can still draw on lexical, typological, and syntactic similarities, such as comparing the word order of their native language and the language they are learning to explain noun-adjective syntagms. Of course, this would require some basic training in linguistics;[237] however, the effect of surprise in class when features from the native languages are embedded in the teaching of the new language is guaranteed. Students would actually be delighted to see that their languages are to some extent acknowledged and valued and would encourage their teacher's attempts to further explore their structures. As for the teachers, demonstrating interest in the learners' languages would show them their willingness to learn more about them, their background, their cultures, and this could boost the learners' motivation, their self-confidence, their interactions, and more generally their wellbeing.[238]

Comparing grammar and lexicon also depends on the students' literacy in their native language(s), and the teacher should be aware

---

[236] AlHammadi, 2016; Chiswick & Miller 2001, 2005; Isphording & Otten, 2014.
[237] Faloppa 2019
[238] Chamorro et al., 2021

that if students have a low-literacy background, due to a non-existent schooling provision in their country of origin, or because their educational path has been discontinuous—as it may happen to unaccompanied minors, for example—they might not even be familiar with the teaching metalanguage (starting from the notions of verb, adjective, pronoun, etc.). Nothing should be taken for granted, and the more information the teachers have about their student education and linguistic background, the more effectively they can diversify teaching methods and approaches.

Apart from the learner's competence and metacompetence in the native language, a teacher could also take advantage from knowing some sociolinguistic information such as what languages the learner speaks at home, with whom, when, for what purpose; or if the learners are attending a language course in community-based schools to consolidate their native language or heritage language(s) to feel closer to their heritage culture(s). Knowing if and to what extent students' can read and write in their native language can also have important implications in terms of new language literacy and school performance,[239] and to advocate for the inclusion of heritage languages in school programs.

From a more practical point of view, in multilingual classes with foreigners, a teacher could easily foster intercultural exchange through code mixing, for pedagogical purposes. For example, the teacher could label all the objects present in the classroom, writing down the words for the different objects in the school language and then ask each students to write down the words they would use for that object in the native language (L1) or, in case of low levels of literacy, to say those loud for another student to write them down. In this way, students can consistently see the word for that object in their native language, in the school language, and in all the other languages (and scripts) present in the classroom. This exercise could also make students work together to scaffold each other's competence and could provide students who are not multilingual or were not raised in a multilingual family with the possibility of coming in

---

[239] Benseman, 2014; Lee, 2017; Windle & Miller, 2012; Woods, 2009

contact with other languages, and potentially activating their curiosity towards other languages and cultures. It would also better reflect the fact that learners' communicative repertoires "are themselves becoming more diverse as they interact in more superdiverse societies",[240] and for many people mixing bits and pieces of different languages in real contexts has become a normal way of communicating (which is very common in migration trajectories).[241]

With such an activity, teachers and students could definitely look at languages not within the native/new language framework, but through *languaging and translanguaging*. These concepts have been introduced exactly to capture the creative dynamic dimension of communication in which people do not just 'use' languages as discrete entities with clear boundaries, but also create language through interactions not discrete entities separated by clear boundaries[242] (see Chapter 10), and to welcome "fluid and dynamic practices" of selecting features from the learners' entire linguistic and semiotic repertoires to create new constructions that cannot be assigned to one or another language.[243] In real life, multilingualism is not just the sum of two or more autonomous language systems "but as one linguistic repertoire with features that have been socially constructed as belonging to two separated languages."[244] In other words, translanguaging is a process through which multilingual speakers can use their full linguistic repertoire as part of the meaning-making process. It emphasizes the transformative nature of language hybridity and creates a (new) social space for language users by "bringing together different dimensions of their pedagogical history, experience, and environment; their attitude, belief, and ideology; their cognitive and physical capacity into one coordinated and meaningful performance."[245]

---

[240] Jones & Themostocleus, 2021: 113.
[241] D'Agostino, 2021.
[242] Swain, 2006.
[243] Garcia & Li Wei, 2013.
[244] García & Li Wei, 2013.
[245] Li Wei, 2018.

'Pedagogical translanguaging' is a learner-centered teaching approach that endorses the support and the development of all the languages used by the students and promotes the development of metalinguistic awareness by "softening of boundaries between languages when learning languages and content"[246] and facilitating the creation of learning spaces among students. Code mixing and translanguaging are common phenomena in popular music, such as Hip Hop: would not be possible for a teacher to use lyrics for seeing translanguaging in action, and then facilitate a creative 'space' in which students mix up their languages to produce their own lyrics?

If applying translanguaging pedagogy in a multilingual primary school, teachers could maybe try to also involve parents in learning activities. For example, they could ask students to find a fairy tale from their parents' country of origin. Following on from the analysis of the plots and general structures of the fairy tales, teachers could invite parents to read the story aloud in class, in the native language. Parental involvement can greatly contribute to the educational achievement of students with migration backgrounds, although several studies often describe communication with families as a challenge. Also, it could emphasize the importance of social practices involving families and communities, and transfer onto them some agency.

Six reasons to advocate for, support, and embed multilingualism in the classroom

In the previous section we have tried to describe some techniques for overcoming potential difficulties in using students' native languages while teaching, especially in contexts in which teachers have no previous knowledge of the learners' native languages or when there is a high number of different languages present in the classroom, mastered at different levels. Despite its potential, this may indeed represent a significant challenge which can prove discouraging for some teachers, especially for those who are not provided with specific training and resources. Teachers however should not forget that they can easily be proactive, as long as they are aware that:

---

[246] Cenoz & Gorter, 2021.

- They play a fundamental role in preserving and promoting the multilingualism of their students; *not* introducing their students' native languages into the classroom because there are 'too many' or because they cannot master them is simply not an option.

- Acquiring advanced knowledge of students' native language is not a requirement for multilingual pedagogy. If teachers are not familiar with the native languages of the students, they can begin with a comparative analysis of syntax and/or grammar in order to seek out differences and similarities between the new language students are learning and their native languages.

- If they do not speak their students' native languages, they can nevertheless begin by searching for information in language textbooks, online or by relying on students' own linguistic knowledge of their native language. Involving parents or promoting peer interaction among students who speak the same language/s can also be a powerful method for allowing students' native languages to emerge during lessons.

- Translanguaging is a valid pedagogical bottom-up approach that can support students' multilingualism in the class, and help teachers in their challenging task, while also contributing to eliminating a monolingual ideology that unfortunately persists within many schools.

- The use of native languages in the classroom represents an issue that is not limited to languages themselves, but also relates to the importance of giving the correct space to each student's culture in an equal way and to nurture students' identities.

- As previously discussed, literacy in the L1 can have important impacts on the literacy of the language students are learning, as well as on students' school performance. Supporting the presence of students' L1 in the classroom can thus boost students' motivation in learning the new language, as well as preserving their knowledge of the L1 and, in some cases, enhancing it.

Conclusion

Teaching in a multilingual and multi-level classroom and trying to use all the languages spoken by the students is extremely challenging but is also the most ethical and rewarding choice. Using multilingual pedagogy in the classroom does not imply for the teacher to be familiar with all the languages spoken in the classroom but provides an invaluable opportunity to open up to language and cultural diversity. Despite the initial challenges, multilingual pedagogy fosters curiosity, open mindedness, mutual understanding and—for the students—participation and recognition. Through this approach, the teacher may acquire a key role not only in enhancing the students' language competence in the L2, but also their awareness of their linguistic resources, and more in general their learning experience. The undeniable emotional bond between any speaker and their language(s) is an additional reason towards the promotion of multilingual pedagogy in the classroom: using the students' languages at school may in fact boost their motivation in learning a new language as well as other topics, and it is a perfect tool for breaking down the identity and societal boundaries based on language hierarchies, prejudice, misconception. Last but not least, behind a student there is always a human being, their family, and their communities: multilingual pedagogy may also be a way to facilitate interaction, provide and acknowledge agency, and foster citizenship and social inclusion.

Chapter 12. Breaking the language barrier: Why embracing native languages in second/foreign language teaching is key

Konstantina Olioumtsevits, Julie Franck, and Despina Papadopoulou

A popular belief in the field of second/foreign language (L2[247]) teaching is that the language classroom should not involve the learners' native language(s). But is the native language really a barrier to second/foreign language learning and what are the origins of this conviction? The goal of this chapter is to demystify the above belief, outlining and discussing scientific evidence which suggests that the principled and systematic use of the native language in the language classroom is actually beneficial for learners.

A practice that has dominated the field of L2 teaching is the evasion of the use of the native or any other language the learners know. This practice has its roots in the belief that the native or the other language(s) will negatively affect the development of the new language. Even when the school curriculum involves the teaching of several languages, connections or comparisons between languages in the classroom are rarely made, or collaboration among language teachers is not encouraged either.[248]

The belief that the L2 classroom should be an 'island', where the sole medium of instruction is the L2, greatly prevails among mainstream language educators; it dates back in the 1970s and is still

---

[247] We will use the terms L2 learning and L2 teaching to refer to second/foreign language learning or teaching, correspondingly.
[248] Arocena, Cenoz, & Gorter, 2015.

widely prominent.[249] The banishment of other languages is the norm, also in bilingual and multilingual educational settings as well as in L2 immersion programs following what has been termed the "two solitudes" assumption,[250] meaning the absolute separation of the languages that are of interest. Although there are several exceptions to these pedagogical practices in Canada, Europe, and the USA, the strict separation of languages still predominates instructional practice.[251]

It therefore comes as no surprise that negative attitudes towards the use of students' native languages at school are quite common among teachers. A group of colleagues conducted a study with primary school teachers in the Netherlands, Italy, and Greece, in order to explore their attitudes towards multilingualism and multilingual practices[252] (see Chapter 10). In the Netherlands, one quarter of the teachers were against allowing children with a migration background who are still in the process of learning the country's language to use their native language, while almost half of them did not support the possibility of a multilingual school library that offers books in the children's native languages. Also, only a small number of teachers in Italy and the Netherlands were in favor of children with a migration background having language lessons for their native languages at school. Although some of the teachers in the three countries expressed more positive attitudes towards multilingual practices, these findings illustrate that the exclusion of the native language from an L2 teaching environment is common in the educational community.

The practice of excluding the learners' native languages from L2 teaching underlies a number of widespread teaching methods. The 'direct method' assumes that L2 learning proceeds similarly to native language acquisition, and thus that learners should receive exposure to ample amounts of L2 input that is directly linked to meaning, without translation into the native language to avoid

---

[249] Moore, Oyama, Pierce, & Kitano, 2020.
[250] Cummins, 2007.
[251] Cummins, 2019.
[252] Bosch et al., 2021.

"contamination." The 'audiolingual' and 'audiovisual' approaches also totally encompass this assumption and banish the use of the native language from the L2 classroom.[253] More recently, the 'communicative approach' also highlights that a learner needs to come into contact with an abundance of linguistic data in order to effectively learn the L2. Even though the communicative approach does not explicitly support the exclusion of the native language, it does not devote any space for it either.[254] Keeping the native language outside of the L2 classroom is also at the core of immersion programs in the USA, which support the rigid differentiation of the taught languages.[255]

But why do these methods promote the exclusion of the native language from L2 teaching? The base of these methods seems to be a fundamental misinterpretation of at least two important findings from empirical research in the field. The first finding highlights the key role of linguistic input in L2 learning: the more and richest the input, the better the learning[256] (see also Chapter 5). However, the fact that the richness of the input has a significant impact on L2 learning does not mean that the inclusion of the native language would penalize learning; empirical findings actually provide no evidence that the use of the native language could negatively affect learning of a L2, merely because those studies did not address this question. The second empirical finding is the massive evidence for 'transfer' from properties of the native language onto the new language being learned:[257] aspects related to the sounds of the native language, its words and even the structure of its sentences were found to "contaminate" L2 learning. The problem is that, although anyone can observe these negative transfers that lead to errors, one does not so easily see the positive transfers arising when learners actually take advantage of their native language to facilitate the learning of what is similar in the new language. For example, when learners have internalized the properties of a verb in their native language, they can

---

[253] Cummins, 2007.
[254] Cummins, 2007.
[255] Cummins, 2019.
[256] Armon-Lotem, & Meir, 2019.
[257] Bardovi-Harlig, & Sprouse, 2018.

transfer these properties to the L2. This knowledge in the native language is precious and can help bootstrap the L2. Unfortunately, the benefits of positive transfers are often invisible, though, since they give rise to correct language use.

Theoretical and empirical research on learning has clearly shown that learning fundamentally proceeds by grounding any new knowledge into knowledge that the learners have already acquired through analogy, namely through the comparison between old and new knowledge.[258] The native language represents learners' prior knowledge upon which they can anchor a new language, a bit like a locomotive pulls the wagons. It is naive to think that the brain would stop proceeding like this if we simply isolated the L2 from the native language in the classroom!

In our own research on L2 learning and teaching with migrant and refugee learners,[259, 260, 261] we witnessed that some teachers were reluctant to make comparisons between the learners' native language and the L2 during teaching. They also advised the families and the learners to avoid using the native language and instead focus on the L2. Needless to say, the teachers—erroneously—believed that this process would help the students learn the L2 better. These attitudes reflect the myth that we have exemplified above. It is interesting to note that, while many learners express the opinion that the lack of reference and comparison with their native language sometimes complicated L2 learning, some claim they would rather avoid using their native language during L2 teaching, echoing what the teacher has told them.

L2 learning benefits from the use of native languages during teaching

Against the traditional view that teachers should avoid the native language during L2 teaching, recent studies suggest that language learning and teaching can actually benefit from the systematic and

---

[258] Donovan, & Bransford, 2005.
[259] Franck, & Papadopoulou, 2022.
[260] Olioumtsevits, Papadopoulou, & Marinis, 2023.
[261] Olioumtsevits, Papadopoulou, & Marinis, 2022.

principled comparison between the native language and the L2. This pedagogical strategy is referred to as 'crosslinguistic pedagogy,' 'multilingual teaching' or also 'pedagogical translanguaging.'[262] Even though there are some subtle and theoretical differences among these approaches, they all have in common the use of instructional techniques and strategies whose design aims to incorporate and exploit a learner's entire linguistic repertoire. For example, translation, multilingual dictionaries, highlighting cognates in different languages as well as comparison of language forms and structures are all teaching practices related to translanguaging pedagogy that teachers along with their students can implement in a classroom.

Let us now discuss in more detail one of the studies showing that pedagogical translanguaging can help L2 learning. The focus of the given study was to explore the efficiency of pedagogical translanguaging in the development of 'morphological awareness', i.e., the ability to recognize the constituents of a word.[263] For example, the word *decolonize* consists of three constituents: the prefix *de-*, the stem *colony,* and the suffix *-ize.* Numerous studies have shown that being aware of these regularities about word formation is beneficial to language learning and language processing. In the study exploring pedagogical translanguaging, a teaching intervention took place with 10-year-old children attending a school in the Basque Autonomous Community in Spain, with the goal to raise their awareness of the words' structure. The teaching intervention consisted of activities in Basque, Spanish, and English and aimed at raising learners' morphological awareness in all three languages. Notice that those children were, most of the time, bilingual speakers of Basque and Spanish, while they learned English as a foreign language. In one of the activities, the learners looked at pictures of different shops and then they wrote the name of the shop in all three languages in order to notice the similarities and differences in the way the words in the given languages are formed. For example, the word

---

[262] See Cummins (2019) for more details on the terminology. Here we will use the term pedagogical translanguaging.
[263] Leonet, Cenoz, & Gorter, 2020.

bookstore is a compound in English, because it consists of two roots, *book* and *store*. The equivalent word in Basque is also a compound (i.e., *liburudenda*), while *librería* in Spanish is the result of derivation, that is we need to attach the derivational suffix *-ía* to the stem *librer-*. The results showed that morphological awareness significantly improved in the learners who attended the pedagogical translanguaging teaching intervention as compared to the control group, which included learners with a similar profile who did not attend the pedagogical translanguaging intervention and instead followed their regular program. Moreover, there were interviews with the learners regarding their perceptions towards translanguaging pedagogy, and they showed enthusiasm for working in all three languages in parallel and comparing them. These findings imply that systematic comparisons among the languages a person learns and/or knows can not only help them improve linguistic awareness and thus benefit language learning, but also make the learning as well as the teaching process more enjoyable.

Emotional consequences of banning the native language from the classroom

Recent research has started to highlight the key role of affective factors in the classroom. The learning process entails emotional involvement to a great degree, as learners face new cognitive challenges and go through tests for their competencies. In the field of language learning, motivation seems to also be a key predictor of L2 learning.[264] Different arguments suggest that the wide adoption of the language separation principle is likely to have a negative impact on the learners' emotional well-being and therefore also on the learning process.

First, when encouraged to discard their native language in the classroom, the learners lose connection with their cultural and linguistic background. The learners are more prone to develop negative feelings towards the L2, while mutual respect and acceptance between the teacher and the learners but also among the learners is more difficult to establish. The feelings of mistrust and

---

[264] Cochran, Mccallum, & Bell, 2010.

rejection may be even greater for learners with a background of forced migration who did not choose to leave their country and who have often experienced traumatic situations during their journey to the host country as well as during their settlement in the new country. These negative feelings may also contribute to the high rates of school dropout, which are often attested for migrant and refugee learners.[265] In contrast, allowing the learners to use their native language plays an important role in the sharing of their experience of migration. The grounding of a new language on a learner's native language contributes to valorizing their linguistic and cultural background, which can lead to significant benefits in terms of well-being in the classroom.[266]

Second, the exclusion of the native language from the L2 classroom does not motivate teachers to familiarize themselves with their students' native languages. This may complicate the teaching process itself and its effectiveness, while the learners feel that their native languages are not welcome.

Ongoing research on the benefits of pedagogical translanguaging

We recently conducted a study to explore what is a good practice to teach vocabulary to children with a refugee background who are still learning the majority language in Greece and have low knowledge of it.[267] Children learned words through three different teaching techniques: cards with images, pantomime, and texts. One thing that was similar for all teaching techniques, though, was the encouragement and support of the use of the young students' native languages. The researchers had included in their own notes the translation of the target words in the students' native languages thanks to the help of translators. When teaching words using cards, for example, the researchers would ask the children to translate each word into their native languages. The children could also write the translation on the card, and this practice had several positive outcomes. On the one hand, the use of the native languages seemed

---

[265] Scientific Committee in Support of Refugee Children, 2017.
[266] Capstick, & Delaney, 2016.
[267] Olioumtsevits, Papadopoulou, & Marinis, 2023.

to motivate and encourage children and increased their participation and engagement in the lesson. On the other hand, we could confirm that the children had understood the word meaning, because we could compare the translation that the children provided with our own notes. Lastly, the mutual gain for both the researchers and the learners was the creation of a bond between them based on the feeling that both sides could contribute to the lesson.

Capitalizing on this experience, we recently started to develop a new tool to teach morphological awareness through pedagogical translanguaging to adult migrants learning the language of the host country. The objectives of this project are to explore on the one hand, whether this pedagogy is an effective teaching method in comparison to a traditional method whose main principle is the separation of languages, and, on the other hand, whether it positively affects learners' emotions. During the pilot phase of the project at the Aristotle University of Thessaloniki and at the University of Geneva, we launched several lessons in which we implemented the method to teach vocabulary and derivational morphology in L2 Greek and French. For example, the Greek word [taksiðévo], meaning *to travel*, consists of the stem *taksið-* and the derivational suffix *-évo*. During the intervention, the learners used google translate to find out the meaning of the word and explored the internal structure of this word in their own language. Through this process, they learned not only new vocabulary but also how to form new words in L2 Greek, since they realized that the derivational suffix *-évo* is present in several verbs. What facilitated this process was comparing the meaning and the morphological structure of the Greek words with the equivalent ones in their native language. Our preliminary observations pointed out that the learners of L2 Greek and French who worked in small groups sharing the same native language enjoyed the entire process of drawing on the knowledge of their native language and creatively employing it in order to acquire knowledge of the L2's morphology. We also learned from this pilot phase of our project that the teachers of Greek who attended the lessons showed positive attitudes towards pedagogical translanguaging. The particularly positive view towards the adoption of multilingual approaches in L2 teaching is probably related to the educational needs that emerged from the large number of migrant and refugee learners in Greece as well as to the intense training that many teachers have attended in order to meet these educational challenges.[268]

Conclusion

In this chapter, we have discussed the popular belief in the field of L2 teaching that it is better and more beneficial to keep the learners' native language(s) outside of the L2 classroom. However, as we showed above through evidence from previous studies as well as our own studies, the inclusion of the native language(s) in the learning process can actually be beneficial on various levels. Both learners and teachers may worry that such pedagogies result in a decline of L2 use. It is important to highlight that inviting learners' native languages in the classroom does not mean shifting away from the language the students need to learn. It is crucial to keep the L2 as the focus of the class and to make it explicit to both learners and teachers that the use of the native language is a bootstrap to facilitate L2 learning, which remains the goal of the teaching program.

A shift is currently taking place in the educational community towards multilingual teaching techniques in Europe, following similar changes in Canada and the USA. This shift becomes apparent through the development of new scientific studies exploring the efficiency of such techniques, the efforts of many teachers in public schools and NGOs to adopt them, and the emergence of teaching materials such as multilingual textbooks and dictionaries.[269] These efforts are particularly valuable, as they take place in contexts that are not always supportive of multilingual approaches. Educators play a key role in developing and promoting this shift, but there should be a greater collaboration among teachers, researchers, and policy makers in order to improve the dialogue between language learning and teaching theories, empirical research, and instructional practices.

---

[268] Bosch et al., 2021.
[269] See the educational material developed for the teaching of Greek as L2: teach4integration.gr/vivliothiki.

Part 5:
Myths on multilingualism and clinical populations

Chapter 13. When less is not more—multilingualism as a resource, not a burden for children with developmental language disorders

Maren Eikerling and Maria Luisa Lorusso

Is a clinical condition concerning a child's language development caused or worsened by his or her multilingual environment? Beliefs about supposed correlations are common, but are they valid? How should multilingualism in the context of developmental language disorders be dealt with appropriately in family, school, and clinical surroundings?

Developmental Language Disorder (DLD) is a neurobiological condition characterized by unexplained and persistent difficulties during language acquisition. It is normally diagnosed in early childhood but usually persists into adulthood. DLD may affect children's abilities to understand and/or use language, e.g., to produce and process sounds, grammar, words, or texts.[270] It is often believed that a multilingual environment can cause or worsen DLD. Many people think that speaking more than one language is a risk factor for DLD. The statements "Being multilingual may cause DLD or increase its severity" and "Children with DLD should be exposed to and use one language only" are myths that we aim to bust in the present chapter: The question "Is multilingualism problematic for children with developmental language disorders?" is crucial to many different professions and stakeholders. It is relevant for clinicians, among them Speech and Language Therapists (SLTs) who diagnose and treat children with DLD as well as pediatricians who also diagnose DLD and prescribe speech and language therapy (SLT). It is also raised by teachers from nurseries over kindergartens and

[270] Bishop et al., 2017.

primary until secondary schools and lastly caregivers of multilingual children.

The answer to the question "Is multilingualism problematic for children with developmental language disorders?" certainly is "No!"—being multilingual does not cause DLD nor does it increase the risk of developing DLD.[271] Consequently, language use of multilingual children with DLD should not be restricted to one language only.[272] However, multilingualism is a challenge for SLTs, teachers and medical staff responsible for DLD diagnosis and intervention and/or prescriptions of the latter. In this chapter, we will illustrate how appropriate methods for the identification of DLD in multilingual children, possibly supported by modern technology, can resolve this apparent dilemma. We will further discuss how the quality rather than the quantity of exposure to the languages may affect language development in multilingual children with DLD.

Language acquisition is not language learning—the monolingual adult perspective is to blame for the myth

For all multilingual children, language performance depends on the duration and intensity of exposure to the languages[273] which results in a wide range of individual language contact patterns and a complex, heterogeneous situation for professionals to take into consideration when working with multilingual children. Some people mistakenly conclude that exposure to only one language is more desirable than exposure to several languages because hearing and speaking more than one language is believed to create confusion and interference among the different ways to produce sounds, name things, and build sentences (see Chapter 1 and 12 of this volume).

The persistence of this myth is understandable when one considers how demanding it is for (monolingual) adults to learn a foreign language. It requires a high level of concentration, good memory and thus a lot of time and energy. Subconsciously, some people put child language acquisition at the level of foreign language

---

[271] Paradis, 2005.
[272] Garraffa et al., 2019.
[273] Treffers-Daller, 2019.

learning and thus consider it effortful. However, language acquisition in children differs from language learning in adults. Adults are not aware that they have acquired their native language(s) automatically and easily because their memory of language acquisition was, so to say, "overwritten" by learning a foreign language, e.g., at school. Thus, the difference between language acquisition and language learning is neglected and it may be erroneously concluded, by intuition, that acquiring an additional language is a problem. Even more so, some people problematize multilingual language acquisition in children with language difficulties and assume that it would be an extra burden for children with language difficulties to grow up in a multilingual environment.

The truth is that it is difficult—even for the best researchers in the field—to empirically investigate whether and to what extent multilingualism causes or worsens a language disorder. For both impaired and unimpaired mono- and multilingual language acquisition, there are a number of influencing factors, such as socio-economic status, the frequency and duration of language exposure, as well as the quality of language input, genetic predisposition, among other, that affect the process of language acquisition and more specifically, the expression of the language disorder.[274] Due to the complex interplay of diverse factors in every multilingual individual, it is very difficult to study the effect of multilingualism in children with a language disorder. However, there is no evidence that multilingualism causes DLD or increases the risk of being affected by it.

Despite this unclear situation, there is no reason to consider it problematic or controversial, because it is possible to answer the question "Is multilingualism problematic for children with developmental language disorders?" clearly with a different approach. If an adult decides not to learn a foreign language, they may not be able to communicate in that language, but they can still get along in society and communicate well in their family context. By not learning a foreign language, they save cognitive and time

---

[274] Sansavini et al., 2021.

resources and are not or only marginally restricted in their everyday communication. We know that for child language acquisition—as opposed to language learning during adulthood—restricting the languages to be acquired is not necessarily an advantage. In multilingual families, limiting the number of languages spoken can mean that in the long run, natural communication either within the family (native language) or in society (societal language) is restricted. However, communication in both above mentioned contexts is crucial for the child's emotional and social development and also to ensure the establishment of relationships and access to education.[275] For multilingual children, linguistic and communicative competence in *all* languages they are exposed to in their everyday life is relevant for their social-emotional development and for their educational and occupational perspectives. Depriving the child of one of these languages would therefore possibly restrict the aforementioned developmental processes.

This reasoning clearly shows that removing a language from multilingual children with a language disorder is not beneficial. However, the misconception persists due to monolingual adults who find foreign language learning challenging and mistakenly compare it to multilingual child language acquisition, perpetuating the myth that "Children with DLD should be exposed to and use only one language." In the context of multilingual language acquisition however, less is *not* more. Children with DLD should be exposed to all the languages they are surrounded by in their everyday life. Acquiring these languages will be crucial for their identity formation and inclusion as well as integration into society. In this sense, multilingualism should be seen as a resource, not a burden for children with DLD. In concrete terms, this implies that language acquisition in these children is favored by hearing rich and correct language, and caregivers and their families should use the language they know best, also when it is not the societal language.

---

[275] Norbury et al., 2016.

Multilingualism in the context of DLD: a challenge for professionals

Following the line of argumentation above, along with the results of scientific studies, language exposure to more than one language cannot be considered a burden for multilingual children with DLD. It has been shown that speaking multiple languages is not directly related to a higher risk of being diagnosed with a DLD. However, multilingualism in the context of DLD is an issue that not only has persistent myths attached to it, but also poses challenges to clinicians and educators, as shown by a variety of surveys[276] as well as policy reports addressed to policy makers.[277] If exposure to more than one language is not the problem concerning multilingual children with DLD—what else is?

The diagnostic dilemma

One of the challenges is the practical difficulty of evaluating language skills when more than one language is spoken. It is difficult to understand whether deviations from monolingual language acquisition can be explained by reduced exposure to the language or DLD. Assessing a multilingual child in one of the languages spoken only does not represent the full scale of their language performance.[278] It is thus recommended to assess all languages spoken.[279] This, however, is difficult to realize due to the variety of languages spoken by the children—it is impossible for clinicians to carry out assessment in all the various languages. The implementation of existing multilingual procedures seems to be associated with too much effort. The evaluation of language performance in a language that clinicians themselves do not speak requires a great deal of time and cognitive effort and often cannot be implemented in everyday clinical practice. Questionnaire studies show that diagnostic procedures are often carried out in the

---

[276] Bloder et al., 2021.
[277] Lorusso et al., 2022.
[278] Core et al., 2013.
[279] Kohnert & Medina, 2009.

surrounding language for reasons of lack of alternatives, indicating that yet, there is no solution to the diagnostic dilemma.[280]

Misdiagnoses

Consequently, some of the difficulties shown in the societal language by multilingual children due to insufficient language exposure to that language can be interpreted as signs of a DLD: some children may be (mis)diagnosed as having a disorder, while they just need more time and more opportunities to learn the language(s). At the same time, misdiagnoses are also made based on the fact that an actual DLD is misinterpreted as an expected result of heterogeneous multilingual language acquisition.[281] In this case, a DLD diagnosis is not made or is made too late and SLT intervention is not initiated early enough. Failure to diagnose DLD and to initiate intervention early increases the likelihood of persistence of DLD and reduces the chances of success of therapeutic intervention.[282]

Overcoming the diagnostic dilemma and misdiagnoses—reaching for Utopia

Although being multilingual does not cause, worsen, or increase the risk of DLD, the situation described above of constant risk of *misdiagnoses* as an expression of the *diagnostic dilemma* is the actual challenge of multilingualism in the context of DLD. Interestingly, a large proportion of clinicians are aware that they should include all languages spoken by their multilingual patients in diagnosis and therapy and that the use of standard test procedures in the societal language must always be related to the quality and quantity of language exposure,[283] but cannot meet these requirements, as it

---

[280] Stankova et al. 2021.

[281] Grimm & Schulz, 2014.

[282] Law, Garrett, & Nye, 2003.

[283] Quality and quantity of language exposure are related to the concepts of Length of Exposure (LoE, i.e., the duration of frequent exposure to (a) certain language(s)), Age of Onset (AoO, i.e., the first time a person is confronted with (a) certain language(s)), frequency (i.e., how often the language is used in everyday life vs. holidays). The quality of language exposure depends on contexts and level of proficiency.

emerges from surveys conducted with SLTs. Thus, there is a gap between clinicians' knowledge and practice.[284]

This gap was impressively demonstrated by a survey of our research group. Similar to preceding studies on the same topic, the data of 300 SLTs from four European countries indicated that they are mostly aware of the specific requirements of diagnosis and intervention for multilingual children with DLD, but do not put them into practice. Despite thorough investigation of this topic, intensive literature work, empirical work, involvement in research networks and training sessions as well as supervision by excellent researchers in the field, SLTs can be confronted with this gap frequently when seeing a multilingual patient to provide SLT, as in the following case example.

A five-year-old boy comes accompanied by his aunt, as she speaks the societal language better than the mother and the mother was said to be very busy looking after his siblings. The father works full time in shifts and cannot accompany his child to therapy. This made it difficult to make an appointment for a parent interview about family language use and to collect anamnestic data. Whether an interpreter is available for parent meetings is decided by the health insurance company on a case-by-case basis—applications and documentation are necessary, a bureaucratic hurdle. A questionnaire on the child's language background that parents can fill out at home is not available in the clinic in the family's language. Clinicians are expected to do their own research on this topic—outside of the paid therapy time. A number of standardized test procedures were performed for lack of alternatives, knowing that without information on language background, those language tests can neither be contextualized nor interpreted and therefore cannot be consulted for diagnosis, therapeutic decision-making, and intervention planning. It was necessary to contact (a) parents for anamnesis and language background, (b) the health insurance for the cost coverage of an interpreter, and (c) the doctors for the diagnoses issued so far. The time spent on this cannot be used to think about relevant observations

---

[284] Marinova-Todd et al., 2016.

in the therapy, such as the interaction in free play, his difficulty in maintaining eye contact and fine motor restrictions, which manifest, for example, when throwing dice.

This personal experience exemplifies that in addition to the knowledge of adequate assessment and treatment options for multilingual children, resources are necessary for the resolution of the diagnostic dilemma and the decision of an appropriate intervention for the multilingual child. There is broad consensus in the research community about what resources are needed. The confrontation of this issue should already begin in SLT training. On the one hand, the theoretical foundation should be laid, and students should be familiarized with the confrontation of other languages because, as our study showed, concrete practical experience with multilingual children is the most influential factor for language-sensitive speech therapy work that includes multilingualism. Beyond the training, however, there should also be sufficient remunerated time in professional practice for dealing with current, possibly foreign-language material or systemic further education and training on these topics. Standardized tests should also not be frowned upon for their use as an orientation method but should contribute to support and therapy planning through contextualization of the test results in relation to language input and exposure patterns—which in turn requires sufficient time for parent consultation. Standardized tests should be seen as a resource, from which, however, a diagnosis cannot be made directly. At the same time, static, computer-based tests that can be administered in different languages and automatically evaluated,[285,286] and more generally, computer-assisted procedures can also reduce the time and effort required for dynamic evaluation.[287] Finally, clinicians in charge of treating and diagnosing multilingual children with DLD should be given the opportunity to exchange information with colleagues on this topic. This also includes a systematic exchange with other professions

---

[285] Eikerling et al., 2022.
[286] Eikerling, & Lorusso, 2022.
[287] Eikerling et al., 2023.

involved in the case and, above all, the possibility to discuss the case with the caregivers without language barriers and to have enough time to do so.

The additional resources required should not, of course, be at the expense of the children concerned or the clinicians treating them. In a society where oral and written communication via advertising, social media and instant messaging is ubiquitous, these resources should be seen by society as a whole.

Although the research community is largely in agreement about what resources are needed, so far factually and situationally appropriate action seems impossible with so many factors that need to be taken into consideration. It is possible that overcoming the diagnostic dilemma remains a utopian, political term, since the resources are not yet available in sufficient quantities. However, such observations should not result in resignation, but rather an effort to prevent it, with the path to adequately assess and treat DLD in multilingual children as the goal. Utopias should not deter.

Conclusion: Less is not more

In the context of multilingualism, the saying "less is more" is not true. Families should make use of the linguistic resources available in the family. The linguistic repertoire should not be limited—the language in which the family can converse most easily and naturally should be the one used. Interacting with the child in the language in which they feel most comfortable ensures that the child receives high quality language stimulation—this is helpful for all children and especially for children with DLD. In this sense, multilingualism can be considered as a resource, not a burden for children with DLD. Which languages are used can vary depending on the context—using one language when reading aloud and another when having dinner with friends is not confusing for children. They usually manage to switch back and forth between languages better than adults and foreign language learners. If children mix these languages, it is absolutely not a sign of confusion (see Chapter 1 of this volume).

The fact that the statement "less is more" is not true in the context of multilingualism and DLD is not only evident in the families, but also in the SLT service. As shown in the case example, language assessment can be somewhat more complex than with monolingual children. There may be more tests and more discussions with the caregivers or interpreters to assess language skills in both languages than with monolingual children. In view of the fact that a correct diagnosis requires the assessment of all languages, it is inevitable to use more diagnostic procedures. In the future, the LITMUS tools (Language Impairment Testing in Multilingual Settings[288]) could be a good resource in this respect.[289] At the same time, it is possible to select specific procedures that are particularly suitable for use in the context of multilingualism, such as the repetition of so-called non-words.[290]

Caregivers and SLTs confronted with multilingualism in children with language difficulties face the difficulty of throwing habitual assumptions overboard. Using different languages even though the child has language problems may seem inappropriate, but it is correct to ensure high qualitative language communication in multilingual families. For multilingual families, the use of fewer languages is *not* desirable, but a restriction in communication within the family and development of linguistic skills.

SLTs also have to break out of habitual ways of thinking, use different and sometimes unfamiliar materials, methods, or technologies, but again, in this way a more comprehensive picture of the child's linguistic abilities can be gained. Also here, less is *not* more—it is worth carefully examining the full scope of resources and needs of a multilingual child with DLD.

---

[288] Armon-Lotem, de Jong, & Meir, 2015.
[289] LITMUS Tools on bi-sli.org
[290] Eikerling, Bloder, & Lorusso, 2022; Bloder, Eikerling, & Lorusso, 2023.

Chapter 14. Don't fall for it! Multilingualism is not a risk factor for dyslexia

Juhayna Taha and Maria Teresa Guasti

Does speaking multiple languages cause language learning disorders, such as dyslexia? Spoiler alert—no, it does not! Let's uncover the origins of this myth and explore how multilingual children learn to read in a new language. Wondering how the reading abilities of multilingual children can be assessed efficiently? We've got that covered too! Plus, we share some tips for teachers and parents to support and empower multilingual children in their journey of learning to read in multiple languages!

Approximately 10% of people have dyslexia.[291] Dyslexia is a specific, unexpected difficulty in learning to read. Children with dyslexia may have a hard time reading quickly and accurately. They might struggle with understanding what they read and make mistakes when spelling words. They might also have trouble with writing and math. While the exact cause of dyslexia is unknown, it tends to run in families, suggesting that it may be genetic. Studies using brain imaging show that dyslexia is linked to problems with the way certain areas of the brain process sound and language. These brain differences lead to difficulties for children with dyslexia to pair letters and the sounds of speech—a crucial skill for reading.

---

[291] The prevalence of dyslexia ranges from less than 5% up to 20%. Estimates vary depending on the population, criteria used to diagnose dyslexia, spoken language, gender, and social class.

Science clearly shows that dyslexia is a brain-based disorder with a genetic basis. Despite this, many people think that speaking multiple languages may cause or increase the risk of dyslexia. However, this isn't true. In this chapter, we attempt to pinpoint the source of this myth. We also compare the reading and reading-related skills of monolingual and multilingual children. We provide research-informed recommendations for teachers and professionals to consider for reading assessment in multilingual children. Lastly, we share some strategies to support multilingual children's reading in the classroom and at home.

Multilingual children are more likely to be wrongly diagnosed with dyslexia

An increasing number of children grow up in households where they acquire one or more languages that are different to the dominant language of society. Thus, upon starting school, these multilingual children need to learn how to read and write in the dominant language. We will use the term additional language (AL) to indicate that the language being learned may not be their second, but could be their third, fourth, or even fifth language! The rate at which these children learn an AL is determined by factors such as the age of the children when they were first exposed to the language, the length of exposure, the context in which they learn the language, and the diversity of language learning experiences they have (reading, storytelling, extracurricular activities, media). This means that the level of AL proficiency not only varies between multilingual children and their monolingual peers but also varies from one multilingual child to another.

Because reading is a language-based activity, it is expected that the reading performance of multilingual children will also vary. This makes it challenging for educators and clinicians to properly assess the reading abilities of multilingual children. When multilingual children struggle with reading in their AL, it is difficult to determine if they are simply having trouble learning a new language or if they have a learning disability. This is further complicated by the stigma surrounding multilingual children's reading difficulties. A lack of understanding of AL reading development may result in viewing multilingual children as being less capable or less intelligent, resulting in an unnecessary diagnosis (overdiagnosis). On the other hand, learning disability such as dyslexia may be overlooked and attributed to the challenges of being multilingual (underdiagnosis).

Here we focus on the overdiagnosis of dyslexia. So why does it happen? Multilingual children's reading abilities are often evaluated using reading tests which are based on monolingual data. Scientists have found that because multilingual children learn more than one language simultaneously, they develop each language at a slower rate than monolinguals.[292] That is, the language and reading skills of multilingual children may differ from those of monolingual children of the same age. Therefore, when multilingual children are compared to monolingual children using monolingual reading tests, multilingual children may obtain lower scores, which may be mistakenly attributed to dyslexia.

Overdiagnosis may occur when the interpretation of test scores does not consider the child's cultural and ethnic background or due to the teachers' or clinicians' lack of understanding of the limitations of the available reading assessment tools and/or insufficient knowledge of the typical course of AL development in multilingual children. As a result, a higher percentage of multilingual children may be inappropriately placed in special education classes. The overrepresentation of multilingual children in special education programs may also result in them being wrongly perceived as less capable and potentially perpetuates broader misconceptions about multilingualism as a disadvantage, rather than a valuable skill. This stigma contributes to the cycle of overdiagnosis, reinforcing the myth that multilingualism is a cause of dyslexia.

---

[292] Hoff & Core, 2015.

Multilingual children may develop reading in an additional language at a slower pace than monolingual peers

As we mentioned earlier, dyslexia causes impairments in accurate and fluent reading, reading comprehension and spelling. Therefore, it is important to understand how multilingual children develop these skills when they learn to read in their AL.

The first aspect of reading we consider is reading accuracy, also known as decoding, i.e., the ability to correctly pronounce written words. After two years of formal reading instruction during primary school, multilingual children can read words and made-up words (nonwords) in their AL just as well as their classmates who only speak one language. Although this is not always the case, some studies have shown this to be true for different languages like English, Italian and Dutch.[293,294,295] But here's something interesting, if multilingual children start learning to read in their AL in secondary school, they might show lower reading accuracy compared to their monolingual peers.[296] This result indicates that multilingual children can achieve monolingual-like reading accuracy as long as they receive AL reading instruction early in school. This applies to multilingual children who were exposed to their AL before the age of three.[297]

Another aspect of reading is reading fluency i.e., being able to read words, sentences, and passages quickly, accurately, and smoothly. Multilingual children in primary school can read words and nonwords in their AL as fluently as their monolingual classmates.[298,299] Some studies suggest that multilingual children might be slower at reading texts in their AL compared to monolingual peers. However, other studies have found that the

---

[293] Geva & Farnia, 2012.
[294] Droop & Verhoeven, 2003.
[295] Papastefanou & Marinis, 2021.
[296] Pasquarella, Gottardo, & Grant, 2012.
[297] Kovelman, Baker, & Petitto, 2008.
[298] Melby-Lervåg & Lervåg, 2014.
[299] Lipka & Siegel, 2012.

reading speed is similar for both groups of children. The reason for these differences might have to do with when the multilingual children were first exposed to the AL, how long they were exposed to it, their reading abilities in their first language, and possibly the system and policy of the educational integration of bilingual children in a given country.

Reading comprehension is all about understanding what you read. Studies have repeatedly shown that, across school grades, bilingual children often have a harder time understanding texts in their AL relative to monolingual children.[300] This is partly because these multilingual children often have smaller vocabularies and weaker grammar skills in their AL. However, research also suggests that when multilingual children get the right kind of instruction in reading comprehension early on, they can catch up to their monolingual peers.[301] It is important to keep in mind that the overall reading comprehension of multilingual children is influenced by many factors, including timing and length of exposure to the AL as well as socio-economic status.

Spelling refers to the ability to form written words with letters. Research suggests that multilingual children tend to struggle with spelling in their AL and underperform their monolingual peers. Recent research suggests that the type and degree of these AL spelling difficulties are influenced by the type of language being acquired.[302] It is important to take this into account when assessing the reading abilities of multilingual children.

Overall, science shows that multilingual children can achieve reading accuracy in their AL similarly to monolingual peers as long as they receive AL reading instruction early in school. However, multilingual children may lag behind their monolingual peers in AL reading fluency, reading comprehension and spelling abilities. The latter skills are linked to the level of AL proficiency. Length of

---

[300] Melby-Lervåg & Lervåg, 2014.
[301] Lipka & Siegel, 2012.
[302] Zhang et al., 2022.

exposure and age of first exposure as well as the type of AL being acquired play a critical role in reading achievement.

Multilingual children develop reading-related cognitive skills at a similar or even faster rate than monolingual peers

Reading is a complex process that relies on different cognitive skills. These are mental abilities that allow us to remember information, reason, control attention, and process information.

Phonological awareness is the ability to hear and play with different parts of spoken language such as words, syllables, and speech sounds. Studies show that children who have strong phonological awareness in kindergarten do better at reading words later on. This is true for different languages. Even better, having strong phonological awareness skills early on can also help with spelling later in school. Some research suggests that multilingual children might be even better at phonological awareness than monolingual children[303] but not always. In general, multilingual children are expected to perform similarly or better than monolingual peers on phonological awareness tasks. It is also interesting to know that how well a child can use their phonological awareness in one language can predict their reading ability in the second language and vice versa. This points to the importance of first language skills in second language reading acquisition. It also implies that phonological awareness skills in one language could be a sufficient indicator of the child's reading ability in both languages.

Rapid automatized naming (hereafter, rapid naming) refers to how quickly you can say out loud the names of familiar things like colors or letters. It's a way to see how fast your brain can process information. This skill is especially important for children who are just starting to learn to read. Studies have shown that how well a child does on a rapid naming test in kindergarten can predict how well they will do at reading later on, especially in reading speed. This is true in many different languages, not just English. But what is interesting is that multilingual children do just as well on this test as their

---

[303] Bialystok, Majumder, & Martin, 2003.

monolingual peers,[304] even if their reading accuracy and fluency are a bit lower than those of monolingual peers.

Executive functions describe the mental processes and skills used to perform tasks, concentrate on new information and negotiate decisions. One of the core executive functioning skills is inhibition control. Inhibition control is the ability to suppress attention and automatic responses to some stimulus, such as ignoring outside noise while listening to the teacher in class or waiting for one's turn to speak during a conversation. Children with better inhibition control skills also have higher reading accuracy and speed and better reading comprehension. Some studies have shown that multilingual children are more efficient than monolinguals in inhibition control. This has been attributed to their experience of inhibiting one or more of their languages while using the other during language production. However, some studies did not find differences between multilingual children and their monolingual peers in inhibition control, questioning the notion of a multilingual advantage.

Working memory is the skill that allows our brain to hold onto information for a brief period while doing something else. Working memory plays some role in reading acquisition: better working memory skills are related to better performance on reading accuracy, reading fluency, and reading comprehension.[305] One of the widely used tasks to assess working memory is nonword repetition. In this task, children are required to repeat words with no meaning. Some nonword repetition tasks are relatively independent of language experience, and many studies show no difference in performance between multilingual and monolingual children. Another often-used task to assess working memory is backward digit recall (repeating numbers backwards). Some studies revealed that by Grade 4, multilingual children perform like their monolingual classmates in backward digit recall tests.[306]

---

[304] Carioti et al., 2023.
[305] Peng et al., 2018.
[306] Farnia & Geva, 2013.

In a nutshell, multilingual children often show similar, or even superior, performance on certain reading-related skills, such as phonological awareness, rapid naming, inhibition control, and working memory.

Approaches to reading assessment in multilingual children

As we discussed previously, multilingual children may show delays in developing AL reading skills. These children may obtain lower scores than their monolingual peers in standardized AL reading assessments. We explained how it is difficult for clinicians to differentiate whether the cause of the AL reading difficulties of multilingual children is due to multilingualism or dyslexia. In this section, we provide recommendations for teachers and clinicians to assess the reading abilities of multilingual children.

Typically developing multilingual children usually have unbalanced language profiles. That is, they may have a certain skill in one language but not in the other. Therefore, it is recommended, when possible, to assess language and reading in the child's home language (L1) and in the language of schooling (AL).[307] This would provide a complete picture of the child's skills because language and reading learning disorders affect all languages the child speaks. Unfortunately, this is not always feasible for several reasons, such as the lack of language assessment tools, time limitations, and lack of interprets/teachers/clinicians with knowledge of the child's L1.[308] Suppose reading is assessed in only one language. In that case, it is important to determine whether the language being tested is the child's dominant or weaker language. Such information will allow us to gain insights into how the child's performance compares to that of peers with similar AL exposure and proficiency. This is particularly useful when monolingual reading assessments are being used. One recommendation for using these tools is to adjust the criteria (i.e., cut-off scores) for classifying typical versus impaired reading performance according to the child's language dominance.

---

[307] Goldstein, 2006.
[308] Thordardottir, 2015.

Information about the child's exposure, proficiency, and use of their languages can be obtained through parental questionnaires. For instance, Q-Bex is a user-friendly, computer-based questionnaire that measures multilingual children's current and cumulative language experiences in up to three languages. This questionnaire is available in 17 languages (see [309] for a list of all available questionnaires).

Alternative approaches to diagnosing dyslexia are based on the assessment of reading-related cognitive skills that are less influenced by the children's language experiences. The language-dependent approach considers tasks that tap into phonological processing and awareness, verbal working memory and speed of naming. Research evidence indicates that 1) these are prerequisite skills for reading development in monolingual and bilingual children, 2) difficulties in these skills characterize dyslexia in monolingual as well as multilingual children, 3) typically developing multilingual children perform similar to, or even better than, monolingual children in tasks tapping into these skills. The evidence suggests that these skills predict reading development and impairment in multilingual children. At the same time, the child's specific language knowledge is less biased.

In a recent study,[310] we examined the potential of a range of linguistic and cognitive reading-related skills in identifying the risk of dyslexia in Italian-speaking monolingual children and multilingual children acquiring Italian as their AL. We found that 9 to 11-year-old poor readers, both monolinguals and bilinguals, underperformed good readers in Italian phonological awareness and nonword repetition tasks. This indicated the potential of phonological processing and verbal short-term memory measures in differentiating poor readers from good readers irrespective of their language experiences.

---

[309] Kašćelan et al., 2022.
[310] Taha et al., 2022.

In another study[311] on Italian, Carioti and her colleagues developed a task assessing the rapid naming of shapes. The task was administered to primary school students in Grades 3, 4 and 5. There were three groups: a group of good monolingual readers, monolingual poor readers, and a group of multilingual minority children. Findings revealed that bilingual children obtained significantly lower scores than good readers on Italian standardized reading tests than monolingual readers. However, both groups performed similarly in the rapid naming task. Monolingual poor readers underperformed multilingual children and good monolingual readers in reading tests as well as in rapid naming. Accordingly, the researchers proposed that, unlike standardized reading tests, rapid naming could be a marker of dyslexia in multilingual children that is unbiased by the child's AL proficiency.

Children with dyslexia show impairments in a range of reading-related cognitive skills, including processing and production of rhythm and executive functions (including attention and inhibition control). The language-independent approach considers these skills which involve minimal or no linguistic knowledge. An example of this approach is the ReadFree tool. This tool is a computerized battery of 12 tasks that tap into a range of reading-related cognitive skills in the visual and auditory domains, including reaction time, beat synchronization (i.e., tapping in time with a beat), timing anticipation, inhibition control, and rapid naming. There is evidence that individual differences in these skills are not related to measures of language exposure. The ReadFree tool was administered to 8 to 13-year-old monolingual good readers, monolingual poor readers, and multilingual children acquiring Italian as their AL. Findings revealed that 6 tasks of the ReadFree tool differentiated good from poor monolingual readers. These tasks measured visual reaction time, auditory beat synchronization, selective attention, rapid naming, and inhibition control (in auditory and visual domains). These outcomes point to the promise of the ReadFree tool for identifying dyslexia. Interestingly, performance on ReadFree tools

---

[311] Carioti et al., 2022.

classified 14.7% of multilingual children as poor readers. In comparison, performance on standardized Italian reading tests classified 23.5% of these children as poor readers. This finding highlights the over-identification of dyslexia in multilingual children when monolingual tools are used. The ReadFree tool has promised to address this issue as performance on the task appears to be less influenced by multilingualism.

Another diagnostic approach that holds promise is dynamic assessment which measures the child's learning potential rather than their current attainment. The usefulness of a dynamic test of decoding skills was examined in 2015.[312] The test consisted of three phases; in the first, children were taught to associate novel letter shapes with their sounds. In the second phase, children learned to put letters together to form invented words and read these words (blending) and in the third phase, children were required to read 12 new invented words. This test was administered to children in kindergarten who were assessed again at the end of Grade 1. The researchers found that the dynamic test performance in kindergarten predicted word reading difficulties at the end of Grade 1, even when other standard predictors of reading were taken into account. These results highlight the potential of dynamic assessment for the early identification of children at risk of dyslexia. The fact that the dynamic test of decoding used artificially invented letters indicates that it does not rely on pre-existing knowledge of a particular language. Accordingly, dynamic assessment is suitable for use with children regardless of AL experience or reading level.

In summary, identifying dyslexia in multilingual children will inevitably rely on comparisons with monolingual reading norms. To achieve an accurate diagnosis, educators and clinicians are recommended to gather information using a combination of different assessment approaches including testing the child's reading ability in L1, obtaining insights about the child's language experiences using parental questionnaires, assessing reading-related language and

---

[312] Gellert & Elbro, 2015.

cognitive skills, and/or dynamic assessment of the child's learning potential.

Strategies to support reading in multilingual children

As we mentioned earlier, multilingual children with typical reading difficulties may be viewed as being less capable or less intelligent, resulting in being incorrectly diagnosed with dyslexia. Unfortunately, this misperception may undermine multilingual children's self-esteem and confidence which can impact their motivation to learn. Teachers may have lower academic expectations for multilingual children resulting in less support being available for these children, hindering their academic progress. Multilingual children may internalize these negative stereotypes and may feel that they are different from their monolingual peers leading to feeling isolated or excluded. The stigma may further impact their cultural identity. In some cases, multilingual children may not accept their linguistic and cultural heritage in an effort to assimilate with their peers and develop a sense of belonging. To address the stigma around multilingualism and reading difficulties, teachers, parents, and caregivers should work together to create inclusive environments to empower multilingual children and support their literacy.

In school, teachers need to adopt a culturally responsive teaching approach that acknowledges and celebrates the linguistic and cultural diversity children bring to the classroom. This includes incorporating topics from various cultures in the curriculum, introducing new vocabulary in the different languages spoken in the classroom, celebrating different cultural holidays, and encouraging multilingual children to use their home language in some activities (e.g., sharing stories or songs). Teachers can develop individualized reading support programs that take into consideration multilingual children's AL proficiency, their strengths and specific learning needs. They use visual aids such as pictures or diagrams to support reading comprehension and learning of new vocabulary.

At home, parents and caregivers should encourage the use of all languages spoken by the child, especially their home language. This not only helps in maintaining and developing multilingual language skills but also allows multilingual children to develop a sense of pride in their linguistic heritage. Parents can also establish a reading routine with their children. Parents can provide reading materials such as books, stories, and magazines in all languages spoken by their children. This is to practice reading and to encourage reading fluency in the different languages used by the child. Parents can also expose their children to multilingual media such as TV shows and educational apps. These activities will enhance vocabulary and grammar which are key to reading fluency and understanding.

Conclusion

Growing up multilingual does not increase the risk of or cause dyslexia. The AL reading abilities of multilingual children are influenced by exposure patterns and proficiency of the AL. Although multilingual children may exhibit early delays in some reading skills, they are likely to catch up with their monolingual peers provided they receive early AL exposure and appropriate reading instructions. Diagnosing dyslexia in multilingual children requires moving beyond comparisons with monolingual children. In addition to monolingual reading tests, the use of tasks that do not rely on previous language experiences is recommended. Multilingual children's reading assessment should take into consideration the exposure patterns to the language of testing, as well as the cultural background, and the educational history of children. Both teachers and caregivers have important roles to address the potential stigma multilingual children with reading difficulties face and use various strategies to support multilingual reading at school and at home.

Chapter 15. The benefits of exploring a foreign language in psychotherapy

Isabel Ortigosa Beltrán and Azucena García Palacios

We tend to do psychotherapy in our native language. But would it be as effective in a foreign language? As we are usually less proficient in a foreign language, we may think it would be less effective than our native language. This issue could depend on factors like the level of proficiency, or the techniques used. However, there are reasons to think that a foreign language could be equally effective as the native one, at least in some specific paradigms. Maybe we should not follow in the wake of the myth that leads us inevitably and almost blindly to seek therapy in our native language, perhaps we should give it a try in a foreign language.

We live in a world in which mobility is rising, from one country to another and even from one continent to another. One of the main consequences of this is the unavoidable incorporation of a foreign language into our daily lives.

A priori, one can sense that most daily tasks, whether it is going to the bank, going shopping, going to the doctor, etc., can be affected or impeded by the use of a language that is not our native language. Indeed, we find it more difficult to cope in these environments in a language we do not master. Especially if the situation we are confronted with involves a lot of language (spoken or written), one may feel some apprehension. This would be the case in psychotherapy, where language is highly involved in the treatment of any kind of disorder or problem. Thus, the widespread and obviously intuitive idea is that using a non-native language in a psychotherapeutic process can be an impediment for the good development of the treatment and, consequently, for the effectiveness of the therapy. 'Psychotherapy in a foreign language is less effective', we might think beforehand.

But how true is this assumption? In this chapter, we will look at this issue from different perspectives in the clinical and scientific field, and then add the conclusions drawn from the experiments carried out within our group. Finally, we will see how much truth or falsehood can be attributed to this curious myth or idea, and what the reader, and citizens in general (migrants in particular), can learn from it in order to transfer it into their lives.

Why is it important to break down the belief that doing therapy in a non-native language can be a handicap?

Imagine a situation in which you find yourself in a foreign country with its particular local language, different from your native one, and you do not have a good command of this language. Over time, you encounter several circumstances in which you are forced to use the foreign language instead of your native one. One of these circumstances may be going to therapy. Given the increase in global mobility and the need to facilitate adaptation to living in new places, messages of normalization in the use of one language or another in the case of bilinguals or multilinguals can contribute to losing the fear of approaching certain services, in this case, mental health services.

Multilingualism and psychotherapy are two worlds that do not meet too often. Admittedly, monolingualism is deeply rooted in psychotherapy. For this reason, a bilingual or multilingual patient having to use his or her foreign language to deal with certain sensitive issues in a therapeutic process can be a great complication. In fact, most multilinguals do not even discuss the possibility of using another language with their therapist. Moreover, multilingual therapists have reported the possibility of a less effective therapy using the patient's foreign language. Hence, the idea that 'If I live abroad, I will have to seek therapy in my own language, otherwise it will not be effective' comes naturally. At least from the patient's point of view. But this does not necessarily have to be the case from the point of view of therapy effectiveness.

The truth is that the use of different languages can influence us to a certain extent and in many ways. From scientific evidence we know that personality and the use of a foreign language are substantially connected, even allowing us to present different parts of ourselves depending on the language we use. Memories of highly emotional experiences and self-identity itself might be notably dependent on cultural and linguistic circumstances. If we have a closer look at the clinical setting, we find several clinical cases collected over the last decades showing patients with a preference for using a non-native language (foreign language) instead of their native one to deal with painful or traumatic memories. It is said that using a foreign language might function as a protector for highly emotional experiences, allowing patients to put some distance and feel safer than in a native language, since it is usually acquired later in life and in a more formal educational setting and 'colder' context. Also, preceding therapists noted that multilingual therapy or the option of switching languages could be used conveniently as an option both by patient and therapist. Switching languages has even been settled as an asset for regulating emotions.

In addition, evidence has shown in several areas a pattern in which the use of the foreign language elicits lower emotional responses than the use of the native one. For instance, advertisements in marketing are perceived as less emotional when watched in a foreign language. Or, rating emotional words in a native and in a foreign language showed a lower recall in the latter. Also, the autonomic response via pupil diameter showed a softer response when reading sentences triggering emotional reactions in a foreign language. Many more studies have been carried out in areas such as decision making. These revealing studies showed intriguing outcomes by playing with material such as moral dilemmas or judgements. We think our moral code is pretty stable and solemn, don't we? What if I told you that it can be distorted by a mere factor such as using another language? It no longer seems as rigorous a code as we thought it was. In one study, participants were asked whether they would push a man onto train tracks to prevent the train from running over five other people. Presumably, our moral judgement would be violated by having to intercede by pushing a life to death despite it being the most life-saving option. As it turned out, people facing this dilemma in a foreign language were substantially more likely to choose the more rational option, that is, to violate our moral prohibition against killing one life in order to save five. Facing this controversial moral dilemma in a non-native language makes you choose the more deliberate and utilitarian option.

Although this milder and 'colder' response in a foreign language is a common finding in research and supports the fact that we can perceive and express ourselves differently in one language or the other, there are many other examples in which the two languages work in the same way. Some studies that have shown lighter levels of arousal or stimulation in a foreign language when performing linguistic tasks, did not find this disparity between languages in the subjective self-ratings. This suggests that although our body may react physiologically differently when using one language or the other, at the behavioral level it may not be so noticeable. So, this shows that even if there are perceptible differences between languages at the physiological level, these can be equally experienced at the subjective level. Transposed to the issue at hand, this would mean that despite the nerves we may feel when using a foreign language, the performance we are confronted with may not be as influenced as we might expect or think. Even so, we are still far from knowing in what circumstances or situations this pattern occurs.

As we have seen, using a non-native language can influence certain aspects of our lives, and it can even influence our behaviors. In short, some of these collected studies are anecdotal rather than empirical. As a result, there is a scarcity of empirical studies that provide a more objective perspective from which to observe the influence of a foreign language on bilinguals and multilinguals while undergoing some specific processes of some psychotherapeutic approaches.

What kind of bilinguals or multilinguals are involved?

Along with the wide range of possibilities within the multilingual world, this particular effect would appear distinctively for bilinguals or multilinguals for whom their foreign language does not reach a proficient level. Especially for people with an intermediate/high level in their foreign language. In other words, with sufficient knowledge to hold a conversation but with a marked difference to the mother tongue. These specific characteristics are very common in people who spend some time abroad or move to another country, or people who are acquiring a new language in an educational setting. The profile of the bilinguals we are referring to is relevant since a non-native language shapes a particular outcome from the individual. As we mentioned, these types of characteristics in a bilingual can influence both decisions and levels of emotionality when facing certain materials or situations, softening our perception, and making it less emotional. However, as we have seen, this is not always the case.

If we delve a little deeper into what is behind this particular effect that the use of a foreign language sometimes has, we find some aspects that result in particular characteristics in these bilinguals for whom their foreign language does not reach a proficient level. The use of a foreign language involves an additional processing required due to the cognitive demand associated with a non-native language. This extra effort demanded by the use of a foreign language and the consequential slower fluency could result in lower emotionality. And this is the effect understood as the 'foreign language effect'. Imagine watching a TV/Netflix series in your native language or watching it in a foreign language. Most likely, if your intention is to improve your level of that foreign language, you will resort to subtitles to learn a bit of it and be able to process conversations and what is happening in a given scene. Whether we like it or not, this makes us uncomfortable, because it requires us to pay more attention to what we are reading than to the scene itself, and this inevitably means more cognitive effort. We may even miss some of the emotional charge of the scene.

The fact that using a language that we do not master demands greater cognitive effort constitutes a barrier. Confronting a situation that requires a great deal of language in a language we do not master inevitably increases anxiety and discomfort. It seems that is how we generally perceive it. And not being able to control the language we need to use in certain situations such as psychotherapy generates this feeling that prevents us from accessing these services. Or at least, we do not approach these services in the same way or with the same peace of mind as we would in our native language.

We carried out our studies with a specific type of bilinguals. The participants were selected according to the peculiar characteristics of the foreign language effect, intermediate/high level in their foreign language. Or to put it another way, bilingual people who had some knowledge of their foreign language but were not proficient and encountered some difficulties in it. So, taking into account the possible outcomes of a foreign language which can influence in some way aspects such as emotionality or decisions, it was important to know how it could have an impact on some of the processes in the field of psychotherapy.

The light our studies shed and the doors they open

A new line of research aimed to explore the foreign language effect in various psychotherapeutic paradigms and the possible effects or implications it may have. Firstly, the foreign language effect was explored in the fear conditioning paradigm, using physiological measures that showed the participants' arousal level. Based on the assumption that fear conditioning could be achieved through verbal instructions without the presence of a real stimulus, participants were conditioned in two groups, one in the native language and the other in the foreign language. The participants were instructed that some images presented on the screen could be associated with an electric shock. Thus, they acquired the emotion of fear during the presentation of the images. Although the process was the same for all participants, it turned out that the fear was more strongly acquired by the group that had received the information and had conducted the experiment in the native language. In other words, the group that completed the experiment in the foreign language showed weaker fear conditioning. This was conceived as a first indication that the foreign language effect might have a modulatory role in emotions within some paradigms in the field of psychotherapy, namely in conditioning processes. This study made it possible to explore whether a different language context other than the native one could make a difference in conditioning processes involving fear.

There are other processes related to fear conditioning and its subsequent depletion or regulation. Some of the main techniques that guarantee competent results in the treatment of fear are extinction or the emotion regulation strategy of reappraisal. Both techniques have proven to be effective in combination with exposure therapy, which constitutes one of the most widely used and effective treatments for anxiety disorders.

Thus, our group continued along these lines and explored the role of foreign language in a subsequent process to conditioning: fear extinction. The purpose of this experiment was to explore the role of a foreign language in extinguishing the emotion of fear. In this study, after a phase of fear acquisition via verbal instructions, a phase of fear extinction was followed, also in an instructed form, either in a native or in a foreign language. In order to have linguistic production (native vs foreign), and in line with the previous study, the task that the participants had to perform consisted of a countdown from 10 to 1 superimposed to them while the stimuli, blue and yellow squares appear randomly on the screen. But in this case the results were somewhat different. We observed that although the group conducting the study in the foreign language showed generally higher levels of activation, fear extinction was achieved with equal effectiveness in both languages, and no differences in the performance.

Undoubtedly, the process of extinction is different from that of conditioning, and this is something to keep in mind when considering or exploring the foreign language effect, since it could be particularly effective in some contexts or processes. This difference between phases may be of great relevance, on the one hand to understand in more depth how a foreign language works in this kind of process, and on the other hand to test how it could be used in the future.

In light of these findings, we then conducted a study that explored one of the main emotion regulation strategies, i.e., reappraisal. Reappraisal consists of the reinterpretation of our thoughts in such a way that the perception of fear or discomfort feels less threatening. This strategy allows the individual to control the intensity and duration of the emotions that are triggered when approaching the phobic stimulus. Thus, this study would allow us to test whether the use of the foreign language within the reappraisal strategy in the exposure to phobic stimuli could affect in any way the functioning of the reappraisal technique. It could also be the case that this effect mentioned above appears, where the use of a foreign language reduces emotionality more than the native language. Would we find this famous 'foreign language effect' when using reappraisal with images that generate fear?

Participants with subclinical phobia to cockroaches were exposed to images of both cockroaches and neutral images of butterflies. During the exposure they had to use the reappraisal technique, some in the native language and some in a foreign language. We used physiological tests of pupil diameter and galvanic skin activity to objectively assess participants' emotional responses as well as fear self-reports. The physiological measures revealed a reduction in fear levels with the use of the reappraisal strategy, and this reduction occurred in both language groups. Again, the effect of a foreign language was once more reflected in higher levels of baseline arousal in that group, but this did not prevent the regulation or reduction of arousal or fear levels when comparing the language groups and the use of the reappraisal strategy.

So now we have an answer to the question above. Did we find the presence of the 'foreign language effect?' Not really. This means that even if the use of a foreign language was noticeable in the levels of arousal of the participants, the regulation of fear was equally accomplished in both languages. Here we can stick exclusively to the fact that, in these particular paradigms, the use of a foreign language is not an impediment to the effective development of the processes of extinction of fear and reappraisal. And this is good news for people in foreign contexts who are kind of scared of confronting situations in their non-native languages.

Conclusion

These two studies show how using a foreign language in these techniques is not a handicap. However, these controlled studies have a number of very particular characteristics, and perhaps by modulating these characteristics we may find different effects. For instance, although we focused on the level of proficiency, there are obviously other factors modulating bilingualism and multilingualism, such as immersion, age of acquisition or frequency of use. They all should be examined, including which language is the foreign language, whether it is a second or third language, and eventually see how to modulate these characteristics in order to discover how a foreign language affects our communication in situations such as a psychotherapeutic context. It would also be good to try these same techniques with other types of stimuli or images and see how participants deal with them in both languages. The same with other types of techniques, as there is a wide range to investigate and see to what extent they can be influenced by the use of a different language.

Likewise, better understanding these characteristics could lead to discovering new ways of using a foreign language. These studies open important 'doors' and bring us closer to options in which the use of a different language is not only a barrier, but can also, perhaps, produce other benefits yet to be investigated. For example, using it as a barrier against situations too emotionally engaging, when used alternately with the native language in certain phases of therapy, or by giving patients the option of choosing what language they prefer. However, we have no information on whether the participants prefer to approach these sessions with their respective tasks in their native language or in the foreign language. The subjective feeling of the patients, in this case of the participants, has an important role to play in assessing to what extent the deliberate choice of one or the other language may be important on a personal or subjective level. This is an 'open door' for future studies in this field. Either way, in order to reach further conclusions, it would be necessary to investigate these ideas from different perspectives, including different treatments, different types of bilinguals, or different stages of therapy in which to introduce one language or the other.

The possibilities are almost endless at this point, as this is still an emerging area of research. In any case, knowing that these novel studies highlight the fact that using a foreign language in certain psychotherapeutic paradigms does not affect the efficacy of the process makes it easier for people to approach mental health services and be willing to start therapy in a non-native language, or to mix them. It remains to be discovered what other paradigms or in what other ways can the use of a foreign language influence. For now, we have the small piece of knowledge that, within these processes studied here, the use of a foreign language does not impede the effectiveness of these techniques. A further challenge would be to transfer this information to all those who live in a bilingual or multilingual context, and to the services and professionals who develop these activities and can facilitate and promote language diversity in therapies.

So, there is still a long way to go before we can say for sure that 'psychotherapy in a foreign language is not less effective.' Yet, we have some first hints or indications that disprove this idea.

Conclusion
Embracing the multilingual mind

*Julie Franck, Federico Faloppa,
and Theodoros Marinis*

As we conclude our journey through the rich tapestry of multilingualism, as illuminated by the EU-funded 'MultiMind' project and by these fifteen chapters, our understanding of language has transformed profoundly. Language emerges not just as a tool for communication but as an integral part of our humanity, influencing our cognitive skills, cultural insights, and neurological development. Throughout the book, a new understanding of multilingualism unfolds. This exploration dispels longstanding myths and sheds light on the extensive benefits of a multilingual mindset, from enhanced cognitive flexibility and executive functions to the fostering of social inclusion and creativity.

Key insights from this exploration include the dismissal of the 'verbal salad' myth, revealing how code-switching can foster cognitive agility. This agility extends beyond linguistic dexterity; it signifies a nimble mind adept at navigating diverse cultural and social landscapes. Another significant revelation is the enduring neuroplasticity in multilingual individuals, challenging the misconception of a rigid adult brain and highlighting that multilingualism enriches our entire spectrum of cognition and social interaction.

The exploration also delves into the positive implications of multilingualism in clinical settings. It reveals how multilingualism can be a valuable resource in addressing developmental language disorders, dyslexia, and in psychotherapy. In the realm of psychotherapy, employing a non-native language can provide patients with psychological distance from traumatic experiences, facilitating more effective therapy.

In the educational context, a shift in perspective is advocated, recognizing and integrating students' linguistic backgrounds as assets. This approach celebrates linguistic diversity and recognizes it as a rich resource, highlighting the benefits of supporting native language development and employing multilingual literacy practices to enhance academic outcomes and foster a sense of belonging.

Reflecting on this wealth of information, it becomes clear that multilingualism is crucial in our globalized society, transcending academic interest to become a vital component of societal progress and personal development. This exploration serves as a guide to understanding the capacity of the multilingual mind for creativity, adaptation, and connectivity, offering insights on harnessing the power of linguistic diversity.

Embracing multilingualism has far-reaching implications, influencing our approaches to education, healthcare, and social interaction. Education systems that integrate multilingualism can better serve diverse student populations, bolstering academic achievement and fostering cultural empathy. In healthcare, particularly in mental health, understanding multilingualism can lead to more personalized therapies. Therapists leveraging patients' multilingual abilities can create nuanced therapeutic environments, enabling deeper understanding and healing.

This exploration also highlights the importance of ongoing research in multilingualism. In our interconnected world, the need for comprehensive insights into multilingual practices is ever-growing. Future research, building on these findings, can explore new intersections of multilingualism with societal and technological changes.

In summary, this journey is not just an exploration of language but an exploration of human potential. The insights offer a roadmap for leveraging the power of multilingualism to create more understanding, creative, and interconnected communities. As we conclude, we are inspired to view multilingualism not as a challenge but as a resource—a resource that enriches our lives, enhances our professional practices, and strengthens the fabric of our societies.

Let us continue to build bridges across cultures, contributing to a richer, more diverse understanding of the world. The path of multilingualism is a journey towards a more inclusive, empathetic, and enriched world, one language, one conversation, one connection at a time.

References

Abutalebi, J. & Green, D. W. (2016). Neuroimaging of language control in bilinguals: neural adaptation and reserve. Bilingualism: Language and Cognition, 19(4), 689-698.

AlHammadi, F. S. (2016). Psycholinguistic determinants of immigrant second language acquisition. Lingua, 179, 24-37.

Alrwaita, N., Houston-Price, C. & Pliatsikas, C. (2022). The effects of using two varieties of one language on cognition. Linguistic Approaches to Bilingualism, 13(6), 830-853.

Amodio, D. M., Devine, P. G., & Harmon-Jones, E. (2008). Individual differences in the regulation of intergroup bias: The role of conflict monitoring and neural signals for control. Journal of Personality and Social Psychology, 94(1), 60–74.

Anderson, J. A. E., Hawrylewicz, K., & Grundy, J. G. (2020). Does bilingualism protect against dementia? A meta-analysis. Psychonomic Bulletin & Review, 27(5), 952–965.

Andersson, I., Gauding, J., Graca, A., Holm, K., Öhlin, L., Marklund, U., & Ericsson, A. (2011). Productive vocabulary size development in children aged 18-24 months – gender differences. Speech, Music and Hearing; Quarterly Progress and Status Report, 51(1), 109–112.

Arias-Trejo, N., Angulo-Chavira, A. Q., Avila-Varela, D. S., Chua-Rodriguez, F., & Mani, N. (2022). Developmental changes in phonological and semantic priming effects in Spanish-speaking toddlers. Developmental Psychology, 58(2), 236–251.

Armon-Lotem, S., de Jong, J., & Meir, N. (Eds.) (2015). Assessing multilingual children: Disentangling bilingualism from language impairment. Bristol: Multilingual Matters.

Armon-Lotem, S., & Meir, N. (2019). The nature of exposure and input in early bilingualism. In A. De Houwer & L. Ortega (eds.)., The Cambridge Handbook of Bilingualism (pp. 193-212). Cambridge: Cambridge University Press.

Arocena, E., Cenoz, J., & Gorter, D. (2015). Teachers' beliefs in multilingual education in the Basque country and in Friesland. Journal of Immersion and Content-Based Language Education, 3(2), 169-193.

Avila-Varela, D. S., Arias-Trejo, N., & Mani, N. (2021). A longitudinal study of the role of vocabulary size in priming effects in early childhood. Journal of Experimental Child Psychology, 205, 105071.

Bardovi-Harlig, K., & Sprouse, R. A. (2017). Negative versus positive transfer. The TESOL Encyclopedia of English language teaching, 1-6. John Wilney & Sons.

Bastiaansen, M. C., Oostenveld, R., Jensen, O., & Hagoort, P. (2008). I see what you mean: theta power increases are involved in the retrieval of lexical semantic information. Brain and Language, 106(1), 15-28.

Bastiaansen, M. C., Van Berkum, J. J., & Hagoort, P. (2002). Event-related theta power increases in the human EEG during online sentence processing. Neuroscience letters, 323(1), 13-16.

Bates, E., & Goodman, J. C. (1997). On the inseparability of grammar and the lexicon: evidence from acquisition, aphasia and real-time processing. Language and Cognitive Processes, 12(5-6), 507-584.

Beaty, R. E., Benedek, M., Silvia, P. J. & Schacter, D. L. (2016). Creative Cognition and Brain Network Dynamics. Trends in Cognitive Sciences, 20(2), 87-95.

Bedoin, N., Brisseau, L., Molinier, P., Roch, D. & Tillmann, B. (2016). Temporally regular musical primes facilitate subsequent syntax processing in children with specific language impairment. Frontiers in Neuroscience, 10, 1–11.

Bellander, M., Berggren, R., Mårtensson, J., Brehmer, Y., Wenger, E., Li, T. Q., Bodammer, N.C., Shing, Y. L., Werkle-Bergner, M., & Lövdén, M. (2016). Behavioral correlates of changes in hippocampal gray matter structure during acquisition of foreign vocabulary. Neuroimage, 131, 205-213.

Benseman, J. (2014). Adult refugee learners with limited literacy: Needs and effective responses. Refuge: Canada's Journal on Refugees, 30(1), 93-103.

Benson, C. (2005). The importance of mother tongue-based schooling for educational quality. Paper commissioned for the Education for All Global Monitoring Report 2005, The Quality Imperative, UNESCO

Bergelson, E., & Swingley, D. (2015). Early word comprehension in infants: Replication and extension. Language Learning and Development, 11(4), 369–380.

Bialystok, E. (2007). Cognitive effects of bilingualism: How linguistic experience leads to cognitive change. International journal of Bilingual education and bilingualism, 10(3), 210-223.

Bialystok, E. (2017). The bilingual adaptation: How minds accommodate experience. Psychological Bulletin, 143(3), 233–262.

Bialystok, E., & Barac, R. (2012). Emerging bilingualism: Dissociating advantages for metalinguistic awareness and executive control. Cognition, 122(1), 67-73.

Bialystok, E., Craik, F. I. M., & Freedman, M. (2007). Bilingualism as a protection against the onset of symptoms of dementia. Neuropsychologia, 45(2), 459–464.

Bialystok, E., Craik, F. I. M., & Luk, G. (2012). Bilingualism: consequences for mind and brain. Trends in Cognitive Sciences, 16(4), 240–250.

Bialystok, E., Luk, G., Peets, K. F., & Yang, S. (2010). Receptive vocabulary differences in monolingual and bilingual children. Bilingualism, 13(4), 525–531.

Bialystok, E., Majumder, S., & Martin, M. M. (2003). Developing phonological awareness: Is there a bilingual advantage? Applied Psycholinguistics, 24(1), 27–44.

Bice, K., & Kroll, J. F. (2019). English only? Monolinguals in linguistically diverse contexts have an edge in language learning. Brain and Language, 196, 104644.

Bishop, D. V. M, Snowling, M. J., Thompson, P. A., & Greenhalgh, T. Adams, C., Archibald, L., Baird, G., G., Bauer, A., Bellair, J., Boyle, C., Brownlie, E., Carter, G., Clark, B., Clegg, J., Cohen, N., ContiRamsden, G., Dockrell, J., Dunn, J., Ebbels, S.,... and the CATALISE2 consortium. (2017). Phase 2 of CATALISE: A multinational and multidisciplinary Delphi consensus study of problems with language development: Terminology. Journal of Child Psychology and Psychiatry, and Allied Disciplines, 58(10), 1068–1080.

Blanco-Elorrieta, E. & Pylkkänen, L. (2007). Bilingual language switching in the laboratory versus in the wild: The spatiotemporal dynamics of adaptive language control. The Journal of Neuroscience : The official journal of the Society of Neuroscience, 37, 9022–9036.

Bleses, D., Makransky, G., Dale, P. S., Højen, A., & Ari, B. A. (2016). Early productive vocabulary predicts academic achievement 10 years later. Applied Psycholinguistics, 37(6), 1461–1476.

Bloder, T., Eikerling, M., & Lorusso, M. L. (2023). Evaluating the role of word-related parameters in the discriminative power of a novel nonword repetition task for bilingual children. Clinical Linguistics & Phonetics, 1-18.

Bloder, T., Eikerling, M., Rinker, T., & Lorusso, M.L. (2021). Speech and language therapy service for multilingual children: Attitudes and approaches across four European countries. Sustainability, 13, 12143.

Bloder, T., Rinker, T., & Shafer V. L. (in preparation). Language input factors and their impact on VOT processing in bilingual

Italian-German and monolingual German children. An electrophysiological study.

Bloomfield, L. (1933). Language. New York: H. Holt and Company.

Boldrini, M., Fulmore, C. A., Tartt, A. N., Simeon, L. R., Pavlova, I., Poposka, V., Rosoklija, G.B., Stankov, A., Arango, V., Dwork, A. J., Hen, R., & Mann, J. J. (2018). Human hippocampal neurogenesis persists throughout aging. Cell stem cell, 22(4), 589-599.e5.

Bonfanti, L. (2016). Adult neurogenesis 50 years later: limits and opportunities in mammals. Frontiers in Neuroscience, 10, 44.

Bosch, J. E., Olioumtsevits, K., Santarelli, S. A. A., Faloppa, F., Foppolo, F., & Papadopoulou, D. (2021). A cross-cultural investigation of teachers' beliefs about multilingualism [paper presentation]. International Conference on Multilingual Learning: Policies and Practices, Tischner European University, Cracow.

Bosch, J. E., Olioumtsevits, K., Santarelli, S. A. A., Faloppa, F., Foppolo, F., Papadopoulou, D. (submitted). How do teachers view multilingualism in education? Evidence from Greece, Italy and the Netherlands.

Bosch, J. E., Tsimpli, I. M. & Guasti, M. T. (2022). How English-medium instruction affects language and learning outcomes of children in the Maldives. Journal of English-Medium Instruction.

Bosch, L., & Ramon-Casas, M. (2014). First translation equivalents in bilingual toddlers' expressive vocabulary: Does form similarity matter? International Journal of Behavioral Development, 38(4), 317–322.

Breadthauer, S., & Engfer, H. (2016). Multilingualism is great- but is it really my business? - Teachers' approaches to multilingual didactics in Austria and Germany, Sustainable Multilingualism, 9, 104-121.

Burgaleta, M., Sanjuán A., Ventura-Campos, N., Sebastián-Gallés, N. & Ávila, C. (2016). Bilingualism at the core of the brain. Structural differences between bilinguals and monolinguals revealed by subcortical shape analysis. NeuroImage, 125, 437–445.

Byers-Heinlein, K. (2020). Challenges of infant language acquisition in bilingual environments.

Byers-Heinlein, K., Tsui, A. S. M., Bergmann, C., Black, A. K., Brown, A., Carbajal, M. J., Durrant, S., Fennell, C. T., Fiévet, A. C., Frank, M. C., Gampe, A., Gervain, J., Gonzalez-Gomez, N., Hamlin, J. K., Havron, N., Hernik, M., Kerr, S., Killam, H., Klassen, K., ... Wermelinger, S. (2021). A multilab study of bilingual infants: Exploring the preference for Infant-Directed Speech. Advances in Methods and Practices in Psychological Science, 4(1).

Calabria, M., Costa, A., Green, D. W., & Abutalebi, J. (2018). Neural basis of bilingual language control. Annals of the New York Academy of Sciences, 1426(1), 221-235.

Canette, L-H., Bedoin, N., Lalitte, P., Bigand, E. & Tillmann, B. (2019). The regularity of rhythmic primes influences syntax processing in adults. Auditory Perception & Cognition, 2(3), 163–179.

Capstick, T., & Delaney, M. (2016). Language for resilience: Supporting Syrian refugees. London: British Council.

Carbonara, V., & Scibetta, A. (2022). Integrating translanguaging pedagogy into Italian primary schools: implications for language practices and children's empowerment. International Journal of Bilingual Education and Bilingualism, 25(3), 1049-1069.

Carioti, D., Desiré, Stucchi, N., Toneatto, C., Masia, M. F., Broccoli, M., Carbonari, S., Travellini, S., Del Monte, M., Riccioni, R., Marcelli, A., Vernice, M., Guasti, M. T., & Berlingeri, M. (2022). Rapid automatized naming as a universal marker of developmental dyslexia in Italian monolingual and minority-language children. Frontiers in Psychology, 13, 783775.

Carioti, Desirè, Stucchi, N., Toneatto, C., Masia, M. F., Monte, M. Del, Stefanelli, S., Travellini, S., Marcelli, A., Tettamanti, M., Vernice, M., Guasti, M. T., & Berlingeri, M. (2022). The ReadFree tool for the identification of poor readers: a validation study based on a machine learning approach in monolingual and minority-language children. Annals of Dyslexia, 73(3), 356-392.

Cason, N., Astésano, C., & Schön, D. (2015). Bridging music and speech rhythm: Rhythmic priming and audio-motor training affect speech perception. Acta Psychologia, 155; 43-50.

Cason, N., Hidalgo, C., Isoard, F., Roman, S., Schön, D. (2015). Rhythmic priming enhances speech production abilities: Evidence from prelingually deaf children. Neuropsychology, 29 1, 102–7.

Castro, S., Bukowski, M., Lupiáñez, J., & Wodniecka, Z. (2023). Bilingualism is related to reduced social biases: The role of cognitive flexibility and motivation to respond without prejudice [Preprint].

Castro, S., Wodniecka, Z., & Timmer, K. (2022). Am I truly monolingual? Exploring foreign language experiences in monolinguals. PLoS ONE, 17(3), e0265563.

Celic, C. M., & Seltzer, K. (2013). Translanguaging: A CUNY-NYSIEB Guide for Educators. New York, NY: CUNY-NYSIEB.

Cenoz, J., Gorter, D. (2021). Pedagogical translanguaging. Cambridge University Press.

Chamorro, G., Garrido-Hornos, M. & Vázquez-Amador, M. (2021). Exploring ESOL teachers' perspectives on the language learning experiences, challenges, and motivations of refugees and asylum seekers in the UK. International Review of Applied Linguistics in Language Teaching. Teaching, 61(2), 201-226.

Chern, A., Tillmann, B., Vaughan, C., & Gordon, R.L. (2018). New evidence of a rhythmic priming effect that enhances grammaticality judgments in children. Journal of experimental child psychology, 173, 371-379.

Chiswick, B. R. & Miller, P. W. (2001). A model of destination-language acquisition: Application to male immigrants in Canada. Demography, 38 (391-409).

Chiswick, B. R. & Miller, P. W. (2005). Linguistic distance: A quantitative measure of the distance between English and other languages. Journal of Multilingual and Multicultural Development, 26 (1-11).

Chow, J., Aimola Davies, A., & Plunkett, K. (2017). Spoken-word recognition in 2-year-olds: The tug of war between phonological and semantic activation. Journal of Memory and Language, 93, 104–134.

Clahsen, H. & Muyske, P. (1989). The UG paradox in L2 acquisition. Interlanguage Studies Bulletin (Utrecht) 5(1), 1–29.

Clahsen, H., & Felser, C. (2006). Grammatical processing in language learners. Applied Psycholinguistics, 27(1), 3-42.

Cochran, J. L., Mccallum, R. S., Bell, S. M. (2010). Three A's: How do attributions, attitudes, and aptitude contribute to foreign language learning? Foreign Language Annals, 43 (4), 566-582.

Collier, V. P., & Thomas, W. P. (2004). The astounding effectiveness of dual language education for all. NABE Journal of Research and practice, 2(1), 1-20.

Cook, V. J. (1992). Evidence for multicompetence. Language Learning. 42, 557–591.

Core, C., Hoff, E., Rumiche, R., & Señor, M. (2013). Total and conceptual vocabulary in Spanish–English bilinguals from 22 to 30 months: Implications for assessment. Journal of Speech, Language, and Hearing Research, 56(5), 1637–1649.

Costa, A., Hernández, M., & Sebastián-Gallés, N. (2008). Bilingualism aids conflict resolution: Evidence from the ANT task. Cognition, 106(1), 59–86.

Costa, F., Guasti, M. T., & Sharley, S. (2020). Double literacy effects on language and reading skills in Italian–English primary school children. Journal of Monolingual and Bilingual Speech, 2(2), 185-218.

Côté, S. L., Gonzalez-Barrero, A. M., & Byers-Heinlein, K. (2020). Multilingual toddlers' vocabulary development in two languages: Comparing bilinguals and trilinguals. Journal of Child Language, 49(1), 114-130.

Craik, F. I. M., Bialystok, E., & Freedman, M. (2010). Delaying the onset of Alzheimer disease: Bilingualism as a form of cognitive reserve. Neurology, 75(19), 1726–1729.

Cristia, A., Lavechin, M., Scaff, C., Soderstrom, M., Rowland, C., Räsänen, O., Bunce, J., & Bergelson, E. (2021). A thorough evaluation of the Language Environment Analysis (LENA) system. Behavior Research Methods, 53(2), 467–486.

Cummins, J. (1979). Linguistic interdependence and the educational development of bilingual children. Review of Educational Research, 49(2), 222-251.

Cummins, J. (2000). Language, Power and Pedagogy: Bilingual Children in the Crossfire. Bristol, Blue Ridge Summit: Multilingual Matters.

Cummins, J. (2007). Rethinking monolingual instructional strategies in multilingual classrooms. The Canadian Journal of Applied Linguistics, 10(2), 221-240.

Cummins, J. (2019). The emergence of translanguaging pedagogy: A dialogue between theory and practice. Journal of Multilingual Education Research, 9, 13.

Cunningham, C. (2019). When "home languages" become "holiday languages": Teachers' discourses about responsibility for maintaining languages beyond English. Language, Culture and Curriculum, 33, 213-227.

Curtiss, S. (1977). Genie: A Psycholinguistic Study of a Modern Day 'Wild Child'. New York, NY: Academic.

Curtiss, S. (1988). Abnormal language acquisition and grammar: evidence for the modularity of language. In F. J. Newmeyer (Ed.), Linguistics: The Cambridge Survey: Volume 2, Linguistic Theory: Extensions and Implications, 96–116. Cambridge University Press.

D'Agostino, M. (2021). Noi che siamo passati dalla Libia. Giovani in viaggio fra alfabeti e multilinguismo. Bologna: Il Mulino.

Datta, H., Hestvik, A., Vidal, N., Tessel, C., Hisagi, M., Wróblewski, M., & Shafer, V. L. (2019). Automaticity of speech processing in early bilingual adults and children. Bilingualism: Language and Cognition, 23, 429–445.

De Anda, S., Cycyk, L. M., Moore, H., Huerta, L., Larson, A. L., & King, M. (2022). Psychometric properties of the English–Spanish vocabulary inventory in toddlers with and without early language delay. Journal of Speech, Language, and Hearing Research, 65(2), 672–691.

De Anda, S., Hendrickson, K., Zesiger, P., Poulin-Dubois, D., & Friend, M. (2018). Lexical access in the second year: A cross-linguistic study of monolingual and bilingual vocabulary development. Bilingualism: Language and Cognition, 21(2), 314-327.

De Angelis, G. (2011). Teachers' beliefs about the role of prior language knowledge in learning and how these influence teaching practices. International Journal of Multilingualism, 8(3), 216-234.

De Houwer, A., Bornstein, M. H., & Putnick, D. L. (2014). A bilingual–monolingual comparison of young children's vocabulary size: Evidence from comprehension and production. Applied Psycholinguistics, 35(6), 1189–1211.

Della Rosa P. A., Videsott G., Borsa V. M., Canini M., Weekes B. S., Franceschini R. and Abutalebi J. (2013). A neural interactive location for multilingual talent. Cortex 49(2), 605–8.

Deluca, V., Miller, D., Pliatsikas, C., & Rothman, J. (2019). Brain adaptations and neurological indices of processing in adult second language acquisition. In J. W. Schwiter & M. Paradis (Eds.), The Handbook of the Neuroscience of Multilingualism.

DeLuca, V., & Voits, T. (2022). Bilingual experience affects white matter integrity across the lifespan. Neuropsychologia, 169, 108191.

Dixon, W. E., & Hull, P. (2000). Links between early temperament and language acquisition. Merrill-Palmer Quarterly, 46(3), 417-440.

Donovan, M. S., & Bransford, J. D. (2005). How students learn - Science in the classroom. Washington DC: National Academy Press.

Droop, M., & Verhoeven, L. (2003). Language proficiency and reading ability in first- and second-language learners. Reading Research Quarterly, 38(1), 78–103.

Duarte, J., & Günther-van der Meij, M. (2020). 'We learn together' —Translanguaging within a holistic approach towards multilingualism in education. In Panagiotopoulou, J. A., Rosen, L. & Strzykala, J. (Eds.), Inclusion, Education and Translanguaging; How to promote social justice in (teacher) education? (pp. 125-144). Springer.

Duff, F. J., Reen, G., Plunkett, K., & Nation, K. (2015). Do infant vocabulary skills predict school-age language and literacy outcomes? Journal of Child Psychology and Psychiatry and Allied Disciplines, 56(8), 848–856.

Eikerling, M., & Lorusso, M. L. (2022). A web-platform for DLD screening in Italian-German-speaking children: preliminary data on concurrent and predictive validity, Lingue e Linguaggio, 11(1), 193.

Eikerling, M., Andreoletti, M., Secco, M., Luculli, B., Cha, G., Castro, S., Gazzola, S., Sarti, D., Garzotto, F., Guasti, M. T. & Lorusso, M.L. (2023). Remote screening for Developmental Language Disorder in bilingual children: preliminary validation in Spanish-Italian speaking preschool children. Applied Sciences, 13(3), 1442.

Eikerling, M., Bloder, T., & Lorusso, M. L. (2022). A Nonword Repetition task discriminates typically developing Italian-German bilingual children from bilingual children with developmental language disorder: the role of language-specific and non-language-specific nonwords. Frontiers in Psychology, 13, 826540-826540.

Eikerling, M., Secco, M., Marchesi, G., Guasti, M. T., Vona, F., Garzotto, F., & Lorusso, M. L. (2022). Remote dyslexia screening for bilingual children. Multimodal Technologies and Interaction, 6(1), 7.

Elmer, S., Hänggi, J., & Jäncke, L. (2014). Processing demands upon cognitive, linguistic, and articulatory functions promote grey matter plasticity in the adult multilingual brain: Insights from simultaneous interpreters. Cortex, 54, 179-189.

European Parliament resolution of 17 December 2020 on the European Citizens' Initiative Minority SafePack.

Faloppa, F. (2019). Brevi lezioni sul linguaggio. Turin: Bollati Boringhieri.

Farnia, F., & Geva, E. (2013). Growth and predictors of change in English language learners' reading comprehension. Journal of Research in Reading, 36(4), 389–421.

Fenson, L., Dale, P. S., Reznick, J. S., Bates, E., Thal, D. J., Pethick, S. J., Tomasello, M., Mervis, C. B., & Stiles, J. (1994a). Variability in early communicative development. In Source: Monographs of the Society for Research in Child Development, 59(5), 1-185.

Fernald, A., & Marchman, V. A. (2012). Individual differences in lexical processing at 18 months predict vocabulary growth in typically developing and late-talking toddlers. Child Development, 83(1), 203–222.

Fernald, A., Marchman, V. A., & Weisleder, A. (2013). SES differences in language processing skill and vocabulary are evident at 18 months. Developmental Science, 16(2), 234–248.

Fibla, L., Kosie, J. E., Kircher, R., Lew-Williams, C., & Byers-Heinlein, K. (2022). Bilingual language development in infancy: What can we do to support bilingual families? Policy Insights from the Behavioral and Brain Sciences, 9(1), 35–43.

Fitch, W. T., Martins, M. D. (2014). Hierarchical processing in music, language, and action: Lashley revisited. Annals of the New York Academy of Sciences, 1316, 87–104.

Fiveash, A., Bedoin, N., Gordon, R. L., & Tillmann, B. (2021). Processing rhythm in speech and music: Shared mechanisms and implications for developmental speech and language disorders. Neuropsychology, 35(8), 771-791.

Floccia, C., Sambrook, T. D., Delle Luche, C., Kwok, R., Goslin, J., White, L., Cattani, A., Sullivan, E., Abbot-Smith, K., Krott, A., Mills, D., Rowland, C., Gervain, J., & Plunkett, K. (2018). Vocabulary of 2-year-olds learning English and an additional language: Norms and effects of linguistic distance. I. Introduction. Monographs of the Society for Research in Child Development, 83(1), 7–29.

Franck, J., & Papadopoulou, D. (2022). L2 French learning by Eritrean refugee speakers of Tigrinya. Bilingualism: Language and Cognition, 25(4), 631-644.

Friederici, A. D., Steinhauer, K. & Pfeifer, E. (2002). Brain signatures of artificial language processing: evidence challenging the critical period hypothesis. Proceedings of the National Academy of Sciences 99 (1): 529–534.

Fuchs, E., & Flügge, G. (2014). Adult neuroplasticity: more than 40 years of research. Neural Plasticity, 541870.

Fung, W., Chung, K. K., & Cheng, R. W. (2019). Gender differences in social mastery motivation and its relationships to vocabulary knowledge, behavioral self-regulation, and socioemotional skills. Early Education and Development, 30(2), 280–293.

Fürst, G. & Grin, F. (2018). Multilingualism and creativity: a multivariate approach. Journal of Multilingualism and Multicultural Development, 39, 341–355.

Gabriele, A., Fiorentino, R., & Bañón, J. A. (2013). Examining second language development using event-related potentials: A cross-sectional study on the processing of gender and number agreement. Linguistic Approaches to Bilingualism, 3(2), 213–232.

Gándara, P., & Escamilla, K. (2017). Bilingual education in the United States. Bilingual and Multilingual Education, 12(1), 439-452.

García-Sierra, A., Ramírez-Esparza, N., & Kuhl, P. (2016). Relationships between quantity of language input and brain responses in bilingual and monolingual infants. International Journal of Psychology: Official journal of the International Organization of Psychophysiology, 110, 1-17.

García, O., & Nelson, F. (2012). Multilingual pedagogies. In M. Martin-Jones, A. Blackledge & A. Creese (Eds.), The Routledge Handbook of Multilingualism (232-246). London: Routledge.

García, O., & Wei, L. (2014). Translanguaging: Language, Bilingualism and Education. Palgrave Macmillan UK.

García, O., (2009). Education, multilingualism and translanguaging in the 21st century. In T. Skutnabb- Kangas, R. Philipson, A.K.Mohanty & M.Panda, Social justice through multilingual education (140-158). Bristol, Blue Ridge Summit: Multilingual Matters.

Garcia-Castro, G., Avila-Varela, D. S., Castillejo, I., & Sebastian-Galles, N. (2023). Cognate beginnings to bilingual lexical acquisition. OSF.

Garraffa, M., Vender, M., Sorace, A., & Guasti, M. T. (2019). Is it possible to differentiate multilingual children and children with Developmental Language Disorder? Languages, Society and Policy.

Gellert, A. S., & Elbro, C. (2015). Does a dynamic of phonological awareness predict early reading difficulties? Journal of Learning Disabilities, 50(3), 227–237.

Genesee, F. (2013). Insights into bilingual education from research on immersion programs in Canada. In Abello-Contesse, C., Chandler, P. M., López-Jiménez, M. D., & Chacón-Beltrán, R. (Eds.), Bilingual and multilingual education in the 21st century: Building on experience (pp. 24-41). Multilingual Matters.

Gennatas, E. D., Avants, B. B., Wolf, D. H., Satterthwaite, T. D., Ruparel, K., Ciric, R., Hakonarson, H., Gur, R.E., & Gur, R. C. (2017). Age-related effects and sex differences in gray matter density, volume, mass, and cortical thickness from childhood to young adulthood. The Journal of Neuroscience: The official journal of the Society of Neuroscience, 37(20), 5065-5073.

Geva, E., & Farnia, F. (2012). Developmental changes in the nature of language proficiency and reading fluency paint a more complex view of reading comprehension in ELL and EL1. Reading and Writing, 25(8), 1819–1845.

Gibbons, P. (2002). Scaffolding Language, Scaffolding Learning: Teaching Second Language Learners in the Mainstream Classroom, Portsmouth, NH: Heinemann.

Gillon-Dowens, M., Vergara, M., Barber, H. A., & Carreiras, M. (2010). Morphosyntactic processing in late second-language learners. Journal of Cognitive Neuroscience, 22(8), 1870-1887.

Giovannoli, J., Martella, D., Federico, F., Pirchio, S., & Casagrande, M. (2020). The impact of bilingualism on executive functions in children and adolescents: A systematic review based on the PRISMA method. Frontiers in Psychology, 11, 574789.

Goldstein, B. A. (2006). Clinical implications of research on language development and disorders in bilingual children. Topics in Language Disorders, 26(4), 305–321.

Gordon, R. L., Shivers, C. M., Wieland, E. A., Kotz, S. A., Yoder, P. J., & Devin Mcauley, J. (2015). Musical rhythm discrimination explains individual differences in grammar skills in children. Developmental Science, 18(4), 635–44.

Greenberg, A., Bellana, B., & Bialystok, E. (2013). Perspective-taking ability in bilingual children: Extending advantages in executive control to spatial reasoning. Cognitive Development, 28(1), 41–50.

Grimm, A., & Schulz, P. (2014). Specific language impairment and Early second language acquisition: The risk of over- and underdiagnosis. Child Indicators Research, 7(4), 821–841.

Grosjean, F. (1989). Neurolinguists, beware! The bilingual is not two monolinguals in one person. Brain and Language, 36(1), 3–15.

Grundy, J. G., Anderson, J. A. E., & Bialystok, E. (2017). Neural correlates of cognitive processing in monolinguals and bilinguals. Annals of the New York Academy of Sciences, 1396(1).

Guiberson, M. M. (2013). Bilingual myth-busters series. Language confusion in bilingual children. Perspectives on Communication Disorders and Sciences in Culturally and Linguistically Diverse (CLD) Populations, 20(1), 5-14.

Güntekin, B., & Basar, E. (2007). Emotional face expressions are differentiated with brain oscillations. International Journal of Psychophysiology, 64(1), 91-100.

Hakuta, K., Butler, Y. G. & Witt, D. (2000). How long does it take English learners to attain proficiency? (Policy Report 2000-1). University of California Linguistic Minority Research Institute.

Hämäläinen, S., Sairanen, V., Leminen, A., & Lehtonen, M. (2017). Bilingualism modulates the white matter structure of language-related pathways. NeuroImage, 152, 249-257.

Hart, B., & Risley, T. R. (2003). The early catastrophe: The 30-million-word gap. American Educator, 27(1), 4–9.

Heard M., & Lee, Y. S. (2020). Shared neural resources of rhythm and syntax: An ALE meta-analysis. Neuropsychologia, 137, 107284.

Heller, M. (2010). The commodification of language. Annual Review of Anthropology, 39(1), 101-114.

Heugh, K., Benson, C., Bogale, B., & Yohannes, M. A. G. (2007). Study on medium of instruction in primary schools in Ethiopia. Report commissioned by the Ethiopian Ministry of Education.

Hoff, E. (2017). How bilingual development is the same as and different from monolingual development. OLBI Journal, 8.

Hoff, E., & Core, C. (2015). What clinicians need to know about bilingual development. Seminars in Speech and Language, 36(2), 89-99.

Hofweber, J., Marinis, T. & Treffers-Daller, J. (2020). How different code-switching types modulate bilinguals' executive functions: A dual control mode perspective. Bilingualism, 23(4), 909-925.

Hornberger, N. H., Jhonson D., C. (2007). Slicing the onion ethnographically: layers and spaces in multilingual language education policy and practice. Tesol Quarterly, 41(3), 509-532.

Hosoda, C., Tanaka, K., Nariai, T., Honda, M., & Hanakawa, T. (2013). Dynamic neural network reorganization associated with second language vocabulary acquisition: A multimodal imaging study. Journal of Neuroscience, 33(34), 13663-13672.

Isphording, I. E., & Otten, S. (2014). Linguistic barriers in the destination language acquisition of immigrants. Journal of Economic Behaviour & Organization, 105, 30-50.

Ito, A., Martin, A. E., & Nieuwland, M. S. (2017). How robust are prediction effects in language comprehension? Failure to replicate article-elicited N400 effects. Language, Cognition and Neuroscience, 32(8), 954-965.

Jisa, H. (2000). Language mixing in the weak language: Evidence from two children. Journal of Pragmatics, 32(9), 1363–1386.

Jones, R., & Themistocleus, C. (2021). Introducing Language and Society. Cambridge University Press.

Kałamała, P., Szewczyk, J., Chuderski, A., Senderecka, M., & Wodniecka, Z. (2020). Patterns of bilingual language use and response inhibition: A test of the adaptive control hypothesis. Cognition, 204, 104373.

Kašćelan, D., Prévost, P., Serratrice, L., Tuller, L., Unsworth, S., & De Cat, C. (2022). A review of questionnaires quantifying bilingual experience in children: Do they document the same constructs? Bilingualism: Language and Cognition, 25(1), 29–41.

Kharkhurin, A. V., & Wei, L. (2015). The role of code-switching in bilingual creativity. International Journal of Bilingual Education. Bilingualism, 18(2), 153-169.

Kharkhurin, A. V., Koncha, V., & Charkhabi, M. (2023). The effects of multilingual and multicultural practices on divergent thinking. Implications for plurilingual creativity paradigm. Bilingualism: Language and Cognition, 26(3), 592-609.

Kim, K. H., & Lee, H. E. (2019). How does bilingualism affect creativity? In Thinking Skills and Creativity in Second Language Education (pp. 17-41). Routledge.

Kohnert, K., & Medina, A. (2009). Bilingual children and communication disorders: A 30-year research retrospective. Seminars in Speech and Language, 30(4), 219–233.

Korenar, M., Treffers-Daller, J., & Pliatsikas, C. (2022). Bilingual switching practices have distinct effects on the volumes of the caudate nucleus and the thalamus. PsyArXiv Preprint.

Korenar, M., Treffers-Daller, J., & Pliatsikas, C. (2023). Dynamic effects of bilingualism on brain structure map onto general principles of experience-based neuroplasticity. Scientific Reports, 13(1), 3428-3428.

Korenar, M., Treffers-Daller, J., & Pliatsikas, C. (2023). Two languages in one mind: Insights into cognitive effects of bilingualism from usage-based approaches. Nase Rec, 106(1), 24-46.

Kotz, S. A., Ravignani, A., & Fitch, W. T. (2018). The evolution of rhythm pocessing. Trends Cognitive Sciences, 22(10), 896–910.

Kotz, S. A. (2009). A critical review of ERP and fMRI evidence on L2 syntactic processing. Brain and language, 109(2-3), 68-74.

Kovács, Á. M., & Mehler, J. (2009). Cognitive gains in 7-month-old bilingual infants. Proceedings of the National Academy of Sciences, 106(16), 6556–6560.

Kovelman, I., Baker, S. A., & Petitto, A. (2008). Age of first bilingual language exposure as a new window into bilingual reading development. Bilingualism (Cambridge, England), 11(2), 203-223.

Kroll, J. F., Dussias, P. E., Bogulski, C. A., & Kroff, J. R. V. (2012). Juggling two languages in one mind: What bilinguals tell us about language processing and its consequences for cognition. The Psychology of Learning and Motivation, 56, 229-262.

Kuhl, P. K., Stevenson, J., Corrigan, N. M., van den Bosch, J. J. F., Can, D. D., & Richards, T. (2016). Neuroimaging of the bilingual brain: Structural brain correlates of listening and speaking in a second language. Brain and Language, 162, 1–9.

Ladányi, E., Lukács, Á., & Gervain, J. (2021). Does rhythmic priming improve grammatical processing in Hungarian-speaking children with and without developmental language disorder? Developmental Science, 24(6), e13112.

Lany, J., Giglio, M., & Oswald, M. (2018). Infants' lexical processing efficiency is related to vocabulary size by one year of age. Infancy, 23(3), 342–366.

Large, E. W., & Jones, M. R. (1999). The dynamics of attending: How people track time-varying events. Psychological review, 106(1), 119.

Lauchlan, F., Parisi, M., & Fadda, R. (2013). Bilingualism in Sardinia and Scotland: Exploring the cognitive benefits of speaking a 'minority' language. International Journal of Bilingualism, 17(1), 43-56.

Law, J., Garrett, Z., & Nye, C. (2003). Speech and language therapy interventions for children with primary speech and language delay or disorder. Cochrane Database of Systematic Reviews, 3.

Lee, Y. S., Ahn, S., Holt, R.F., & Schellenberg, E. G. (2020). Rhythm and syntax processing in school-age children. Developmental Psychology, 56(9), 1632–1641.

Lee, K. (2017). Using collaborative strategic reading with refugee English language learners in an academic bridging program. TESL Canada Journal, 33, 97-108.

Legacy, J., Zesiger, P., Friend, M., & Poulin-Dubois, D. (2018). Vocabulary size and speed of word recognition in very young French-English bilinguals: A longitudinal study. Bilingualism (Cambridge, England), 21(1), 137–149.

Lehtonen, M., Soveri, A., Laine, A., Järvenpää, J., de Bruin, A., & Antfolk, J. (2018). Is bilingualism associated with enhanced executive functioning in adults? A meta-analytic review. Psychological Bulletin, 144(4), 394–425.

Lenneberg, E. H. (1967). The biological foundations of language. Hospital Practice, 2(12), 59-67.

Leonet, O., Cenoz, J., & Gorter, D. (2020). Developing morphological awareness across languages: Translanguaging pedagogies in third language acquisition. Language Awareness, 29(1), 41-59.

Li, W. (2018). Translanguaging as a practical theory of language. Applied Linguistics, 39(1), 9–30.

Lindsey, E. W., & Mize, J. (2001). Contextual differences in parent-child play: Implications for children's gender role development. Sex Roles, 44(3-4), 155-175.

Lipka, O., & Siegel, L. S. (2012). The development of reading comprehension skills in children learning English as a second language. Reading and Writing: An Interdisciplinary Journal, 25(8), 1873–1898.

Lorusso, M. L., Eikerling, M., Bloder, T., Rinker, T., Guasti, M. T., Marinis, T. (2022). How to improve assessment and treatment of multilingual children with language and reading disorders.

Lövdén, M., Wenger, E., Mårtensson, J., Lindenberger, U., & Bäckman, L. (2013). Structural brain plasticity in adult learning and development. Neuroscience and Biobehavioral Reviews, 37(9), 2296–2310.

Macedo, D. (2019). Decolonizing Foreign Language Education: The Misteaching of English and Other Colonial Languages. Routledge.

Mancilla-Martinez, J., & Vagh, S. B. (2013). Growth in toddlers' Spanish, English, and conceptual vocabulary knowledge. Early Childhood Research Quarterly, 28(3), 555–567.

Marchman, V. A., & Fernald, A. (2008). Speed of word recognition and vocabulary knowledge in infancy predict cognitive and language outcomes in later childhood: Fast-track report. Developmental Science, 11(3), F9-F16.

Marian, V., Blumenfeld, H. K., & Kaushanskaya, M. (2007). The Language Experience and Proficiency Questionnaire (LEAP-Q): Assessing language profiles in bilinguals and multilinguals. Journal of Speech, Language, and Hearing Research, 50(4), 940–967.

Marinova-Todd, S. H., Colozzo, P., Mirenda, P., Stahl, H., Kay-Raining Bird, E., Parkington, K., Cain, K., Scherba de

Valenzuela, J., Segers, E., MacLeod, A. A., & Genesee, F. (2016). Professional practices and opinions about services available to bilingual children with developmental disabilities: An international study. Journal of Communication Disorders, 63, 47–62.

Mårtensson, J., Eriksson, J., Bodammer, N. C., Lindgren, M., Johansson, M., Nyberg, L., & Lövdén, M. (2012). Growth of language-related brain areas after foreign language learning. NeuroImage, 63(1), 240-244.

Martin, C. D., Thierry, G., Kuipers, J. R., Boutonnet, B., Foucart, A., & Costa, A. (2013). Bilinguals reading in their second language do not predict upcoming words as native readers do. Journal of Memory and Language, 69(4), 574-588.

Marzecová, A., Bukowski, M., Correa, Á., Boros, M., Lupiáñez, J., & Wodniecka, Z. (2013). Tracing the bilingual advantage in cognitive control: The role of flexibility in temporal preparation and category switching. Journal of Cognitive Psychology, 25(5), 586–604.

Mayberry, R. I. (1993). First-language acquisition after childhood differs from second-language acquisition: the case of American sign language. Journal of Speech, Language, and Hearing Research, 36(6), 1258–1270.

Melby-Lervåg, M., & Lervåg, A. (2014). Reading comprehension and its underlying components in second-language learners: A meta-analysis of studies comparing first- and second-language learners. Psychological Bulletin, 140(2), 409–433.

Metz, M. (2018). Challenges of confronting dominant language ideologies in the high school English classroom. Research in the Teaching of English, 52(4), 455–477.

Midobuche, E., Benavides, A. H. & de Guyenne, W. d. R. (2010). Perceptions, attitudes, and the identification of dispositions for teachers of English language learners. Teacher Education and Practice, 23(2), 181–93.

Mohamed, N. (2013). The challenge of medium of instruction: A view from Maldivian schools. Current Issues in Language Planning, 14(1), 185-203.

Moore, D., Oyama, M., Pierce, D. R., & Kitano, Y. (2020). Plurilingual education and pedagogical plurilanguaging in an elementary school in Japan: A perspectival origami for better learning. Journal of Multilingual Theories and Practices, 1(2), 243-265.

Morales, M., Mundy, P., Delgado, C. E. F., Yale, M., Neal, R., & Schwartz, H. K. (2000). Gaze following, temperament, and language development in 6-month-olds: A replication and extension. Infant Behavior and Development, 23(2), 231-236.

Morgan, P. L., Farkas, G., Hillemeier, M. M., Hammer, C. S., & Maczuga, S. (2015). 24-month-old children with larger oral vocabularies display greater academic and behavioral functioning at kindergarten entry. Child Development, 86(5), 1351–1370.

Morgan-Short, K. (2020). Insights into the neural mechanisms of becoming bilingual: A brief synthesis of second language research with artificial linguistic systems. Bilingualism: Language and Cognition, 23(1), 87-91.

Navarro, E., & Conway, A. R. (2021). Adult bilinguals outperform monolinguals in Theory of Mind. Quarterly Journal of Experimental Psychology, 74(11), 1841–1851.

Navarro, E., Deluca, V., & Rossi, E. (2022). It takes a village: Using network science to identify the effect of individual differences in bilingual experience for Theory of Mind. Brain Sciences, 12(4), 487.

Norbury, C. F., Gooch, D., Wray, C., Baird, G., Charman, T., Simonoff, E., Vamvakas, G., & Pickles, A. (2016). The impact of nonverbal ability on prevalence and clinical presentation of language disorder: Evidence from a population study. Journal of

Child Psychology and Psychiatry, and Allied Disciplines, 57(11), 1247–1257.

OECD. (2019). What students know and can do. PISA 2018 Results (Volume 1).

Olioumtsevits, K., Papadopoulou, D., & Marinis, T. (2023). Second language grammar learning in refugee children: Is group dictation an effective teaching technique? Pedagogical Linguistics, 4(1), 50-76.

Olioumtsevits, K., Papadopoulou, D., & Marinis, T. (2022). Vocabulary teaching in refugee children within the context of the Greek formal education. Languages, 8(1), 7.

Osterhout, L., Poliakov, A., Inoue, K., McLaughlin, J., Valentine, G., Pitkanen, I., Frenck-Mestre, C., & Hirschensohn, J. (2008). Second-language learning and changes in the brain. Journal of neurolinguistics, 21(6), 509-521.

Pagliarini, E., Scocchia, L., Granocchioa, E., Sarti, D., Stucchi, N., & Guasti, M. T. (2020). Timing anticipation in adults and children with Developmental Dyslexia: evidence of an inefficient mechanism. Scientific Reports, 10(1), Article 1.

Papastefanou, T., Marinis, T., & Powell, D. (2021). Development of reading comprehension in bilingual and monolingual children—effects of language exposure. Languages, 6(4), 166.

Paradis, J. (2005). Grammatical morphology in children learning English as a second language. Language, Speech, and Hearing Services in Schools, 36(3), 172–187.

Pasquarella, A., Gottardo, A., & Grant, A. (2012). Comparing factors related to reading comprehension in adolescents who speak English as a first (L1) or second (L2) language. Scientific Studies of Reading, 16(6), 475-503.

Patel, A. D. (2008). Music, Language, and the Brain. Oxford University Press.

Peng, P., Barnes, M., Wang, C. C., Wang, W., Li, S., Swanson, H. L., Dardick, W., & Tao, S. (2018). Meta-analysis on the relation between reading and working memory. Psychological Bulletin, 144(1), 48–76.

Petersson, K. M., Folia, V., & Hagoort, P. (2012). What artificial grammar learning reveals about the neurobiology of syntax. Brain and language, 120(2), 83-95.

Pliatsikas, C., Johnstone, T., & Marinis, T. (2014). Grey matter volume in the cerebellum is related to the processing of grammatical rules in a second language: A structural voxel-based morphometry study. The Cerebellum, 13(1), 55–63.

Pliatsikas, C. (2020). Understanding structural plasticity in the bilingual brain: The Dynamic Restructuring Model. Bilingualism: Language and Cognition, 23(2), 459-471.

Pliatsikas, C., Johnstone, T., & Marinis, T. (2014). fMRI evidence for the involvement of the procedural memory system in morphological processing of a second language. PloS one, 9(5), e97298.

Pliatsikas, C., DeLuca, V., Moschopoulou, E., & Saddy, J. D. (2017). Immersive bilingualism reshapes the core of the brain. Brain Structure and Function, 222(4), 1785–1795.

Pliatsikas, C., Moschopoulou, E., & Saddy, J. D. (2015). The effects of bilingualism on the white matter structure of the brain. Proceedings of the National Academy of Sciences, 112(5), 1334-1337.

Prior, A., & Gollan, T. (2011). Good language-switchers are good task-switchers: Evidence from Spanish-English and Mandarin-English bilinguals. Journal of the International Neuropsychological Society, 17(4), 682–691.

Prior, A., & Macwhinney, B. (2010). A bilingual advantage in task switching. Bilingualism: Language and Cognition, 13(2), 253–262.

Rinker, T., Alku, P., Brosch, S., & Kiefer, M. (2010). Brain & language discrimination of native and non-native vowel contrasts in bilingual Turkish-German and monolingual German children: Insight from the Mismatch Negativity ERP component. Brain and Language, 113(2), 90–95.

Roncaglia-Denissen, M. P., Schmidt-Kassow, M., Heine, A., Vuust, P., & Kotz, S. A. (2013). Enhanced musical rhythmic perception in Turkish early and late learners of German. Frontiers in psychology, 4, 645.

Rosenthal, R., & Jacobson, L. (1968). Pygmalion in the classroom. The urban review, 3(1), 16-20.

Rossi, E., & Prystauka, Y. (2020). Oscillatory brain dynamics of pronoun processing in native Spanish speakers and in late second language learners of Spanish. Bilingualism: Language and Cognition, 23(5), 964-977.

Rossi, E., Kroll, J. F., & Dussias, P. E. (2014). Clitic pronouns reveal the time course of processing gender and number in a second language. Neuropsychologia, 62, 11-25.

Rossi, S., Gugler, M. F., Friederici, A. D., & Hahne, A. (2006). The impact of proficiency on syntactic second-language processing of German and Italian: Evidence from event-related potentials. Journal of Cognitive Neuroscience, 18(12), 2030-2048.

Rothman, J. (2008). Why not all counter-evidence to the critical period hypothesis is equal or problematic: Implications for SLA. Language and Linguistics Compass, 2(6), 1063–1088.

Ruiz-Felter, R., Cooperson, S. J., Bedore, L. M., & Peña, E. D. (2016). Influence of current input-output and age of first exposure on phonological acquisition in early bilingual Spanish-English-speaking kindergarteners. International Journal of Language and Communication Disorders, 4, 368–383.

Sabourin, L., Stowe, L. A., & De Haan, G. J. (2006). Transfer effects in learning a second language grammatical gender system. Second Language Research, 22(1), 1-29.

Sansavini A., Favilla M.E., Guasti M.T., Marini A., Millepiedi S., Di Martino M.V., Vecchi S., Battajon N., Bertolo L., Capirci O., Carretti B., Colatei M.P., Frioni C., Marotta L., Massa S., Michelazzo L., Pecini C., Piazzalunga S., Pieretti M., ... Lorusso, M. L. (2021). Developmental Language Disorder: Early predictors, age for the diagnosis, and diagnostic tools. A scoping review. Brain Sciences, 11, Article 5.

Schroeder, S. R. (2018). Do bilinguals have an advantage in Theory of Mind? A meta-analysis. Frontiers in Communication, 3, Article 36.

Scientific Committee in Support of Refugee Children. (2017). Refugee education project: A. Assessment report on the integration project of refugee children in education (March 2016-April 2017) B. Proposals for the education of refugee children during the 2017-2018 school year. Athens: Ministry of Education, Research and Religious Affairs.

Singh, L., Quinn, P., Qian, M., & Lee, K. (2020). Bilingualism is associated with less racial bias in preschool children. Developmental Psychology, 56(5), 888–896.

Slater, J., & Kraus, N. (2016). The role of rhythm in perceiving speech in noise: a comparison of percussionists, vocalists and non-musicians. Cognitive processing, 17, 79–87.

Smithson, L., Paradis, J., & Nicoladis, E. (2014). Bilingualism and receptive vocabulary achievement: Could sociocultural context make a difference? Bilingualism: Language and Cognition, 17(4), 810–821.

Stankova, M., Rodríguez-Ortiz, I. R., Matić, A., Levickis, P., Lyons, R., Messarra, C., Kouba Hreich, E., Vulchanova, M., Vulchanov, V., Czaplewska, E., Ringblom, N., Hansson, K., Håkansson, G., Jalali-Moghadam, N., Dionissieva, K., Günhan Senol, N. E., & Law, J. (2021). Cultural and linguistic practice with children with developmental language disorder: findings from an international practitioner survey. Folia Phoniatrica Et Logopaedica, 73(6), 465–477.

Stein, M., Federspiel, A., Koenig, T., Wirth, M., Strik, W., Wiest, R., Brandeis, D., & Dierks, T. (2012). Structural plasticity in the language system related to increased second language proficiency. Cortex, 48(4), 458-465.

Steinhauer, K., White, E. J., & Drury, J. E. (2009). Temporal dynamics of late second language acquisition: Evidence from event-related brain potentials. Second Language Research, 25(1), 13-41.

Stolarova, M., Wolf, C., Rinker, T., & Brielmann, A. (2014). How to assess and compare inter-rater reliability, agreement and correlation of ratings: an exemplary analysis of mother-father and parent-teacher expressive vocabulary rating pairs. Frontiers in Psychology, 5, 81818.

Surrain, S., & Luk, G. (2019). Describing bilinguals: A systematic review of labels and descriptions used in the literature between 2005–2015. Bilingualism: Language and Cognition, 22(2), 401–415.

Swain, M. (2006). Languaging, agency and collaboration in advanced second language proficiency. In H. Byrnes (Ed.), Advanced Language Learning: The Contribution of Halliday and Vygotsky (pp. 95-359). Continuum.

Szagun, G., Stumper, B., & Schramm, S. A. (2009). Fragebogen zur frühkindlichen Sprachentwicklung (FRAKIS). Pearson Assessment.

Taha, J., Carioti, D., Stucchi, N., Chailleux, M., Granocchio, E., Sarti, D., De Salvatore, M., & Guasti, M. T. (2022). Identifying the risk of dyslexia in bilingual children: The potential of language-dependent and language-independent tasks. Frontiers in Psychology, 13.

Thordardottir, E. (2015). Proposed diagnostic procedures for use in bilingual and cross-linguistic contexts. In S. Armon-Lotem, K. de Jong, & N. Meir (Eds.), Assessing multilingual children: Disentangling bilingualism from Language impairment (pp. 331–355). Multilingual Matters.

Toivainen, T., Papageorgiou, K. A., Tosto, M. G., & Kovas, Y. (2017). Sex differences in non-verbal and verbal abilities in childhood and adolescence. Intelligence, 64, 81–88.

Trakulphadetkrai, N. V., Courtney, L., Clenton, J., Treffers-Daller, J., & Tsakalaki, A. (2017). The contribution of general language ability, reading comprehension and working memory to mathematics achievement among children with English as additional language (EAL): An exploratory study. International Journal of Bilingual Education and Bilingualism, 23(4), 473-487.

Treffers-Daller, J. (2019). What defines language dominance in bilinguals? Annual Review of Linguistics, 5(1), 375–393.

Treffers-Daller, J. (2009). Code-switching and transfer: an exploration of similarities and differences. In Bullock, B. E., & Toribio, A. J. (Eds.), The Cambridge handbook of linguistic code-switching (pp. 58-74). Cambridge University Press.

Tsimpli, I. M., Balasubramanian, A., Marinis, T., Panda, M., Mukhopadhyay, L., Alladi, S. & Treffers-Daller, J. (2020). Research report of a four-year study of multilingualism, literacy, numeracy and cognition in Delhi, Hyderabad and Patna. The British Council.

Tu, L., Zhou, F., Omata, K., Li, W., Huang, R., Gao, W., Zhu, Z., Li, Y., Liu, C., Mao, M., Zhang, S., & Hanakawa, T. (2022). Increased gray matter volume induced by Chinese language acquisition in adult alphabetic language speakers. Frontiers in Psychology, 13.

Van de Putte, E., De Baene, W., García-Pentón, L., Woumans, E., Dijkgraaf, A., & Duyck, W. (2018). Anatomical and functional changes in the brain after simultaneous interpreting training: A longitudinal study. Cortex, 99, 243–257.

van Hell, J. G. & Witteman, M. J. (2009). The neurocognition of switching between languages: A review of electrophysiological studies. In L. Insurin, D. Winford, & K. de Bot (Eds.),

Multidisciplinary approaches to code switching (pp. 53-84). John Benjamins.

van Hell, J. G., & Tokowicz, N. (2010). Event-related brain potentials and second language learning: Syntactic processing in late L2 learners at different L2 proficiency levels. Second Language Research, 26(1), 43-74.

Vidal, N. (2016). Neurophysiological correlates of English vowels /I/ and /e/ in monolingual and bilingual 4 and 5-year-old children. City University of New York, ProQuest Dissertations Publishing.

Whelan, B. M., Murdoch, B. E., Theodoros, D. G., Darnell, R., Silburn, P., & Hall, B. (2004). Redefining functional models of basal ganglia organization: role for the posteroventral globus pallidus in linguistic processing? Movement Disorders: Official Journal of the Movement Disorder Society, 19(11), 1267-1278.

Will, A.-K., (2019). The German statistical category "migration background": Historical roots, revisions and shortcomings, Ethnicities, 19(3), 535–557.

Windle, J., & Miller, J. (2012). Approaches to teaching low literacy refugee-background students. Australian Journal of Language and Literacy, 35(3), 317-333.

Woodruff Carr, K., White-Schwoch, T., Tierney, A. T., Strait, D. L., & Kraus, N. (2014). Beat synchronization predicts neural speech encoding and reading readiness in preschoolers. Proceedings of the National Academy of Sciences, 111(40), 14559–14564.

Woods, A. (2009). Learning to be literate: Issues of pedagogy for recently arrived refugee youth in Australia. Critical Inquiry in Language Studies, 6(1-2), 81-101.

Yakoumetti, A. (2007). Choice of classroom language in bidialectal communities: To include or to exclude the dialect? Cambridge Journal of Education, 37(1), 51-66.

Yates, K. M., Moore, D. R., Amitay, S., & Barry, J. G. (2019). Sensitivity to melody, rhythm, and beat in supporting speech-in-noise perception in young adults. Ear and hearing, 40(2), 358.

Yee, J., Yap, N. T., Korenar, M., Saddy, J. D., & Pliatsikas, C. (2023). Subcortical restructuring as a function of multilingualism: insights from monolinguals, bilinguals, trilinguals and quadrilinguals. Bilingualism: Language and Cognition, 1-14.

Zhang, S., Breuer, E. O., Grünke, M., & Joshi, R. M. (2022). Using spelling error analyses to examine individual differences in German students from diverse linguistic backgrounds: A latent class approach. Journal of Learning Disabilities, 55(2), 123–137.

About the authors

Daniela S. Avila-Varela, a researcher at the University of Lisbon (Portugal), focuses on morphological processing in second-language speakers. Originally from Santiago del Estero (Argentina), she pursued her studies in Psychology and completed her master's in psychology of health at the University of Granada (Spain). Her Ph.D. in infant word recognition and learning was accomplished at Georg-August University in Goettingen (Germany). As a part of the MultiMind project, she investigated word recognition in young bilinguals while working as a researcher at Pompeu Fabra University (Spain). Proficient in Spanish, English, and German, she enjoys spending quality time with friends and family.

Theresa Bloder is currently working at nyra health, exploring the use of artificial intelligence in the diagnosis and treatment of speech and language disorders following brain injury. She completed her BSc in Speech-Language Pathology at the FH JOANNEUM Graz (Austria), her M.Sc in Language Sciences (with a specialization in language development) at University College London (UK), and her Ph.D. in German as a Second and Foreign Language at the Catholic University Eichstätt-Ingolstadt (Germany). Within the MultiMind project she used EEG to investigate the relationship between multilingual language input and the neural processes underlying speech perception in children. In her free time, she enjoys hiking, yoga, and reading.

Jasmijn Bosch works as a postdoctoral researcher at the University of Amsterdam, where she investigates the use of multilingual book clubs and L1 literacy to stimulate reading motivation in adolescents. She studied Liberal Arts and Sciences at University College Utrecht (The Netherlands), after which she did the Research Master Linguistics at the University of Amsterdam (The Netherlands). Within the MultiMind project, she completed her Ph.D. in psycholinguistics, on language processing in multilingual children, at the University of Milan-Bicocca (Italy). She has investigated several topics related to education, including English-medium instruction and teachers' attitudes towards multilingualism. In her free time, Jasmijn likes to read, travel and have long dinners with friends.

Sofía Castro is an Early-Stage Researcher part of the MSCA ITN MultiMind, as well as a Ph.D. candidate in Psychology at Jagiellonian University (Poland). She holds a bachelor's degree in Speech and Language Therapy from the University of A Coruña (Spain) and a master's degree in Cognitive and Behavioral Neuroscience from the University of Granada (Spain). Within the Multimind project, she investigated the relationship between multilingualism and social biases, as well as the linguistic experiences of multilinguals and monolinguals. In addition, she has professional experience as a Speech and Language Therapist, working with children and adults. You can find her often practicing various sports, such as Olympic Weightlifting or bouldering.

Grazia Di Pisa is a UX/QA Project Manager at Testbirds. She received her B.A. in Applied Linguistics from the University of Palermo (Italy), her M.Sc in Cognitive Neuroscience from the University of Nijmegen (The Netherlands), and her Ph.D. in Linguistics from the University of Konstanz (Germany). Her Ph.D. project that was part of MultiMind studied how adult multilingual speakers acquire and process grammatical gender. She has been involved in projects related to education, language development, and teaching in multilingual contexts. In her free time, she likes taking pictures, going on long walks with her dachshund Spikkel, watching old movies, and collecting antiques.

Maren Rebecca Eikerling is a post-doc at Martin-Luther-University in Halle (Saale) (Germany) on virtual round tables and digitized interdisciplinary collaboration in the field of child language development and impairment. She studied Clinical Linguistics in Bielefeld (Germany) before starting her Ph.D. at Bicocca university in Milan (Italy) within the MultiMind International Training Network. As a MultiMind early-stage researcher, she worked on a screening platform for risk identification of language and reading disorders in multilingual children at IRCCS Medea in Bosisio Parini (Italy). Maren now contributes to university teaching with seminars on multilingualism and also works in the university SLT clinic. She likes to practice and learn languages while traveling.

Federico Faloppa is a Professor of Italian Studies and Linguistics at the University of Reading, where he is the director of the M.A. Migration and Intercultural Studies. His research focuses on the construction and representation of otherness in language, on the media representation of migrants and minority groups, on multilingualism in borderscapes, on hate speech and language discrimination. In his free time, he likes walking, going to art exhibitions, and strolling around to buy second-hand records from the 1970s and 1980s.

Francesca Foppolo is Associate Professor of Psycholinguistics in the Department of Psychology of the University of Milan-Bicocca (Italy). She studies language processing and comprehension in typically and atypically developing children, bilinguals, and adults by means of different techniques, particularly eye-tracking in visual contexts and reading. She collaborates in several national and international projects and is an Associate Editor of Applied Psycholinguistics. In her free time, Francesca likes travelling and visiting friends around the world, hiking and watching movies.

Julie Franck is Lecturer in Psycholinguistics at the University of Geneva and head of the Language and Cognition unit. Her work focuses on grammar learning, representation and processing in babies, children, and adults, capitalizing on variations across languages. More recently, she started to study foreign language learning by children and adults, with a focus on refugee learners. In her free time, she develops and contributes to social justice and bonding projects like the Solidarity cafés, where members of the University and migrants meet every Wednesday morning to get to know each other.

Gonzalo Garcia-Castro earned his Psychology degree from the University of Oviedo (Spain) and pursued his master's at the University of Barcelona (Spain). Presently, he is a Ph.D. candidate at Universitat Pompeu Fabra (Spain) under the supervision of Prof. Nuria Sebastian-Galles. His research deals with how bilingual toddlers develop their vocabulary through experimental and observational techniques. He is interested in language acquisition, developmental psychology, and methodologies in infant research. In her free time, Gonzalo likes learning about programming languages and statistics. On Twitter (@gongcastro), he shares research findings, programming tips, and data visualizations.

Maria Teresa Guasti is a Professor of Linguistics and language acquisition in the Department of Psychology of the Università degli Studi di Milano-Bicocca. She holds a Ph.D. from the University of Geneva and held positions at MIT, Boston, École des sciences de l'homme, Paris, University of Siena. She studies language acquisition in various populations of children and is the author of more than 100 articles and 4 books. She has recently participated in Multimind and is currently PI of the ERC-Synergy project, Realizing Leibniz's Dream [leibnizdream.eu]. With Professor Franca Garzotto (Politecnico of Milan), she is developing tools using interactive technologies to promote communication skills in children. In her free time, she practices yoga and climbs mountains.

Dávid György is a researcher at the University of Geneva. His interests include the processing of linguistic syntax, prosody, musical rhythm, and how exposure to multiple languages changes the brain. He received his B.A. in French Studies and his M.Sc in Language Sciences from University College London (United Kingdom) and is currently finishing his PhD in Neuroscience at the University of Geneva (Switzerland). His MultiMind project focuses on the overlap between rhythm, syntax, and multilingualism. He enjoys teaching and is committed to sharing information in a clear and interactive manner. In his free time, he is an avid gamer, reader, puzzle-solver, and cat worshipper.

Michal Korenar is an Assistant Professor in the Department of Dutch Studies at the University of Amsterdam, and he also works at Amsterdam University Medical Centers. He earned his master's degrees in Dutch Language and Literature, as well as Linguistics, from Charles University (Czechia), and his Ph.D. in Neuroscience from the University of Reading (UK). In MultiMind, Michal focused on the neuroscience of creativity and multilingualism. Several personal grants have enabled him to continue working on these topics across various research labs worldwide. Beyond his academic pursuits, Michal finds solace and joy in music, being a member of a choir.

Tanja Kupisch is Professor of Linguistics at the University of Konstanz and Professor II at UiT The Arctic University of Tromsø. Her research is concerned with multilingualism from various angles, including child bi- and trilingualism, adult second and third language acquisition, bilectalism and language policy. She is a founding Member of the Cluster of Excellence *The Politics of Inequality*, where she collaborates in interdisciplinary projects with political scientists. In her free time, she enjoys long distance hikes, swimming, and cooking.

Maria Luisa Lorusso is head of the Unit of Neuropsychology of Developmental Disorders at Scientific Institute IRCCS Medea in Bosisio Parini, Italy, where she conducts both clinical and research activity. She graduated in General and Experimental Psychology in Padova and in Clinical Linguistics in Groningen, where she also got her PhD in Developmental Neuropsychology. Her interests mainly concern reading and language disorders in children, their causes and remediation, and new technologies. She collaborates in various projects addressing individual and environmental factors in neurodevelopmental disorders. She is a passionate traveler.

Theodoros Marinis is Professor of Multilingualism at the University of Konstanz (Germany) and the Director of the Center for Multilingualism at the University of Konstanz. His research focuses on language acquisition and processing across populations of typically and atypically developing learners and aims to understand how language develops as a cognitive system and the way it is processed across the lifespan. He was the coordinator of the Innovative Training Network 'The Multilingual Mind'. In his free time, he does cycling, swimming, and scuba diving.

Konstantina Olioumtsevits uncovered her passion for linguistics during her BA in Philology at the Aristotle University of Thessaloniki (AUTh; Greece). She subsequently graduated from the European Master's in Clinical Linguistics, jointly completed at the universities of Groningen (The Netherlands), Potsdam (Germany), and Eastern Finland (Finland). Finally, she returned to the AUTh as a Ph.D. Candidate and the main researcher in a large-scale EU funded project on second language acquisition and teaching in migrant children within MultiMind. Recently, she was also awarded a Ph.D. in Linguistics from AUTh. In her free time, she loves walking and playing with her dog, dancing, painting, and hiking.

Isabel Ortigosa is a Psychologist and Neuropsychologist. She received her B.A. in Psychology from the University of Valencia (Spain), her M.Sc in Cognitive Neuroscience from the University of Sussex (England), and her Ph.D. in Biomedicine from the Pompeu Fabra University (Spain). Her Ph.D. project, as a part of MultiMind, explored the use of a foreign language in several psychotherapeutic technics such as cognitive reappraisal and fear extinction. She has been doing psychotherapy with patients and involved in different groups of psychological and neuropsychological supervision, learning, and contributing with creative ideas. In her free time, she likes doing sports, especially martial arts, writing poetry and fiction stories, and enjoys a good red wine with friends.

Leticia Pablos-Robles is an assistant professor at the Leiden University Centre for Linguistics (The Netherlands) who is passionate about interdisciplinary research at the crossroads between linguistics, psychology, and cognitive neuroscience. Since 2009, she is based at Leiden University where she has worked on projects that examined the mental processes internal to language use by focusing on different aspects, such as linguistic prosody, syntax-semantics phenomena, language control, language learning and code-switching. Aside from that, she enjoys singing, attending music concerts, watching movies, and taking walks in nature.

Azucena García Palacios is Professor of Psychopathology in the Department of Basic and Clinical Psychology and Psychobiology at the Universitat Jaume I. The line of research in which she has developed most of her clinical and research tasks has been the study and treatment of cognitive-behavioral perspectives of various psychological disorders. She has mainly investigated emotional disorders, personality disorders and chronic pain. She is also Director of the Laboratory of Psychology and Technology (Labpsitec) at the Universitat Jaume I, a center dedicated to research on new information and communication technologies within Clinical Psychology.

Despina Papadopoulou is Professor of Linguistics at the Aristotle University of Thessaloniki. Her research focuses on bilingual/multilingual development, second/foreign language acquisition and processing, and second/foreign language teaching. Recently, a considerable amount of her research and teaching has been devoted to migrant education, with particular emphasis on L2 learning and teaching. She also collaborates with UNICEF in the implementation of teacher training programs for educators who work with migrant populations. In her free time, she does voluntary work for NGOs and likes swimming and reading.

Christos Pliatsikas is an Associate Professor in Psycholinguistics in Bi-/Multilinguals at the School of Psychology and Clinical Language Sciences, University of Reading, UK, and the Chair of the International Symposium on Bilingualism (ISB). He is on the Editorial Board of *Bilingualism, Language and Cognition*, and of *Frontiers in Language Sciences*, section *Bilingualism*. His work focuses on experience-based neuroplasticity, with a primary interest on the effects of bi-/multilingualism on brain structure and function, including in brain development and ageing.

Tanja Rinker is professor for German as a Second and Foreign Language at the Catholic University Eichstätt-Ingolstadt. Her research focuses on multilingual child language development, inside and outside the classroom, as well as on developmental disorders. Since 2022, she has been the third director of Bilingualism Matters Ltd, a partner of MultiMind. She is raising her own children bilingually and likes yoga and travel (or best both together).

Jason Rothman is Professor of Linguistics at the UiT, the Arctic University of Norway in Tromsø and Senior Researcher at the Nebrija Research Center in Cognition at the Universidad Nebrija in Madrid. His work includes linguistically-focused research on the acquisition and processing of mainly morphosyntax in bi-/multilingual children and adults as well as interdisciplinary work seeking to unpack and understand how bi-multilingual language experience changes/shapes the mind (cognition) and brain. During his free time, he enjoys walking his dalmatian, hiking in the Norwegian mountains and binging seasons of TV shows.

Doug Saddy is the founding director of the Centre for Integrative Neuroscience and Neurodynamics at the University of Reading. His own research combines behavioral, neuroimaging and computational modelling techniques to understand typical and atypical language and cognition in children and adults. Work related to the present chapter includes how multilingualism shapes the brain, how the mind extracts hierarchical dependencies from sequential stimuli and what role rhythm plays in this process. In his spare time, he champions research that integrates Humanities, Social Sciences and STEM disciplines and plays his 1964 Telecaster.

Solange Santarelli is a teacher of Italian involved in different projects for migrants in Palermo. She received her B.A. in Asian Studies from Ca' Foscari University (Venice, Italy), her Research Master in Asian studies from Leiden University (The Netherlands) and her Master for teaching Italian to foreigners from the University of Milan (Italy). She has been a Multimind early-stage researcher, and her work focused on multilingual practices for migrants' linguistic education in Palermo, Italy. For the last six years she has been involved in projects related to education in multilingual settings. In her free time, she likes travelling.

Niels O. Schiller is a professor of psycho- and neurolinguistics at the Leiden University Centre for Linguistics and the Leiden Institute for Brain and Cognition (The Netherlands). His research interests include aspects of the neurobiology of language, such as grammatical, morphological, and phonological encoding. Currently, his interests focus particularly on the representation and processing of syntactic features, such as grammatical gender, classifiers, and number, in mono- and multilingual settings. In his spare time, he likes hiking and running, as well as (live) music, and he likes to spend time on food and wine.

Valerie Shafer has a M.A. and Ph.D. in Linguistics from the University of Buffalo and is currently Professor in the Ph.D. Program in Speech-Language-Hearing Sciences at The Graduate Center, City University of New York. Her research focuses on the neurobiology of first and second language development and language disorders, primarily using EEG and behavioral measures. For MultiMind, her focus has been on training students in the use of EEG methods for studying child language and multilingualism. In her free time, she likes to hike and garden.

Nuria Sebastian-Galles is a professor in the information technology department at Pompeu Fabra University (Spain). She directs the SAP (Speech Acquisition and Processing) Research Group at the Center for Brain and Cognition at UPF. Her scientific interests focus on understanding the brain mechanisms that make language learning possible, especially in bilingual contexts. Her studies of how babies growing up in bilingual environments learn languages have been pioneering in the field. Her research is characterized by interdisciplinary work since she combines fundamental psychology, neuroscience, and linguistics concepts.

Sergio Miguel Pereira Soares is a postdoctoral researcher at the Max Planck Institute for Psycholinguistics (The Netherlands). He received his B.A. in Biology and M.Sc. in Neuroscience from the

University of Zurich (Switzerland). He was awarded a Ph.D. in Linguistics from the University of Konstanz (Germany) in 2022. His Ph.D. project was couched within the MultiMind network and focused on the links between the brain, multilingual language acquisition and processing in adult populations. He has also been involved in several projects related to language teaching in bilingual and multilingual contexts. He likes to spend his free time outside, either doing some type of physical activity or just relaxing in the garden.

Antonella Sorace is Professor of Developmental Linguistics at the University of Edinburgh. The main topics of her interdisciplinary research are gradience in natural language at the syntax-discourse interface and bilingualism across the lifespan. She is also committed to communicating research on bilingualism in all sectors of society: she is the founding director of the non-profit organization Bilingualism Matters, which has a wide international network of branches all over the world. She enjoys spending her free time with her family.

Juhayna Taha is a lecturer in language development at University College London's Institute of Education. She received her B.A. in Speech Therapy from Birzeit University (Palestine), her M.Sc in Psycholinguistics from Edinburgh University (Scotland), and her Ph.D. in Clinical Language Sciences from Reading University (England). As a postdoctoral researcher within MultiMind at Milano-Biccoca University (Italy), she examined the rhythm-language-reading link in linguistically diverse children with and without dyslexia. She is passionate about science communication and has delivered public lectures and workshops and co-founded an online platform to raise awareness of developmental language disorders in the Arab world. In her free time, she creates digital art, experiments with recipes, and visits art exhibitions.

Jeanine Treffers-Daller is Professor Emerita in the Department of English Language and Applied Linguistics at the University of Reading. She has published widely about multilingualism, with a specific focus on code-switching, language dominance and motion event construal. She has recently co-edited an Article Collection for *Frontiers in Psychology* and one for *Languages* on Code-switching and Language Switching. She is on the Editorial Board of Bilingualism, Language and Cognition, as well as the International Journal of Bilingualism.

Sarah von Grebmer zu Wolfsthurn is a researcher and lecturer at Leiden University (The Netherlands). She obtained her BSc in Psychology and her MSc in Neuropsychology from the University of Bristol (United Kingdom), and her MSc in Clinical Psychology and her PhD in Psycho- and Neurolinguistics from Leiden University (The Netherlands). Her PhD project was part of the "MultiMind" project and investigated cross-language interactions and their impact on the multilingual brain. For her project, she also completed research stays in Spain, Germany and Mozambique to work with local multilingual communities. In her free time, she is a dedicated volleyball player and runner, and has a fascination for Roman history and food markets.

Zofia Wodniecka is an associate professor at the Institute of Psychology at Jagiellonian University in Krakow. Her research topics include multilingual language processing and development, consequences of multilingualism, individual variation in multilingualism experience, neurocognitive functions underlying use of more than one language, as well as the consequences of second language learning on first language processing and other aspects of cognition. She is also involved in public engagement as a director of Bilingualism Matters Krakow and a partner on the TEAM outreach project (Teacher Education about Multilingualism). Her hobbies include hiking and spending time outdoors.

Ngee Thai Yap is an Associate Professor in the English Language Department, Faculty of Modern Languages and Communication, Universiti Putra Malaysia (UPM). Her work primarily involves second language speech perception and speech production particularly on the intelligibility of non-native accented speech, vocabulary acquisition and language processing among bi-/plurilinguals. More recently, she has been exploring the relation between multiliteracy, working memory, and cognitive control capacity among bi/plurilinguals. She binges on Korean and Chinese dramas in her free time, plays *mahjong* whenever possible and enjoys travelling and exploring unique food and culture.

Jia'en Yee is a postdoctoral researcher at the National Institute of Education (Singapore). She received her B.A. in Psychology from Nanyang Technological University (Singapore) and her M.Sc. in Applied Neuropsychology from the University of Bristol (United Kingdom). She completed her doctoral studies at Universiti Putra Malaysia while contributing as an early-stage researcher with Multimind. During which, she explored the influence of multilingualism and multiliteracy on language processing, cognition, and brain structure, using behavioral and neuroimaging techniques. In her free time, she indulges in her passion for photography and enjoys travelling to capture the essence of new places and people.

About TBR Books

TBR Books, a program of the Center for the Advancement of Languages, Education, and Communities, publishes works by researchers and practitioners focusing on education, languages, cultural history, and social initiatives. We aim to engage diverse communities and extend our reach by translating our books into various languages.

BOOKS FOR A GENERAL AUDIENCE *(in several languages)*

Guiding Teachers into Bilingual Education edited by V. Fialais & R. Streb
Speaking the World: Multilingualism and Cultural Fluency in the Professional World, edited by M. Lazar & F. Jaumont
Mosaic of Tongues: Multilingual Learning for the Arabic-speaking World, edited by C. Allaf, F. Jaumont, & S. Talha-Jebril
Bilingual Children: Families, Education, Development by E. Bialystok
A Bilingual Revolution for Africa edited by C. Hager & F. Jaumont
The Heart of an Artichoke by L. Phillips Ashour and C. Lerognon
French All Around Us: French Language and Francophone Culture in the United States edited by K. Stein-Smith & F. Jaumont
Navigating Dual Immersion: A Teacher's Companion by V. Sun
Conversations on Bilingualism by F. Jaumont
Can We Agree to Disagree? by S. Landolt & A. Laurent
Salsa Dancing in Gym Shoes by T. Oberg de la Garza & A. Lavigne
Beyond Gibraltar; The Other Shore; Mamma in her Village by M. Lorch
One Good Question. How Countries Prepare Youth to Lead by R. Broussard

The Clarks of Willsborough Point by D. Hale
The English Patchwork by P. Tozzi & G. de Lima
The Hummingbird Project by V. Frémont
Peshtigo 1871 by C. Mercier
The Word of the Month by B. Lévy, J. Sheppard, & A. Arnon
The Gift of Languages by K. Stein-Smith & F. Jaumont
Two Centuries of French Education in New York by J. Flatau Ross
The Bilingual Revolution: The Future of Education is in Two Languages by F. Jaumont

BOOKS FOR CHILDREN *(in several languages)*
My Granny Lives in the Tablet by C. Hélot
Sara, Roumaine en France, Française en Roumanie by C. Houée
Lapin is Cold; Lapin is Hungry by T. Czajka & O. Czajka
The Bilingual Diaries by A. Moreau
Biscotte by K. Cohen-Dicker & A. Angeles
My Garden is a Square by B. Schindelhauer & M. Hansen
Regards sans complexe by B. Tchoumi
Zenzi and the Talking Bird by F. Gwaradzimba & T. Simpson
Franglais Soup e by A. Mei
Morgan; Rainbows, Masks, and Ice Cream by D. Sobel Lederman
Super Korean New Years with Grandma by M. Kim & E. Feaster
Math for All by M. Hansen
Rose Alone by S. Decosse
Uncle Steve's Country Home; The Blue Dress; The Good, the Ugly, and the Great by T. Moja
Immunity Fun!; Respiratory Fun!; Digestive Fun! by D. Stewart-McMeel
Marimba by C. Hélot, P. Velasco, & A. Kojton

Visit our website for a complete list of TBR Books' publications, series information, and author submission guidelines. Our books are available in paperback and e-book formats on our website and major online bookstores, with some titles translated into 20+ languages.

www.tbr-books.org

About CALEC

The Center for the Advancement of Languages, Education, and Communities (CALEC) is a nonprofit organization focused on promoting multilingualism, empowering multilingual families, and fostering cross-cultural understanding. The Center's mission is in alignment with the United Nations' Sustainable Development Goals. Our mission is to establish language as a critical life skill, by developing and implementing bilingual education programs, promoting diversity, reducing inequality, and helping to provide quality education. Our programs seek to protect world cultural heritage and support teachers, authors, and families by providing the knowledge and resources to create vibrant multilingual communities.

The specific objectives and purpose of our organization are:

- To develop and implement education programs that promote multilingualism and cross-cultural understanding, and establish an inclusive and equitable quality education, including internship and leadership training. [SDG # 4, Quality Education]

- To publish and distribute resources, including research papers, books, and case studies that seek to empower and promote the social, economic, and political inclusion of all, with a focus on language education and cultural diversity, equity, and inclusion. [SDG # 10, Reduced Inequalities]

- To help build sustainable cities and communities and support teachers, authors, researchers, and families in the advancement of multilingualism and cross-cultural understanding through collaborative tools for linguistic communities. [SDG # 11, Sustainable Cities and Communities]

- To foster strong global partnerships and cooperation, and mobilize resources across borders, to participate in events and activities that promote language education through knowledge sharing and coaching, empowering parents, and teachers, and building multilingual societies. [SDG # 17, Partnerships for the Goals]

SOME GOOD REASONS TO SUPPORT US

Your donation helps:

- develop our publishing and translation activities so that more languages are represented.
- provide access to our online book platform to daycare centers, schools, and cultural centers in underserved areas.
- support local and sustainable action in favor of education and multilingualism.
- implement projects that advance dual-language education.
- organize workshops for parents, conferences with large audiences, meet-the-author chats, and talks with experts in multilingualism.

DONATE ONLINE

For all your questions, contact our team by email at contact@calec.org or donate online on our website:

www.calec.org

www.ingramcontent.com/pod-product-compliance
Lightning Source LLC
Chambersburg PA
CBHW021146160426
43194CB00007B/707